Shelagh Rowan-Legg is a writer and filmmaker. She is a programmer for FrightFest, an associate editor and film critic for *Screen Anarchy*, and a critic for *Sight & Sound*. Her short films have played at festivals in North America, Asia and Europe. She has a PhD in Spanish fantastic film from King's College London.

TAURIS WORLD CINEMA SERIES

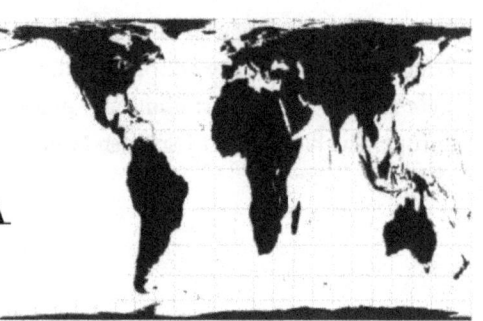

Series Editors:
Lúcia Nagib, *Professor of Film at the University of Reading*
Julian Ross, *Research Fellow at the University of Westminster*

Advisory Board: Laura Mulvey (UK), Robert Stam (USA), Ismail Xavier (Brazil), Dudley Andrew (USA)

The *Tauris World Cinema Series* aims to reveal and celebrate the richness and complexity of film art across the globe, exploring a wide variety of cinemas set within their own cultures and as they interconnect in a global context. The books in the series will represent innovative scholarship, in tune with the multicultural character of contemporary audiences. Drawing upon an international authorship, they will challenge outdated conceptions of world cinema, and provide new ways of understanding a field at the centre of film studies in an era of transnational networks.

Queries, ideas and submissions to:

Series Editor: Professor Lúcia Nagib –
  l.nagib@reading.ac.uk

Series Editor: Dr. Julian Ross –
  rossj@westminster.ac.uk

Cinema Editor at I.B.Tauris,
  Maddy Hamey-Thomas –
  mhamey-thomas@ibtauris.com

'*The Spanish Fantastic* brings a highly informed critical perspective to key works from one of the most exciting production cycles in recent Spanish cinema. From Guillermo del Toro and Álex de la Iglesia, to lesser-known genre specialists Jaume Balagueró and Paco Plaza, the author's range is unsurpassed and her approach expertly informed.'

Andy Willis, University of Salford, UK

'Shelagh Rowan-Legg's innovative monograph eschews the normal auteurist and nationalist approaches to Spanish cinema to offer a series of excellent close readings of genre films, many of them little known.'

Paul Julian Smith, City University of New York (CUNY)

THE SPANISH FANTASTIC

CONTEMPORARY FILMMAKING IN HORROR, FANTASY AND SCI-FI

SHELAGH ROWAN-LEGG

I.B. TAURIS
LONDON · NEW YORK

Published in 2016 by
I.B.Tauris & Co. Ltd
London • New York
www.ibtauris.com

Tauris World Cinema Series

ISBN: 978 1 78453 677 0
eISBN: 978 1 78672 078 8
ePDF: 978 1 78673 078 7

A full CIP record for this book is available from the British Library
A full CIP record is available from the Library of Congress

Library of Congress Catalog Card Number: available

Printed and bound by CPI Group (UK) Ltd, Croydon, CR0 4YY

MIX
Paper from
responsible sources
FSC   FSC® C013604
www.fsc.org

Table of Contents

List of Figures

Acknowledgements

First, a big thank you to Anna Coatman, who first read the proposal of this book and embraced it with great enthusiasm. Thanks also and just as much to my editor, Madeleine Hamey-Thomas, for her insight. And to the entire team at I.B.Tauris for their hard work.

Thank you to Sophie Mayer, not only for her copyediting skills, but also for her friendship, and endless cups of tea poured out over sage advice.

To Belén Vidal, my PhD supervisor, who advised and guided me, and who watched countless horror films even when they made her cringe. Thanks to the faculty and students at King's College London, especially Jinhee Choi, Sarah Cooper, Lilly Husbands, Ed Lamberti, Luke Robinson, and Catherine Wheatley. Thanks to Agustín Rico-Albero and Alejandro Melero Salvador, academics and friends, for their advice, and to Antonio Lázaro-Reboll and Paul Julian Smith, whose notes on my viva were invaluable.

To Mike Hostench, Ángel Sala, and everyone at Sitges International Fantastic Film Festival of Catalonia, where the idea for this book began. Thank you to the directors, producers, screenwriters, and industry professionals who gave their time in interviews: Mikel Alvariño, Gaz Bailey, Jaume Balagueró, Rafael Cabrera, Nacho Cerdà, Rodrigo Cortés, Mateo Gil, Adrian Guerra, Gabe Ibáñez, Nahikari Ipiña Sadaba, Enrique López Lavigne, Miguel Martí, Eugenio Mira, Paco Plaza, Koldo Serra, Antonio Trashorras, and Nacho Vigalondo.

Thank you to my friends and colleagues on the fantastic film festival circuit, and from *Screen Anarchy*, who often had to listen to me talk endlessly about my love of Spanish fantastic film: Ryland Aldrich, Kristen Bell, Todd Brown, Pierce Conran, Mitch Davis, Mattie Do, Evrim Ersoy, Can Evrenol, Colin Geddes, Jason Gorber, David Hall, Jen Handorf, Eva Herrero, Kier-la Janisse, Alan Jones, Peter Kuplowsky, Tim League, Annick Mahnert, James Marsh, Peter Martin, Paul McEvoy, Nicole McControversy, Jordan McGrath, Juan Carlos Medina, Katherine O'Shea, James Pearcey, Maria Reinup, Ailsa Scott, Joakim Sten, Alice Waddington, and Russell Would.

And last, but most important, never-ending thanks to my mother Judi and my sister Lorna, for their endless support and encouragement.

Acknowledgements

An earlier version of some of the material on *Sexykiller* in Chapter 6 was previously published in 'Deadly Hybridity: *Sexykiller*, the Female Serial Killer & The New Spanish Horror Film', in Duncan Wheeler and Fernando Canet (eds), *(Re)viewing Creative, Critical and Commercial Practices in Contemporary Spanish Cinema* (Intellect, 2014), and is reprinted here by kind permission of Intellect.

An earlier version of some of the material on *[REC]* and *[REC]2* was previously published in 'Don't Miss a Bloody Thing: *[REC]* and the Spanish Adaptation of Found Footage Horror', *Studies in Spanish & Latin American Cinemas* 10/2 (2013), which is also reprinted here by kind permission of Intellect.

Introduction

Bastard Sons: Contemporary Spanish Fantastic Film

In 2008, I attended a screening of *Sexykiller* (*Sexykiller: morirás para ella*, Miguel Martí, 2008) at the Toronto International Film Festival (TIFF). I had always made a point of seeing the Spanish films that played in the Midnight Madness section of that festival, such as *Mutant Action* (*Acción Mutante*, Álex de la Iglesia, 1993), *Killer Tongue* (Alberto Sciamma, 1996), and *The Abandoned* (Nacho Cerdà, 2006), and fantastic films from other sections, such as *The Devil's Backbone* (*El espinazo del diablo*, Guillermo del Toro, 2001) and *The Orphanage* (*El orfanato*, Juan Antonio Bayona, 2007). But it was not until viewing *Sexykiller* that something clicked in my brain. Like most of the audience that night, I laughed and cheered at *Sexykiller*'s title character Bárbara as she slashed her way through her victims while providing fashion tips and generally putting to test the iconography of slasher killers in horror films. The film was brightly coloured in a way often seen as typical for a Spanish film, given the popularity of Pedro Almodóvar, but *Sexykiller* was also violent in the manner of Álex de la Iglesia, while at the same time referencing both US and European horror films.

What was it about Spanish fantastic film that made its output so varied, despite coming from the same country? Why did some of these films seem to be commenting on their own society and culture, while others seemed to have little to do with Spain other than language? Why did the only other Spanish fantastic films that were popular among genre fans date from more than 30 years ago, in the era of Jesús Franco and Paul Naschy? Why was it only since the early 1990s that Spanish fantastic film apparently had taken over genre festivals, with films from this southern European nation lauded as some of the best in the world?

My curiosity was piqued: a few days later, I went to the library to find a history of Spanish fantastic film. At the time, I was an undergraduate student at the University of Toronto, and interested in pursuing a master's degree in cinema

1

studies. I was quite dismayed to find that there were no books exclusively on this topic. The few English-language books on Spanish film history made brief mention of directors such as Franco, Naschy, de la Iglesia and Alejandro Amenábar, but these were cursory glances. More mention was made of directors such as Franco and Naschy in books on horror films, but without much concern for their national film context.

In 2009, in my capacity as programmer for Toronto After Dark Film Festival, I attended the Sitges International Fantastic Film Festival of Catalonia, considered the most important genre festival in Europe. At this point, I had started my master's degree, and my thesis would eventually investigate Guillermo del Toro's Spanish Civil War films, so I was already moving in a Spanish direction. That year, as well as showing new and varied Spanish fantastic films such as *Hierro* (Gabe Ibáñez, 2009), *Carriers* (David Pastor and Àlex Pastor, 2009), and *[REC]2* (Jaume Balagueró and Paco Plaza, 2009), the festival also showcased classic films *The Spirit of the Beehive* (*El espíritu de la colmena*, Victor Erice, 1973), *The Mad Monkey* (Fernando Trueba, 1989), and *Dead Mother* (*La madre muerta*, Juanma Bajo Ulloa, 1993). These films (different in theme, tone and presentation) were frequently mentioned by my cinephile friends as being some of the most important among Spanish fantastic films. But it seemed to me that there was a new wave that warranted exploration, especially given its popularity, and proliferation, since the early 1990s, and influence on worldwide fantastic film.

It really has been from the early 1990s until the present that Spain has seen this increase in the production and popularity of fantastic films. Films such as *The Day of the Beast* (*El día de la bestia*, Álex de la Iglesia, 1995), *The Others* (Alejandro Amenábar, 2001), *Pan's Labyrinth* (*El laberinto del fauno*, Guillermo del Toro, 2006) and *Timecrimes* (*Los cronocrímenes*, Nacho Vigalondo, 2007) have expressed the cultural outlook of a new generation of filmmakers, and have gained popularity through productions aimed at national and international audiences. This new generation of Spanish filmmakers, or those with Spanish connections, was mainly raised after, or immediately before, Spain became a democracy in 1978. This coincided with the widespread introduction of home theatre technology in the 1980s, which gave spectators (and future filmmakers) more ready access to cinema from around the world. Starting in the 1990s, and continuing today, the cost of filmmaking has been reduced through the development of digital technology. In addition, changes to government funding including subsidies for national film productions, the rise of film festivals, and availability of films via the Internet and video on demand, have created what could be called a postnational cinema culture.

While English-language films dominate movie theatres around the world, box office records show that an overwhelming number of fantastic films, such as *Star Wars Episode IV: A New Hope* (George Lucas, 1977), *E.T. the Extra-Terrestrial* (Steven Spielberg, 1982), and *The Hunger Games* (Gary Ross, 2012), are consistently some of the most popular internationally. As fantastic films share aspects that are not culturally specific, they suggest a body of cinema that can be defined as postnational. Postnational cinema combines that which is nationally specific – either within a film in terms of cultural references or symbolism, or in terms of production with a creative team of a single nation – with that which is not nationally specific, such as tropes recognized across cultures, or having international financing and/or an international creative team.

While Spain's cinema history contains the fantastic, such films are rarely considered part of the national cinema canon. But what or who defines a film as part of a nation's cinematic canon? Is it drama or comedy that purports to display life as it is lived in the nation? Is it experimental, avant-garde, or art cinema? Or is it any film that, either directly or indirectly, reacts to and reflects on national cultural, social and/or political conditions? In the 1980s, the Spanish film industry moved to reclaim a cinema of quality that had a strong basis in realism. But since the mid-1990s, the fantastic genres have been recycled and reshaped by a new generation of Spanish filmmakers. These films are part of a current movement of postnational cinema.

Spanish films are no longer solely to be considered within a national context; instead, the turn to postnational cinema brings with it a move to examine all expressions that emerge from Spain, whether that be a film which examines the political, social or cultural context of the contemporary period or the past, or is simply a film by a Spanish filmmaker. The national is neither abandoned nor promoted; rather, it can be both, though arguably some films have more nationally-specific markers than others. The aesthetics and experimentation within fantastic films involves both the cultural diversity of Spain, and divergence from other national cinemas' fantastic films. All genres, not just social realism, can be an expression of a national culture, and the fantastic genres introduce influences both within and without the national. Much of previous scholarship on Spanish film identifies the Spanish Civil War, the Fascist dictatorship and the transition periods as crucial events that are frequently represented. However, for contemporary Spanish fantastic filmmakers, these events (while not necessarily ignored or excluded) are less significant to their postnational cultural outlook.

Barry Keith Grant writes that genre movies 'are secular stories that seek to resolve the basic problems and dilemmas of contemporary life'.[1] As the term 'fantastic' is understood and used today, by fans and festivals that focus on such cinema, fantastic films generally fall under one or more of following genres: horror, science fiction, fantasy, and thriller. The word 'fantastic' in relation to film tends to bring an assumption that something within the narrative or stylistic elements will be unrealistic or highly improbable within our empirical understanding of the world: a mysterious intrusion into the context of real life, a confrontation with the inexplicable, or a break with the acknowledged order. This can mean the supernatural, abnormal psychic states, delusion, or the extreme. In her work on fantastic literature, Rosemary Jackson points out that these works cannot be separated from the social context in which they were written, and the author must be placed within their historical, social and political determinants.[2] This can also be applied to film. Vicente Rodríguez Ortega writes that genre negotiates 'between the global appeal of certain generic mechanisms and modes of address… and the emphasis on extremely specific cultural markers'.[3] While any fantastic film may have specific cultural markers, the generic mechanisms of the fantastic can be extrapolated and interpreted without intimate knowledge of the originating culture.

As Antonio Lázaro-Reboll and Andrew Willis point out, until recently, '[c]urrent and past methodologies of Spanish film studies have remained primarily aesthetic, auteurist and nationalist in their purview'.[4] Spanish fantastic film has suffered from a history of omission; that is to say, it has not often been mentioned, and frequently only in a few paragraphs, in texts on Spanish films. One of the first Spanish-language books on the subject, *Cine español: cine de subgeneros*, published in 1974, dismisses horror cinema outright, believing these films to be mere imitations of American horror films, aimed at international markets.[5] While neither of these statements is entirely untrue, the dismissal of said cinema was premature. *Historia del cine español* by Román Gubern, an extensive Spanish-language work, also mentions directors such as Franco and Eugenio Martín when discussing commercial cinema, but does not expand on genre film.[6]

Essays and scholarly articles on a number of the more popular films, such as the work of del Toro and Amenábar, can be found in numerous journals and books, some focusing on textual analysis, some on production context, and some looking at the national cinema contexts of their films. More recent books on Spanish film are likely to include chapters or sections on fantastic film in general, or focus on specific fantastic films. General guides such as *Contemporary Spanish Cinema* by Barry Jordan and Rikki Morgan-Tamosunas, *Spanish Cinema* by Rob Stone, and *A Companion to Spanish Cinema* by Bernard Bentley, do not devote much space to fantastic film as such, serving instead as overviews of all of Spanish film. However, each of these volumes mentions important fantastic filmmakers of the late twen-tieth century such as Amenábar and de la Iglesia. In her book *Spanish National Cinema*, Núria Triana Toribio links filmmakers such as de la Iglesia to what she terms the 'new vulgarities' cinema seen in films such as *Airbag* (Juanma Bajo Ulloa, 1997) and *Torrente, The Dumb Arm of the Law* (*Torrente, el brazo tonte de la ley*, Santiago Segura, 1998). But she is careful to point out that this link is perhaps super-ficial due to the films' use of black humour and what she calls 'puerile' [sic] jokes, and notes that de la Iglesia's work thus far was highly self-conscious and an attempt at reflecting Spanish culture and society as much as any social realist film.[7] Triana Toribio in effect begins to establish a methodology for understanding contemporary Spanish cinema as postnational, noting how filmmakers are drawing on other cul-tural influences.

This position leads to the early twenty-first-century shift towards examin-ing Spanish film, not from a strictly auteurist or national cinema perspective, but by integrating other theories such as transnationalism, and genre cinema. *Contemporary Spanish Cinema and Genre*, published in 2008 and edited by Jay Beck and Rodríguez Ortega, is one of the first collections to look at the importance of genre theory in connection to Spanish cinema, and contains some essays that focus specifically on Spanish fantastic films, reading more carefully into the texts to argue for how they can be interpreted through Spanish culture and changes in the Spanish film industry.[8] The introduction by the editors makes a point of emphasizing the importance of studying Spanish film through genre theory, espe-cially in light of growing transnational and postnational cinema trends.[9] This approach has informed my book due to its stressing the importance of engag-ing with Spanish film from a genre perspective, understanding cross-hybridity of genre use, new methods of production, and the growing importance of trans/postnational cinema.

Many recent works have pointed out not only the importance of looking at Spanish film through genre theory, but also through theories of transnational-ism and postnationalism. Willis points out that 'while there may be generic codes and conventions that are reproduced across national borders, horror cinema pro-duced within particular national contexts will differ in significant ways'.[10] This can be applied to all subgenres of fantastic film, and points to the necessity for new examinations of Spanish fantastic film both within and beyond the national con-text. As Ann Davies notes, while national cinema studies are not defunct per se (as even this book is studying films from a single nation), a canonical approach can be limiting.[11] While certain directors included in this book are arguably estab-lished auteurs (notably Amenábar, de la Iglesia, del Toro, and Jaume Balagueró), to limit them to their national auteur status means ignoring cinematic influences that suggest the postnational industrial and creative environment in which they work. Recent works by Davies, such as *Spanish Spaces: Landscape, Space and Place in Contemporary Spanish Culture* and *Spain on Screen: Developments in Contemporary Spanish Cinema* (which she edited) have devoted more space to fantastic films.

More recently, some Spanish-language books dedicated to Spanish fantastic film have emerged. Carlos Águilar has edited two general overviews on Spanish fantastic and terror films (*Cine fantástico y de terror español 1900–1983* and *Cine fantástico y de terror español 1984–2004*), which examine the films and eras in question. Ángel Sala's book *Profanando el sueño de los muertos: la historia jamás contada del cine fantástico español* is a history of Spanish fantastic film from its beginnings until the present; each chapter covers approximately ten years and discusses the various films made during that period, the filmmakers and their influences, Spanish filmmakers' work outside of Spain, and non-Spanish filmmakers' work inside Spain. The two largest chapters, one covering 1968–1975 and the other 1997–2010 (which together form more than half of the book), reflect on the importance of these two eras and the sheer volume of fantastic films produced therein. As well, a second Spanish-language book on fantastic film, *Silencios de pánico: historia del cine fantástico y de terror español, 1897–2010*, by Diego López and David Pizarro, has added to Sala's book in information and context. All of these books provide evidence that, while in certain eras Spanish fantastic film might have been somewhat light in volume, it did exist, and that both the Spanish horror boom of the late 1960s and the current era are of increasing importance and relevance both for international genre film and Spanish film.

Also recent is Lázaro-Reboll's 2012 book *Spanish Horror Film*, the first critical study of this subject in English, looking at seminal films and filmmakers, their cult audiences, and contexts of reception. As he points out, 'Spanish horror film is visually categorized and discussed as part of a wider "Eurohorror" tradition', as opposed to being included as part of Spanish national cinema.[12] He emphasizes the need to integrate Spanish horror into the general discussion of Spanish cinema, and his book looks at the history and development of Spanish horror in relation to Spanish cultural history. He investigates the institutions, technologies, genre users and consumers that shape and participate in the process of genre classification and reconfiguration of the horror genre.[13] He notes also that it is only in the past 20 years that critics have embraced genre cinema, largely due to its international festival and box office success.[14] While he focuses more on fan culture and its importance and influence than this book will, his approach to textual analysis and production is highly informative. I have drawn on all of these books for their extensive look at Spanish fantastic film history, and the attention given therein to transnational and postnational film theories, alongside the aforementioned scholarly work on general Spanish film history, genre theory, and postnational cinema theory.

This recent and increasing interest in contemporary Spanish fantastic film by academics and critics, as stated, is most likely due, at least in part, to an increase in film production. However, with the exception of *Spanish Horror Film* (which is limited to that one genre), none of these studies address the specificity of the fantastic genre and its place in contemporary Spanish film. This book examines the unique approach of the Spanish filmmakers to their work, the semantics of the fantastic genres as they are reused and adapted, and the spectrum of the films' connections to their Spanish roots. The recent Spanish proliferation of the fantastic makes for an interesting case study of the development of the fantastic genres, and the place of the fantastic within national and postnational cinematic canons. But more importantly, contemporary Spanish fantastic film has become increasingly important in world fantastic cinema. This is in part due to filmmakers such as Balagueró, de la Iglesia, and del Toro; in part due to the importance of and publicity surrounding film festivals, both in Europe and around the world; and in part due to the increased availability and access to films through video on demand and other home entertainment platforms. The increasing globalization of the film industry means we need to look at Spanish fantastic film not just from a national perspective, but a generic and postnational one.

Spanish Fantastic Film before the 1990s

Until the early 1990s, there were fewer fantastic films produced in Spain than in other western nations such as the United States, the United Kingdom, and France. These countries had continuous (though different) cycles of fantastic films; for example, the US had the Universal Studios era of monster films in the 1930s and later the science fiction cycle of the 1950s; and the UK had several gothic horror films in the 1950s followed by the Hammer Films era of the 1960s. Spain, however, only briefly had a prolific era of horror film in the late 1960s and early 1970s. While Spanish fantastic film might have been sparse before the late twentieth century, the historical circumstances of its production are important in understanding the current movement.

In his book on fantastic film in Spain, Sala notes that its history cannot be paralleled with other European nations, due mainly to government censorship of the mid-twentieth century and the control of the Catholic Church over the arts and education.[15] No mysteries or supernatural beings, save those of the Catholic faith, were permitted representation. And this was not only true of film; throughout its history, most of Spanish art and literature was based in the realist tradition. It is the exceptions to this, curiously, that are the most familiar to international audiences: *Don Quixote* by Miguel de Cervantes parodies fantastic elements found in the chivalric novel, and Spanish artists such as Francisco de Goya and Pablo Picasso are mainly known for their more surreal (bordering on fantastic) work.

Certainly, like many other European nations, Spain had a strong cinematic tradition before the Civil War; however, it was not necessarily consolidated into a national cinema.[16] One of the earliest Spanish cinema pioneers was Segundo de Chomón, who worked with Georges Méliès in Paris in the early twentieth century. Many of his short films were of a macabre nature, and de Chomón was interested in special effects and creating camera tricks, seen in *La dernière sorcière* (1906) and *El hotel eléctrico* (1908).[17] As the film industry grew in the 1910s and 1920s, other filmmakers continued to explore the fantastic mode, particularly in Barcelona, which housed the majority of film production at that time. The film industry became more active in the early 1930s, and by 1935 there were 11 studios in Spain.[18] Much of this early cinema comprised adaptations of novels, plays and musical theatre, and Sala admits that during this time, there were not many fantastic films, and of course fewer films overall once the Civil War began in 1936.[19] The situation did not improve after the war, for fantastic films or otherwise, until the 1960s; government censorship did not approve of the fantastic, as it was not in keeping with the promotion of the governing ideology. The government wanted films that exalted Catholic values and fought foreign influences.

Between 1939 and 1959, film production centred on a few genres: civil war films, historical extravaganzas, religious films and folk musicals, which promoted the values of the state and the Catholic Church. Directors of fantastic films had to find ways to work around the censors, often presenting images of the idealized life in combination with fantastic elements.[20] Edgar Neville (who worked both in Spain and Hollywood) made films such as *The Tower of the Seven Hunchbacks* (*La torre de los siete jorobados*, 1944) and *Sunday Carnival* (*Domingo de carnaval*, 1945), which showed a particularly Spanish combination of black comedy and horror. As well, director Carlos Serrano de Osma, in films such as *Embrujo* (1947) and *La sirena negra* (1947) combined influences from early silent film with the fantastic, utilizing characters and situations such as dancers and flamenco with a style that suggests surrealism.

In 1962, José María García Escudero was appointed Director of the Department of Film and Theatre, and he began to champion what became known as *el Nuevo Cine Español* or NCE. Lack of economic growth forced the Spanish government to open the industry to more foreign investment, which meant a certain relaxation of censorship restrictions and the possibility of the use of the fantastic genres. The NCE was meant to produce a new wave of quality cinema, more in line with trends in other European nations such as France and Italy, who were achieving critical success with the New Wave and neo-realist movements. García Escudero modified funding so as to encourage this quality cinema, though this was as much to help the faltering Spanish economy as it was about a more open film industry. However, this modification (which included credit protection and government grants) ultimately created debt that led to García Escudero's dismissal in 1968, though horror films managed to survive due to their popularity both nationally and internationally.[21]

Another reason that horror films managed to survive both funding changes and censorship policies was that they were usually coded as 'foreign': the actors were dubbed, the action frequently took place outside of Spain, and there was (at least overtly) nothing recognizable as Spanish in the characters or story. During this time, many British actors known for their work in horror, such as Christopher Lee and Peter Cushing, worked with Spanish directors. Lee starred in Franco's films *The Castle of Fu-Manchu* (1968) and *The Bloody Judge* (1970), and both Lee and Cushing starred in Martín's film *Horror Express* (1972). Due to the use of international stars and settings, and international co-production status, films such as these were labelled as 'foreign' and therefore able to slip past the censors.

The most notable filmmakers to come out of this era (commonly referred to as the Spanish Horror Boom), were Franco, Naschy, and Narciso Ibáñez Serrador. Arguably the first of the Horror Boom films is Franco's *The Awful Dr Orlof* (*Gritos en la noche*), from 1961. Franco made 55 films in the last six years of the Fascist regime, mostly in the horror genre, and his and Naschy's importance in the history of horror and cult cinema has been widely recognized by both scholars and cinephiles. Ibáñez Serrador wrote and directed the popular television series *Historias para no dormir*, which ran from 1966 to 1968, as well as one of the most famous films of the era, *The House that Screamed* (*La residencia*) in 1969, and is cited as influential by several contemporary directors including Balagueró and Eugenio Mira.[22] These films, while frequently financially successful, were dismissed by critics at the time as unrefined and unworthy of attention. This attitude was not shared by the audience: indeed, Ibáñez Serrador (popularly known as 'Chico') was viewed as the 'Alfred Hitchcock' of

9

Spain, and his television series was so popular that it spawned a book series and fanzines on horror film.[23] Making horror films proved inexpensive, allowing Spain to gain a foothold in the film market and engage in co-productions with other European nations.

In 1975, General Francisco Franco died and the Fascist regime fell. In 1977, new legislation abolished film censorship and a new board of classification was established, as well as new quotas for the distribution of national films.[24] However, according to Triana Toribio, very little happened in the film industry between 1977 and 1982, as the newly open Spanish film market became flooded with foreign films, especially from Hollywood.[25] While it was at this time that festivals such as Sitges, and specialist fanzines such as Terror Fantastic, gained a cult following, that following would remain on the margins for some time. Hollywood cinema dominated the world, and most Spanish films tended to be sex comedies, cheap horrors, and a small number of arthouse films.[26] In 1982, a left-leaning government was elected, which viewed film as an instrument of emancipation and investigation of the past. At this point, many filmmakers wanted to make films that openly examined Spanish history, religion, family, sexuality, and other topics that were either banned or censored under Fascism.[27]

Pilar Miró, who had been an oppositional filmmaker during the later Fascist years and whose film *The Cuenca Crime* (*El crimen de Cuenca*, 1979) was at first refused a distribution license, was given the task of revitalizing the film industry, as Directora General de Cinematografía from 1982 to 1985.[28] In 1983, she introduced *La ley Miró* or the Miró law, which, among other benefits, would pay subsidies in the amount of up to 50 per cent of costs to certain productions, to be determined by arbitrators of the Film Protection Fund.[29] Sally Faulkner writes that some described the policy as 'the encouragement of quality cinema, a preference for literary adaptations and an eye for international distribution and festivals'.[30] This fund would generally only finance so-called 'approved' films that were meant to reflect the Spanish character and be 'good' for Spanish audiences. The policy was designed to promote a smaller number of productions, those with high production values, but also to favour high-culture cinema, encouraging experimental work.

Voices in favour of the new policies and the films it generated were in the minority; the majority condemned it as defacto censorship and for its favouritism toward certain kinds of films, its presentation of a homogeneous Spanish culture, and its lack of variety. Triana Toribio interprets the official policy as supporting films that 'function as an international calling card, a sample of the new cinema that could call itself legitimately Spanish and even serve as an enticement to foreign distributors'.[31] Jordan and Morgan-Tamosunas write that the law 'favoured projects which could best be described as safe, middle-brow, arthouse films' that seemed to ignore the viewing interests of Spanish audiences.[32] Bentley also notes that the policy ignored what were considered lowbrow genre films, which included the fantastic.[33] This is not to say that there were no fantastic films made during this time; there were several, such as *Operación mantis* (Paul Naschy, 1984), *Alien Predator* (Deran Sarafian, 1985), and *Slugs* (Juan Piquer, 1987). In 1985, an attempt was made at a large and expensive fantastic film production with an international cast. *Star Knight* is a gothic science fiction film about a medieval village and the abduction of a girl by aliens, directed by Fernando Colomo, and starring Miguel Bosé and well-known actors Harvey Keitel and Klaus Kinski. Unfortunately, it failed both with critics and at the box office, further damaging the reputation of the Spanish fantastic.[34]

However, a few films managed to slip through the cracks. Agustí Villaronga's *In a Glass Cage* (*Tras el cristal*, 1987), which told the story of a former Nazi war criminal and paedophile, and Bigas Luna's *Anguish* (1987), about a serial killer in a movie theatre, embraced art cinema, Hollywood cinema, and a darker side of Spanish cultural representations that went beyond the boundaries of traditional social realism, and depicted violence in ways that had before not been seen in Spanish cinema outside the horror films by Franco and his contemporaries. Films such as these helped younger filmmakers see the potential of the fantastic, and helped lead to the current renaissance of the fantastic film in contemporary Spain.

The Spanish Fantastic New Wave

During the transition period of the early 1980s, filmmakers in their 30s and older were interested in reflecting on their youth, lost to Fascism. This was in contrast to those in their 20s, for whom this time period brought some level of ambivalence at the entire process of democracy and an exposure to the wider world that their elders had never enjoyed. This younger generation was a part of what has since been named *la movida*, a 1980s subculture that emerged out of Madrid, influenced by British punk, new wave, and comics, whose films, music and literature reflected the underground culture that was ignored and marginalized by the cultural elite.

As Spain moved into the 1990s, the youth were seemingly more affected by cultural influences of other countries than by their own country's history, which in a sense made them no different from youth in other western nations. John Hopewell writes that since the late twentieth century, 'Spanish film directors have haltingly sought to appeal more broadly to a new generation of audiences for whom the Spanish Civil War is as distant as the Siege of Troy'.[35] This generation was as much influenced by American popular culture, and fantastic films from Asia, as it was by the film history of Spain. Directors such as Rodrigo Cortés, Miguel Martí, Paco Plaza, and producer Nahikari Ipiña Sadaba all cite the influence of American popular cinema of the 1980s.[36] George Lucas, Steven Spielberg, Chris Columbus, and others who made films across the range of fantastic genres – horror, science fiction, adventure – showed Spanish filmmakers the variety and potential of fantastic films, not only in reaching larger audiences, but expressing their worldview, which neither they nor audiences were seeing in the majority of Spanish cinema at the time.

By the early 1990s, it had become clear that the Miró law, with a few exceptions, was a failure. Spanish audiences had little interest in their national cinema, and young filmmakers were rebelling against the strict criteria of what constituted a worthy Spanish film. In late 1994, the then Minister of Culture, Carmen Alborch, changed film funding to a system that favoured subsidies based on box office receipts; these subsidies were not tied to any criteria of so-called 'national interest' of the film. By the mid-1990s, those filmmakers coming of age and those who had settled into adulthood were no longer interested solely in classical filmic references or literary adaptations. The popular and mass culture of Europe and North America, and the continuing popularity of television, had created a new generation of artists: the *hijos bastardos del posmodernismo de los ochentas*, or bastard sons of eighties postmodernism, who were creating a de-ideologized and apolitical cinema.[37]

Filmmakers such as Amenábar, de la Iglesia, and Juanma Bajo Ulloa looked outward as much as inward for their inspiration. Young filmmakers were tired of restrictions that made European art films the only option for receiving funding. Now that the benchmark was removed, many diverse films that either were of the fantastic genres or had connections to the fantastic were produced. Films such as *Mutant Action, Dead Mother* and *Airbag*, Santiago Aguilar and Luis Guridi's *Justino (Justino, un asesino de la tercera edad,* 1994), and Amenábar's *Thesis (Tesis,* 1996), began to prove that there was a place for the Spanish fantastic. In an interview, Mateo Gil (co-screenwriter of *Thesis*) says that for the younger filmmakers in the 1990s, 'it was very important… to change the traditional Spanish film image. We didn't want the realism, the dark Spain. We wanted to make moderns movies, with big cities, and North American-like backgrounds'.[38] These filmmakers were not afraid of utilizing the fantastic genres, or to include explicit sexual or violent content, and to give such content thematic importance.

Mike Hostench, co-director of the Sitges festival, and Adrià Monés, a producer with Filmax, both highlight the importance of international co-productions with countries such as France, Portugal, Mexico and the UK in revitalizing the Spanish fantastic film industry.[39] These co-productions – for example *The Backwoods* (Koldo Serra, 2006), *Intruders* (Juan Carlos Fresnadillo, 2011), and *Pan's Labyrinth* – have received wider distribution. Monés states that the film industry has been long politicized; many conservative politicians did not like to support an industry that it felt often made political films counter to the government, nor did they want the films to receive financial support.[40] For industry professionals, this comes from a widespread misconception as to the extent of government support for film and Spanish film revenue. Many in Spain compare the Spanish film industry to the US (or more specifically Hollywood), which is seen as profitable and therefore does not need government assistance, or to France, which has a long tradition of funding policies that support the national film industry. Indeed, when the conservative political party, Partido Popular, was in power between 1996 and 2004, a change in film support policy meant cutbacks on state subsidies in order to let commercial forces take their course.[41] Given that Hollywood cinema dominated the box office, this made it more difficult for Spanish films to succeed. In response, international co-productions became more common.

Another reason for the move towards the fantastic was the creation of Fantastic Factory, a production company from Barcelona that devoted itself to the production of fantastic film, utilizing Spanish talent and pursuing co-productions with groups within and outside of Spain. Begun by Julio Fernández of Filmax and American director Brian Yuzna, the label set out to produce English-language horror and science fiction films of low-to-mid budget, bringing together Spanish and English-language talent. It was an attempt to find a space between traditional European art cinema and popular Hollywood cinema. The company produced several films, including *Faust: Love of the Damned* (Brian Yuzna, 2001), *Romasanta: The Werewolf Hunt* (Paco Plaza, 2004) and *The Nun* (Luis de la Madrid, 2005), before being folded into Filmax in 2005. Filmax has continued the spirit of The Fantastic Factory with production of Spanish-based horror films, such as the *[REC]* series. Rafael Cabrera, from Spain's Ministry of Culture, adds that Fantastic Factory made a point not only of making international co-productions, but also of shooting films in English to capture the international market.[42] These films have found popularity in the Spanish movie houses as well. In 2004, seven of the top 25 grossing national films in Spain can be considered fantastic. The late 1990s and early 2000s proved not only was there a national market for these films, but an international one.

In 2014, the Spanish film industry received €50.8 million in subsidies, far less than the average €770 million in France and €120 million in the UK.[43] But these are countries that, as stated, have far more support both financially and from national public attendance. Many Spanish production companies, especially those specializing in the fantastic, are now turning to production and distribution companies from outside of Spain, for financial support and sales. Many of these sales take place at festivals, furthering the importance of fantastic films for the international market.

Between 1990 and 2001, 251 Spanish filmmakers made their first feature film.[44] These filmmakers do not come from any one particular school, nor do they necessarily share common interests, or address or show any explicit thematic interest in their nation's history. They are not interested in making 'art' films, but they are not necessarily turning their back on their Spanish identity. Rather, their films are an amalgam, allowing many of them to enter into the global film culture while still remaining relevant in their native country. Enrique López Lavigne, producer of films such as *Lovers of the Arctic Circle* (*Los amantes del Círculo Polar*, Julio Medem, 1998) and *28 Weeks Later* (Juan Carlos Fresnadillo, 2007), as a child would spend hours at the cinema watching horror B-movies both from Spain and abroad, films that would become available on VHS in the 1980s. According to him, it was these kinds of films that drew the new wave filmmakers away from the realism that dominated Spanish cinema during the transition and early 1980s, and into the fantastic.[45] As Carmen Herrero writes, 'new wave filmmakers… are distinguished by their desire and capacity for working in-between cultures and industries'.[46] For many filmmakers, this in-between space is found in the fantastic, which combines the universal with the local.

A general growing interest and access to popular visual culture coincided with (and contributed to) the growth of popularity of the fantastic. This new wave of Spanish fantastic films manifests in an incredible heterogeneity and chaotic eclecticism, influenced by American cinema, action comics, hard rock music, video games, and the Internet. From the early 1990s, the creation of a national fantastic cinema, successful with the public and critics, and capable of producing and maintaining a successful industrial and commercial infrastructure, allowed a new generation of filmmakers to create the films they wanted. The rise in the popularity of these films internationally can be linked to the proliferation and influence of film festivals. Since the mid-1990s, the growing popularity of film festivals, and those dedicated to the fantastic genres, such as the Sitges, Fantasia International Film Festival in Canada, and Fantastic Fest in the US, has allowed for greater exposure to and of the new Spanish fantastic cinema.

The Rise of Fantastic Film Festivals

According to the European Coordinator of Festivals, the number of festivals on the continent rose from 76 in 1995 to 154 in 2000.[47] Kenneth Turan gives the key causes of this proliferation to younger, more active filmmakers who wanted to reach a wider audience, audiences that wanted to see films outside of mainstream fare, and the ability of smaller producers and distributors to get exposure for their films.[48] While most of the long-running festivals, such as Berlinale and Venice International Film Festival, have general programmes with a wide variety of films, in the latter half of the twentieth century, and continuing today, there are more festivals specifically devoted either to a mode, subject, or social/cultural group. Festivals are now seen as an alternate method of distribution, particularly for smaller films that likely will not get a theatrical release. Part of the global cachet and appeal of festivals for both filmmakers and audiences is the ability to showcase and view work that might not otherwise be seen, either theatrically or in one's home.

Many new fantastic film festivals, such as Bucheon International Fantastic Film Festival in the Republic of Korea, Saskatoon Fantastic Film Festival in Canada, and Strasbourg European Fantastic Film Festival in France, have been founded over the past two decades, and this increase can be attributed to the rise in festivals in the previous decade, the readier availability of cheap filmmaking equipment which allowed more people to make films, and the growth of social media and networking that allowed for cheaper promotion of films and festivals. In addition, while larger, more prominent festivals such as Cannes Film Festival or TIFF, require premiere status, most genre film festivals do not, or at least only a local premiere. This allows fantastic films to travel a festival circuit for several months, with increasing publicity if they are well received by critics and/or fans. In the world of cinephiles, films that fall under categories such as 'midnight madness', 'extreme visions', or any fantastic-type category, had often been the unwelcome elephant in the proverbial room at festivals. In large part due to a devoted audience, however, such is the current popularity of genre film that in 2009, TIFF introduced a separate audience award for the Midnight Madness programme. Dirk Van Extergem notes that 'contemporary [genre] audiences... adopt movies, create cults around them, tour through them'.[49] This is not to suggest a homogeneous audience, but rather a commitment to the fantastic that is not found in the audience of other types of cinema. Contemporary Spanish fantastic filmmakers have taken advantage of this circuit, gaining publicity and audiences for their films as an alternative to national theatrical distribution.

Fantastic film festivals often stand out from general festivals, in no small part by virtue of their audiences. These audiences can be as varied as the films shown. Hostench notes that the audience for films at Sitges can range from young people who are interested in the latest trends in fantastic films, to those who focus on Asian cinema, to older spectators interested in documentaries or the more cerebral films, to fans that only come out to see some of the big-budget blockbuster films.[50] These types of festivals also tend to draw together fans that are not just there to see films, but also to interact with each other as a community. Gaz Bailey of Abertoir Wales' International Horror Festival, has found that for his audience, 'it's about seeing familiar faces year after year, being able to talk to other people about the films you've just seen, and the shared experience of watching the same films as everyone else for the duration of the festival'.[51] Many fans will return to one or a few of the same festivals every year, and so become familiar with a festival's particular programming.

Bailey has noted at his festival, that there is 'a sense of ownership among the fans. We like to include audiences as much as possible to create a warm and welcoming event, and we've noticed that people feel they are part of the festival themselves, rather than just a customer'.[52] Hostench also notes that, as more films are available on VOD and DVD, audiences are far more knowledgeable, and therefore more demanding about quality films. But with the rise of VOD especially, and a concurrent decline in DVD sales, many films (especially fantastic films) might never have a legal release in a particular country, and therefore festivals are the only potential (legal) means of seeing them. This continues to strengthen the sense of community for fans of fantastic films.

These developments have made it possible for Spanish fantastic films to adopt established formulae from countless preceding films from around the world, reinforced by the use of English, international financing and casts, and locations outside of Spain, making them postnational almost by default. Whether horror, science fiction, fantasy or thriller, these films have certain attributes that audiences have come to recognize. These attributes can be narrative, stylistic, or thematic, and while certain trends or tropes may be established within generic frameworks, the border between genres is not firm. While not alone in this, Spanish filmmakers have used genre hybridity to establish their cinema.

Genre and Intertextuality

Genre and its definition(s) have been seen as a triangle formed between the film-maker, the industry, and the spectator, with a specific set of linguistic and semiotic signifiers. But these signifiers can vary from film to film, and so too can their meaning, especially in different cultures. Stephen Neale writes:

> Genres do not consist only of films: they consist also, and equally, of specific systems of expectation and hypothesis that spectators bring with them to the cinema and that interact with film themselves during the course of the viewing process. Those systems provide spectators with a means of recognition and understanding.[53]

In other words, genres are formed both within and without the film; audiences determine a genre as much by expectation and by accumulation of knowledge through viewing as a filmmaker does through use of certain tropes. Films are classified within genres because they share certain themes, typical actions, characteristic mannerisms and intentions. Thomas Sobchack writes that a 'genre film... still differs fundamentally from other films by virtue of its reliance on preordained forms, known plots, recognizable characters and obvious iconographies'.[54] Rick Altman notes that a cinema based on genre depends on an audience that is knowledgeable of genre systems and trained to recognize generic plots and cues.[55] To arrive at a definition of a particular genre, a certain number of films that have similar conventions must be examined; but in order to choose those films, there must first be a definition by a generic connection. This apparent contradiction means that a film can often fall under several genre categories.

Cultural influences cannot be discounted in considering why and how certain genres are used in a given nation or culture. Andrew Tudor writes that the 'crucial factors which distinguish a genre are not only the characteristics inherent to the films themselves; they are also dependent on the particular culture within which they are operating'.[56] Genre is not only a product of the abstract filmmaker and/or spectator, but of an actual filmmaker and/or spectator, each of who is part of a particular culture, and will bring to any particular genre traits and attitudes towards what and how the expression of each genre manifests. For Raphaëlle Moine, genres are often carriers of ideology; she uses the example of Hollywood horror films of the 1930s, which evacuated social problems to an imaginary level through use of monsters such as Dracula and Frankenstein.[57] As noted, Fascist ideology meant that Spanish fantastic films of the 1960s had to avoid implicating Spain or the

Spanish people as the villain, and much of the 1980s saw a rejection of fantastic cinema as inappropriate for what was then a desire for a more realist cinema. In this case, it could be argued that the creation and proliferation of Spanish fantastic film was actually going against the governing ideology by its very existence.

As stated, when one introduces the word fantastic, it tends to bring an assumption of some kind of supernatural element, or something within the narrative or aesthetics of a film that is unrealistic in relation to an empirical understanding of the world. Bruce Kawin writes that genres are determined not only by their various elements, but also by the attitude towards those elements, and how they are 'deployed and interrelated'.[58] The fantastic genres differentiate themselves because of their attitude towards the unknown and fantastic genre filmmakers are more open in their curiosity towards realizing those attitudes in a direct manner.[59] In his work on the fantastic, Tzvetan Todorov considered any literary work fantastic if it followed three criteria:

1. The reader must consider the world presented in the book as concrete and hesitate between a natural and supernatural explanation of events.
2. This hesitation must also be experienced by the character(s).
3. The reader must reject all allegorical interpretations.[60]

He then created four subcategories of fantastic, which depend on the outcome of the story. An uncanny story has some hesitation and a rational conclusion, while the marvellous is a story in which the conclusion proved the existence of the fantastic.[61] Todorov did not, however, take into account the culture from which the fantastic emerged, a point to which Jackson takes exception. In her work, she writes that 'fantasy is produced within, and determined by, its social context'.[62] Jackson wishes to define the fantastic as a mode as opposed to a genre; from this mode emerge related genres. She defines three states of reality as they appear in literature:

1. The ordinary: a mimetic interpretation of the world
2. The eerie: a transitional or fantastic world
3. The trance-like, an imaginary or marvellous world

For Jackson, the fantastic exists in 'the hinterland between real and imaginary'.[63] She writes that the fantastic pushes toward non-signification; but this could be slightly reinterpreted, in that the fantastic is able to have local cultural significance, as well as content that can be interpreted and understood by an audience outside of the culture of origin, but one familiar with the fantastic genres. Jackson's definition of the fantastic as per the preceding list would apply to those films that do not present any supernatural elements but rather what she calls a general understanding of the fantastic as presenting 'some kind of existential anxiety and unease'.[64]

As Altman points out, the history of genre theory has trained critics to study a frequently predetermined corpus of films in order to discuss genre.[65] This approach can be limiting, however, as even within predetermined genres there can be great variety, and it fails to account for genre development. For Barry Langford, genre is a process, 'one in which different perspectives, needs and interests can and do deliver widely varying outcomes'.[66] For example, *Dracula* (Tod Browning, 1931) and *Buffy the Vampire Slayer* (Fran Rubel Kuzui, 1992) are both Hollywood vampire films, but because the horror genre has progressed over time, the films vary greatly in iconography and tone. Langford sees genre as a form of social practice, of ritual, myth or ideology, which 'broadly designates the ways in which genres rehearse and work through... shared cultural values and concerns by rendering them in symbolic narrative'.[67]

In his work on genre theory in the late 1990s, Altman examines two approaches to genre definition: the semantic and the syntactic. To define a genre by its semantics means to depend on a list of common iconography, traits, characters, shots, locations and sets – what Altman calls a genre's building blocks – that can be broadly applied. Meanwhile, the syntactic definition of genre favours the narration, themes, and aesthetic arrangement of these traits, which gives a film its explanatory power.[68] A given film could be placed in one genre or another, or a combination, by virtue of its semantics or syntax. The semantic approach uses easily identifiable qualities and vocabulary, and might apply to a larger number of films: the genre label 'science fiction' could be any film set in outer space or the future, or dealing with technology. By these criteria, for example, *Timecrimes* would be considered science fiction, as it involves time travel. The syntactic approach would look to the lexical arrangement of the narrative and themes, the meaning of its structure, and involve what Altman refers to as 'extratextual syntactic patterns' such as history or myth. By these criteria, *Timecrimes* might be considered a thriller, as it is syntactically arranged through its story of solving a mystery.

Altman proposes that genre can also be applied to a film when both semantics and syntax are accounted for and examined simultaneously, and it is this combination that can more fully explain the workings of genre within a given text; either there are a stable set of semantic meanings with changing syntax, or a syntax adopts different or new semantic traits.[69] To this, I would add that semantics and syntax can change not only in relation to the development of a genre, but according to the nation or culture in which a given film is produced, especially when considering how often a particular genre is used and how it is used. The semantic-syntax pairing has variations throughout film history. As genres develop over time and in different nations and cultures, so too the meanings of the semantics change and adapt with new syntaxes, or syntaxes can adopt different semantics and by extension change their meanings.

While fantastic films from around the world have had influence on the Spanish new wave, all of these films are connected by the fantastic genre's relatively stable set of semantics, which have syntactical variation in different nations and cultures. For example, from the Spanish Horror Boom era, Franco's *The Awful Dr Orlof* was in part inspired by French horror cinema such as *Eyes Without a Face* (*Les yeux sans visage*, Georges Franju, 1960), and *Nights of the Werewolf* (*Las noches del Hombre Lobo*, René Govar, 1968) took cues from Hammer and Universal monster films. *The Others* and *Darkness* (Jaume Balagueró, 2002) feature the semantic trope of the haunted house. But *The Others* draws inspiration for the representation and meaning of the haunted house from British gothic literature and cinema such as *The Innocents* (Jack Clayton, 1961), whereas *Darkness* turns more to Hollywood and American horror cinema, such as *Poltergeist* (Tobe Hooper, 1982).

I would argue that certain elements can be more or less stable in their association with certain genres, especially the fantastic, given the common usage of certain semantic tropes in fantastic cinema from around the world. But there can be adjustments to the meaning and representation of semantic elements, which I argue is part of a syntactical imposition. That is to say, part of a genre's development comes from changes made to semantics in different national cinemas and cultures, which form part of its syntactical arrangement. In light of the inconsistent development of Spanish fantastic film, contemporary works become open to wide interpretation and are formed by a multitude of generic influences.

If genre mixing has been a part of filmmaking since its inception (with western musicals, comedy romances, etc.), we might be entering a post-genre era. As Willis has pointed out, when the Spanish fantastic new wave began to rise, many critics and academics did not know how to classify these films that often did not adhere to traditional genre boundaries; nor did older audiences.[70] But the mixing of genres was and is a main feature of Spanish fantastic film. With an increase of intertextuality (references in one film to other films through narrative, themes, or tropes), comes the more difficult task of defining a film within a single, or even two or more, generic categories. Genres ebb and flow in popularity, especially those, such as the fantastic, that rely on specific signifiers. Combining different elements from each not only creates new hybrids, but also challenges the idea of grouping films together by genre classification, or least, obvious groupings, such as only films set in outer space, or only films set during the Spanish Civil War. Certainly, film promoters have used several genre terms to advertise and define films since the early twentieth century, and a film may be studied under one or more generic categories, but as its genre category may not be fixed, so its study cannot be fixed. Any and all cultural products, be they film or television, literature or music, high or low culture, refined or popular, and from any nation or culture, are open to reference, recycling, and rearticulation. With access to all comes incorporation of all; contemporary filmmakers working in the fantastic (and arguably non-fantastic) genres are no longer tied to previous classical forms of narration and representation, which keep generic semantics fixed.

This is also a factor in the rise in international co-productions. While these types of productions are common across genres, fantastic films often benefit the most due to greater exposure through the fan and festival systems. It also leads to what could be called a postnational cinema.

Postnational Cinema

There are several theories on the meaning of postnational cinema. For Jo Labanyi, 'the new postnational order means the definitive end of monolithic versions of national culture, dominated by the bourgeois canon of "good taste".[71] For Ulf Hannerz, postnationalism is a kind of cosmopolitanism, which in part is based on aesthetics and experimentation, involving an appreciation of cultural diversity.[72] For Pietari Kääpä, postnational cinema can either present new values, ideas and representations of a nation outside of its traditions, or explore them in presentation to a global audience.[73] With changing industrial and cultural conditions, such as international co-productions and influence from international cinema, traditional definitions of national cinemas must change as well.

Certainly, transnational film production is increasingly common and more often than not expected, particularly in a world culture where film festivals have become extremely important in promoting and distributing non-Hollywood cinema. The film website IMDB now lists the dates a film played at a festival; even though these are not technically release dates (at the moment, that term is still reserved for theatrical release), it indicates the importance of festival screenings. As discussed before, festivals are sometimes the only point of distribution for a film, or at least, lead to VOD, DVD and/or theatrical distribution. Many European co-productions of the mid-twentieth century were based around popular genres such as horror, spy films and spaghetti westerns, which are seen as more internationally viable due to lack of national specificity. In a world of increasing international co-production, is there such a thing as a national cinema, if companies from many nations produce a film? If a film is able to circulate around the world via the film festival network, for example, with which country will it be identified, or can any film with international production funding arguably be inherently postnational?

There are semantics and syntax that cross national borders or even cannot always be readily identified with a single national culture. Especially in the internet age, national borders cannot contain political and economic developments, cultural practices and identity. Contemporary cultures, especially those with open cultural borders, can become hybrid as they ingest cultural forms and norms from other nations. From a film's creative perspective this is true, though in terms of production and finance, many films are still produced solely within a single nation, such as *The Orphanage* and *Hierro*. But more than this, these hybrid cultural formations are constantly changing and adapting, and through that opportunity for adaptation, come different uses of semantics and syntax.

Thomas Elsaesser has written that there is no longer an entity that can strictly be called 'European Cinema', meaning that there is such diversity of culture within not only the continent, but individual countries, making it impossible to discuss them as a singular entity other than by their geographical location.[74] Studies of European cinema have traditionally focused on specific film movements within individual nations, such as the Czech New Wave or Scandinavian neo-noir. To this can be added the issue of genre; as most art cinema has been deemed to be expressive of national identity and culture, especially in the mid-twentieth century, much of genre film has been discounted from studies of European cinema, unless a specific movement, such as Italian giallo or the Hammer films from the UK, came from a single nation. Fantastic film is frequently considered a category unto itself, and thus not often mentioned or represented in national cinema studies; it is what Tim Bergfelder refers to as the supranational. Bergfelder writes that in order 'to establish a national identity for a particular film culture, features which transcend or contradict [realist] identity formations have either been neglected or marginalized, but also viewed as threatening'.[75] Horror, science fiction, fantasy and thriller films are frequently seen as mass-produced and consumed, and therefore inferior to high culture, upon which a national cinema is based. This is especially true of the fantastic in Spain, where it is seen as an imported genre. But imported culture can also be indigenized, given new meaning and significance, recycled and adapted for use in a new culture. In Spain, the fantastic genres are reinterpreted and recycled for both local and global consumption. I argue that these types of films have more universally recognizable semantics, and such semantics can be inflected with a culturally-specific syntax.

Postnational cinema is part of its national culture, and has a style that is translatable and understandable by a world cinema audience. The contemporary Spanish fantastic film can be considered national, in that its roots can be found through its cultural syntax, and postnational, in that it is a product of local, national and global forces and influences.

Outlining The Spanish Fantastic

The majority of films examined in this book were produced between 2001 and 2012, as this has been a particularly prolific period for Spanish fantastic film. The films are placed in thematic, as opposed to chronological, order. While a certain kind of development of the Spanish fantastic might be discernible from a chronological overview, a focus on the use of the fantastic genres through the semantic/syntactic lens affords a deeper perspective on how the different films and filmmakers are approaching the fantastic film.

Five of the chapters are devoted to directors whose work has been of particular influence and importance in the development and recognition of Spanish fantastic film. De la Iglesia, Amenábar, Balagueró, del Toro and Nacho Vigalondo all have different approaches to fantastic cinema, and styles that differ widely. Four of the chapters examine specific, important films from the contemporary period, paired through similar themes and/or motifs, such as the image of the haunted house, female protagonists, and the found-footage mode.

Film titles are given in English, with their original language title (if not English) afterwards. For those films never released outside of Spain, only the original Spanish title is listed. All box office figures come from Box Office Mojo, IMDB, and/or Spain's Ministry of Culture database.

1

Álex de la Iglesia: The Father of a Generation: *Mutant Action* and *The Day of the Beast*

In the early 1990s, it seemed that Spain had emerged from the shadow of the Fascist era. The economy was stable, and various sporting and cultural events in 1992, such as the Barcelona Olympics, the World's Fair in Seville, and the designation of Madrid as the European Capital of Culture, announced that the nation was now integrated into the democratic western world. It was this new Spain that cried out in a roar for a new cinema, one that challenged not only the dominant middle-of-the-road comedies and dramas of the 1980s, but also the vision of Spain perpetuated by those films. It was the dawn of a new era, where popular genre forms could be appropriated and put to use in Spanish cinema. At the forefront of this era was Álex de la Iglesia.

Born in 1965 in Bilbao into a middle-class family, de la Iglesia grew up as one of five children; his father was a professor of sociology, and his mother a painter. Their left-leaning ideology meant that de la Iglesia grew up exposed to a wide range of cultural influences. As a child, he watched Japanese animation and old movies, both Spanish and international, on television. He was as obsessed with Godzilla and Tintin as he was with Alfred Hitchcock and Luis Buñuel. He loved role-playing games and was fascinated by the African battles of World War II. At 13, inspired in part by the magazine 'Famous Monsters of Filmland', he began drawing comic books, which he would photocopy at school and give out to his friends. He took philosophy at university, but claims that he frequently fell asleep in class; his desire to compare the ancient Greek philosophies of Plotinus with Marvel comics found little support. He continued to work in the underground comic scene in Bilbao, and eventually found his way into art design and set decoration in television, working with Enrique Urbizu, and on short films, including Pablo Berger's 'Máma' (1988). De la Iglesia made his first short, 'Mirindas asesinas', in 1991, and it was popular enough to catch the attention of Pedro Almodóvar.

It was the cultural influences of underground comics and heavy metal music in his native Bilbao, with their 'fondness for gory violence, two-dimensional characterization, improbably proportioned women, and a generalized non-realist aesthetic', that lead to de la Iglesia's rejection of the dominant cinema of that time.[1] Although the themes and characters of their films are extremely different, Almodóvar saw a kindred spirit in de la Iglesia, who, like him, was challenging the hegemony of arthouse cinema, and wanted to use popular genre forms in new ways. El Deseo, Almodóvar's production company, was branching out to produce films not directed by Almodóvar, and wanted to get behind films that stretched the boundaries of Spanish cinema. El Deseo would become the initial production company behind *Mutant Action*.

De la Iglesia was not interested in what he described as the contemporary 'conspiracy of boredom' he saw in most mainstream Spanish film of the 1980s,[2] and combined cinematic influences from around the world. He would never deny the influence of non-Spanish filmmakers on his work, and often cites popular cinema directors such as Steven Spielberg and George Lucas, as well as auteur directors such as Ingmar Bergman. As for Spanish filmmakers, the influence of horror directors such as Jesús Franco and Paul Naschy can be seen, as well as Luis Berlanga and Juan Antonio Bardem. Certainly, de la Iglesia has adapted both early Spanish motifs and genres, and various foreign influences, to his particular brand of cinema, and he was prepared to wage an intellectual battle for the importance of fantastic cinema.

The fantastic in Spain has manifested over the centuries in forms that may be designated grotesque. Painters such as Diego Velázquez and Francisco de Goya created works that modern art historians have labelled grotesque: the former in his paintings of fools and dwarves of the seventeenth-century Spanish court, and the latter in his black paintings and *Capricho* prints.[3] During the nineteenth century, several Spanish authors wrote naturalist novels, which aimed to represent that which was repugnant to the senses, with descriptions of the vile and miserable; much of this work was found offensive by the traditionalist and religious establishment of Spain at the time.[4] Philip Thomson writes that the 'grotesque mode in art and literature tends to be prevalent in societies and eras marked by strife, radical change or disorientation'.[5] For many artists, the grotesque was viewed as 'an appropriate expression of the problematic nature of existence'.[6] Modernist artists used the grotesque through experimental and dislocated language, dissolution of personal identity, emphasis on discourse over story, and philosophical speculation.[7] Painters such as Salvador Dalí and Pablo Picasso explored the surreal (connected to the grotesque through themes and styles of dislocation and experimentation), as did Luis Buñuel and writer Federico García Lorca.

In Spain in the 1920s, a dramatic form called *esperpento* emerged, created by playwright Ramón del Valle-Inclán. Valle-Inclán's plays were affected by and reflected concerns over post-war trauma, social and political problems, industrial strife, and the shift to a more secular culture. He was criticizing the political practices and social decadence of his age through esperpento, which was 'the first attempt to convert the disparate tendencies of the grotesque into a genre', and included an 'absurd, deformed caricature [and] deranged vision of the human condition'.[8] It used grotesque characters, situations and language, but was also meant to be rooted in everyday experience. Esperpento is 'a concave mirror [that] catches, distorts, and ridicules appearance, so the dramatist reflects in a grotesque framework an imaginative elaboration of reality'.[9] Rather than an abandonment of realism, it is a deformation of realism. Most importantly, this deformation is meant to be both farcical and tragic.

Spain's postmodernist cultural era coincided with the introduction of democracy in 1977 and its integration into the European Union in 1986. The fantastic films that followed would frequently manifest parody and pastiche. Linda Hutcheon calls postmodern parody the mode of the ' "ex-centric"... of those who are marginalized by a dominant ideology'.[10] She writes that parody is part of a dialogical relationship between identification and distance; a parody might echo the past, but it also changes the past to suit its contemporary culture. De la Iglesia's films are what Ángel Sala refers to as 'neo-esperpento', updating its themes and style to a postmodern perspective, to represent the contemporary filmmaker and be applicable to a contemporary spectator.[11]

De la Iglesia and co-writer Jorge Guerricaechevarría made a point of avoiding themes that had dominated Spanish cinema in the 1980s, such as the Civil War and post-war era, realistically-portrayed social problems, and the recreation of childhood trauma. Like Valle-Inclán in his time, de la Iglesia looks at Spanish culture of the late twentieth century as a strange carnival, a mix of both the disparate regional cultures within Spain and the mainstream versus subcultures, with influence from Europe and North America. Jordi Sánchez Navarro writes that the 'cinema of Álex de la Iglesia is purely postmodern in its irreverent fusion of genres, a reinvention of film tradition and a hyperconscious appeal to pop culture'.[12]

De la Iglesia frequently collaborates with the same people, both behind and in front of the camera, such as Guerricaechevarría and actors Santiago Segura and Álex Angulo, which suggests their like-minded perspective and desire to bring certain themes and ideas of their generation to the screen. De la Iglesia's cinema is a fusion of the influences of popular culture combined with a sharp, critical eye on Spanish cinema and society that propelled him and his first two feature films into cult status.

Mutant Action

De la Iglesia and Guerricaechevarría showed their script for *Mutant Action*, at first a short film, to Almodóvar in 1991; it was Almodóvar who suggested that they make it into a feature. It was another two years before the film went into production, financed by El Deseo and CIBY 2000. At the time, they envisioned it as the nerviest, 'cheekiest' film in Spanish history. It was a moderate success at the Spanish box office, grossing a little under €1 million. But it went on to win three Goya Awards, for Best Production Design, Best Special Effects, and Best Make-Up. While some critics at the time wrote that it was empty of content, despite its appearance as a pastiche and homage to extreme genre cinema, the film is arguably criticizing not only 1990s Spanish society, but also the homogenous film culture it produced.

Set in a dystopian future, *Mutant Action* is the frenetic tale of a ragtag group of terrorists and their attempt to extort money through kidnapping Patricia, the daughter of a wealthy businessman. Their leader Ramón, recently released from prison, leads his mutant group in the slaughter of a wedding party and the kidnapping. Successful in their capture of Patricia, they set out to a distant planet to exchange her for the ransom. While en route, Ramon kills all but one of the mutants in turn in order to keep the ransom money for himself. Crash landing on the planet, now with a willing hostage, Ramon fights off both her father and the galactic military in a shoot-out in an Old West bar.

The film combines the semantics of several genres, including horror, science fiction, and western, through tropes of violence and murder, a futuristic setting both on Earth and in outer space, and its main characters who refuse civilization in favour of barbarism. The syntactical connection between semantic staples such as spaceships, saloons, and mutants highlights the film's intertextual references to other films in which those semantics usually appear. According to de la Iglesia, 'Science fiction was a reference to create a comedic situation… a way to make a savage comedy with black humor, very bloody, with hyperviolence, with a look between madness and filth'.[13] Peter Podol points out that black humour and the grotesque are often 'characterized by an inherent dialectical quality which is generally expressed in an extremely visual manner'.[14] The esperpento, as a distortion of realism, can be expressed through a combination of disparate visual elements that enhances the grotesquerie.

In her examination of contemporary Spanish film, Cristina Moreiras Menor sees postmodern Spanish culture as embracing image and appearance as a way of selling itself to Europe.[15] She interprets this through Fredric Jameson's theory of postmodernism, and specifically through three conditions of the relationship between the subject and their experience that she sees as characteristic of postmodernism:

1. A privileging of the culture of image and simulacrum
2. A lack of historicity
3. A waning of affect[16]

In *Mutant Action*, the first condition would seem to be met: the emphasis is placed on spectacle, images of violence, and the intertextuality of esperpento with the semantics of the various genres, privileging images and imagery through an emphasis on the body politic. The spectator is meant to engage with the visual flamboyance as much as the story. The second condition might seem to be met at first glance, given that the story is set in an unspecified future in a non-specific location. However, the presentation of the characters, and the deliberate use of and engagement with television within the story, belies this. The film is deliberately engaging with imagery found in contemporary Spanish culture and television, distorting it for political engagement.

The third condition is met in part: the excessive violence and its almost nonchalant portrayal suggests the waning of violence's effect on the contemporary spectator. However, it is not entirely met; Jameson might view postmodernism as ahistorical, but de la Iglesia is in part creating a history of the present. By setting the film in a dystopian future, as opposed to the present, de la Iglesia is making a critical point as to the ways in which contemporary Spanish film frequently ignores the more frivolous excesses of its society. It is both nonchalant in its portrayal of violence and excess, and making a critical point of both Spanish society's dismissal of underground culture and Spanish film's disdain for popular culture through that nonchalance. De la Iglesia is critically revisiting representations of Spanish society through the fantastic neo-esperpento mode.

The opening of the film suggests science fiction, given its futuristic setting as indicated through mise-en-scène, and also black comedy, given the absurdity of the opening actions and situation. Yet it also a heist, as indicated by the kidnapping and request for ransom, and a western, shown in the planet to which they travel, its desert setting, and the barbaric characters the mutants encounter there. De la Iglesia mutates (pun intended) traditional genre semantics, imposing a syntactic resignification on spectacle. Barry Keith Grant writes, '[g]enre movies may reflect, reinforce, question or subvert accepted ideology, but viewers enjoy them *as* movies whether they fulfill, violate or thwart conventions and expectations'.[17] While genre mixing does not in and of itself thwart expectations, the particular combination, representation and extremes of the film can be considered as a challenge to the dominant cinema of the 1980s rejected by de la Iglesia.

In classical realist cinema, production design is constructed so that the spectator may focus on the narrative. If a film is set in the present, production design elements such as set decoration are made to be 'invisible', meeting expectations so that they can be ignored in favour of character and action. However, in a fantastic film, the setting is frequently different from empirical reality, and the production design must create this fantastic world so that it can be understood in the context of the story. The production design in *Mutant Action* is retro-futurist (a mixture of future and contemporary signifiers), reminiscent of *Blade Runner* (Ridley Scott, 1982): the mutants drive their van beneath bridges, through a concrete jungle, which is filled with refuse both inanimate and human. Both films showing grungy streets populated by the underclasses juxtaposed against the extravagance of the rich, and indicators of both the imagined future (advanced technology) and the contemporary (parking meters). The design of the spaceship is similar to that in films from the 1970s, such as *Alien* (Ridley Scott, 1979), where the ships are dirty and their inhabitants seen performing crude maintenance (also associated with retro-futurist production design). In *Mutant Action*, the spectator would actively register the production design as part of the narrative, which connects more to a generic verisimilitude of past science fiction films, representing the retro-futuristic vision of science fiction that is both imagining the future, yet analogous to the present. The bright, pastel-coloured world of the wedding party and the dank, claustrophobic spaceship are exaggerated for contrasting effect, relating not only to the symbolism embedded in the narrative, but to the world on which it might be based, a neo-esperpentic distortion of contemporary Spanish culture.

Douglas Pye writes that tone, usually understood as a linguistic device of interpretation of words, translates to film through 'the various interrelated modes of... address and our response to them'.[18] The tone of *Mutant Action* is set in the first ten minutes. First, a scream is heard over a black screen. Then, an image appears of a man with an orange stuffed into his mouth. As the camera pans out, the screen shows a group of deformed men perpetrating this crime. Their physical appearance, their argument over what to do with the body, and their ineptitude are all exaggerations beyond both empirical reality and generic expectations, thus setting the comedic tone. As the mutants are leaving the crime scene, non-diegetic music plays: it is the theme song from the US television show *Mission: Impossible* (CBS, 1966–73). This reference juxtaposes a show that featured attractive government agents performing illegal yet necessary activities, against a decidedly unattractive group of mutants performing illegal and unnecessary activities, again emphasizing the comedic tone. The rap-rock theme song that plays over the credits is accompanied and juxtaposed by images showing the mutant gang attempting to look tough and failing. In addition, the intermedial use of the television news programme before and after the credits emphasizes the mutants' lack of beauty and monstrous activities in a 'factual' manner. The combination of the physical beauty of the victims from the opening scene, and the depraved manner of their death, invites a reading of the grotesque and the horror genre, while the tone is set as comedic.

From the screams of the mutants' murder victims, to the bright colours of the upper-class world, to the dark corridors of the spaceship, to the inescapable shoot-out in a bar, the violence in the film is spectacular in its excess, and yet represents a functional relationship with the ideological implications of the film's genres and themes. This is a comment not only on the social and cultural life of Spain at the time, where those on the margins were ignored, but also the state of film, in which such excesses were frowned upon. There are very few wide shots or long takes in the film, and almost all the settings, even those outdoors, give a feeling of claustrophobia, as if trapping the spectator within the represented violence. It is not necessarily the amount of violence that is at issue, but its context and portrayal. The humour that surrounds the horrifying events suggests a detachment from the violence exerted by the characters.

Wes Gehring identifies film parodies as dealing with cinematic norms as opposed to social norms; films dealing with the latter being what he would call satire.[19] If this is the case, *Mutant Action* can be identified as both a parody, as it thwarts expectations of cinematic norms through its unusual combination of semantics, and as satire, as it is arguably attacking social norms. Gehring also identifies two different kinds of parodies, one of which takes a subdued approach 'that manages comic deflation with eventual reaffirmation of the subject at hand'.[20] This can be applied to *Mutant Action*: the characters are not the ones being parodied, but rather doing the parodying. Hutcheon writes that parody 'is a form of imitation, but imitation characterized by ironic inversion not always at the expense of the parodied text'.[21] She characterizes this as repetition with critical distance, so it is the differences, and the meaning of those differences, that are emphasized. The

Fig. 1.1 The mutants plan their attack, *Mutant Action* (Metrodome, 2008)

film is not parodying either the genre semantics in use or the characters at their expense, but rather highlighting their usage through parody.

Valle-Inclán apparently meant his esperpento plays to be performed by puppets, to enhance the comic aspects of the tragedy.[22] This attempt at detachment from reality not only in the narrative but the aesthetic of the theatre genre suggests dehumanization, which is explored in *Mutant Action*. Ramón reminds the gang that, before he organized them, they were 'hospital refuse' and now they are 'mutants' [See Figure 1.1]. These two concepts are not far apart, but in the narrative, the former is given a negative connotation, and the latter a positive one. The giant's, the dwarf's and the conjoined twins' physical state may be natural, but it is rare and thereby grotesque and unacceptable. The mechanic wears a brace that limits the movement of his arms; César uses a hovercraft to travel and has a chest full of explosives; Ramón wears a mask that hides the half of his head that is without skin and partially covered by metal. Each of them is in effect de-humanized.

In her analysis of grotesque realism, Vivian Sobchack writes:

> Excessive representations of the body and its messier aspects might be read as containing critical and liberating potential – this, not only because certain social taboos are broken, but also because these excessive representations of the grotesquerie of being embodied are less 'allegorical' and fantastic than they are exaggerations of concrete conditions in the culture of which they are a part.[23]

For Sobchack, the concrete conditions of culture include a technologized view of the body, with cosmetic surgery and fitness centres representing this society's idea of the maintenance and repair of the perfect human body, away from an inherent grotesquerie. The mutants' grotesquerie, their dehumanization and the comedy it creates, is part of the esperpentic distortion of reality. De la Iglesia often uses masks and mannequins in his cinema; this is another example of his break from realism, and by extension from humanism. The gang is a metaphor for this dehumanization of the body: since they are not allowed in mainstream culture because of their deformities, they set out to destroy it. Bodybuilders, fitness instructors, and the wedding guests who parade around in high fashion and scream in terror at all that is not perfection, are also in part victims of the mechanization of the body, but they have triumphed socially, and so the mutants retaliate. During the 1980s, Spanish visual media seemed obsessed with physical beauty, and television shows stressing the importance of possessing a perfect body were ubiquitous.[24] To show the grotesque attacking the beautiful goes far beyond allegory to become a direct reflection on the contemporary Spanish society of the 1990s.

This spectacle is further emphasized by the use of news programmes and reality television that feature the mutants' actions, providing another point of intermediality between cinema and television. The engagement between cinema and television plays with the perception of the medium within the story, and how by extension it affects the spectator's conception of a story. De la Iglesia uses television to highlight the obsession with beauty and perfection, and society's obsession with the televising of violent events. In the second scene of the film, a news reporter relates the terrorist activities of the mutants. Rather than the footage featuring in a corner of the screen with the television news studio occupying the frame, the footage takes up the entirety of the screen, with the reporter's image in one corner. The audience is the spectator of the film, but also the society in the film that watches this news. In the final shoot-out, the news crew arrives before Orujo. As Ramón and Orujo argue, the film crew pans back and forth between the two; this is a parody not only of news, but also of so-called reality television shows, which, like esperpento, distort reality in order to appeal to the spectator's desire for spectacle. The spectator witnesses the spectacle, and the creation of the spectacle. Through its different manifestations of cinema spectatorship, the scene forces the spectator to confront and question that relation.

Mutant Action does not seek to hide its parody and satire of cinematic or social norms. As an intertext of generic semantics from science fiction, western, horror and action films, and through the inclusion of intertextuality with television, the film arguably began the contemporary Spanish fantastic film renaissance. It bypasses the dominant narrative themes and style of much of 1980s Spanish film in favour of a postmodern parody in order to approach and critique, from the outside, mainstream Spanish culture and cinema.

The Day of the Beast

When *The Day of the Beast* was released in 1995, many Spanish critics dismissed it as 'a shallow inquiry into the mid-1990s sociocultural milieu'.[25] That criticism fell on deaf ears. The film was a hit in Spain, speaking to a generation who finally saw themselves represented on screen. It was viewed by more than one million people in its home country, and won several Goya awards, including Best Director, and Best New Actor for Santiago Segura. Disaffection with the government and the Catholic Church, high youth unemployment through the 1980s, and growing concerns over the corruption and criminality of city life, combined with what was often seen as the slow dilution of Spanish national identity and the absorption into European and international consumer market, found a means of expression in the postmodern, grotesque humour of filmmakers such as de la Iglesia.

The idea for the film was actually conceived by de la Iglesia and Guerricaechevarría before they began *Mutant Action*. The script went through four drafts, and had begun with a much darker and more violent tone, eventually moving more towards comedy. With no big-name stars and subject matter that would be far more disagreeable to many in political power, it was arguably a far bigger risk than de la Iglesia's first feature. As a vision of something between *Vertigo* (Alfred Hitchcock, 1958) and Franz Kafka, its esperpentic comedy is a searing portrait of contemporary Madrid and Spain, an infernal vision of apocalypse toned as much for laughter as horror.

The Day of the Beast follows Father Ángel, a Jesuit theologian and priest, who discovers that the Antichrist will be born in Madrid on Christmas Day. In order to stop the destruction of the world, he goes to Madrid and proceeds to commit evil deeds to get the attention of the Devil and thus defeat him. José María, who introduces himself as a 'metal head and Satanist', gleefully agrees to help Father Ángel perform a satanic ritual to make contact with the Devil. Father Ángel forcibly recruits Cavan, the popular host of a television show on the occult, to his endeavour. After performing the ritual, the three men make their way to a tower block to confront Satan. While Father Ángel believes he sees Satan in the flesh, it might also be a projection of his mind onto a man who is actually just a criminal thug. While Father Ángel shoots Satan/the thug, and apparently saves the world, he and Cavan are left as homeless bums.

The Day of the Beast became a representation of the conflict of tradition versus modernity, rural versus urban values, and the past versus the future. By situating the film in its contemporary time, using characters who could easily be identified – the country priest (representing the old Spain and the power of the Church), the urban freak (representing the underground culture of new urban life), and the television opportunist (representing the greed and commercialism of the new era) – and setting it in Madrid, de la Iglesia and Guerricaechevarría made a film not only for their immediate circle of colleagues and fans, but for the larger public. The esperpentic tradition that seeks to reflect and critique on politics, culture and society is updated and transferred to the screen and to different generic conventions.

The original target audience for the film was likely one that had not seen itself reflected in the dominant Spanish cinema of the 1980s and early 1990s. And yet, this film is exploring many of the same themes as that cinema: the decay of the urban centre, the collapse of the influence of the Catholic Church, the dominance of trash television, and the rise of crime, but this time it uses and adjusts the semantics of horror and comedy in its representation. According to Rosanna Maule, the violence of the new generation is often categorized as exploitative, commercial, non-political and non-social in its critique of contemporary society.[26] That is to say, it is not a form of anti-Francoism or exploration of personal or historical trauma, as was much of the violence in films of the previous decade, but rather a reaction to how that violence was portrayed, and the lack of attention to spectators from more underground and youth cultures. Marsha Kinder would connect the roots of this aesthetic to the violence depicted by Goya in the eighteenth century, which was a form of social critique, specifically questioning the glorification of heroes or the rationalization of violence.[27] Violence in twentieth-century Spanish cinema is often associated with an anti-Franco perspective, such as in *Poachers* (*Furtivos*, José Luis Borau, 1975), which explores rural family violence in the 1970s, and *Lovers: A True Story* (*Amantes*, Vicente Aranda, 1990), which explores sexual violence in the 1950s. The combination of violence and comedy has a history in Spanish art, of both high and low cultural status. By eroding the distinction between high and low culture, popular cinema can examine social issues, much as Valle-Inclán used the grotesque in his esperpento plays as social commentary.

The opening scene of *The Day of the Beast* is reminiscent of 1970s horror films that dealt with religion and/or had Catholic priests as main characters, such as *The Exorcist* (William Friedkin, 1973) and *The Omen* (Richard Donner, 1976). The first scene shows Father Ángel entering a church; he tells his superior that he has uncovered some biblical code, and he must commit evil in order to meet the devil and thereby stop a greater evil. A moment later, a giant cross flattens his superior to death, again reminiscent of scenes from *The Omen* where anyone who would stand in the way of Satan is killed. And yet, even in a moment of horror, the tone of the scene is deliberately comic, in direct parody of the films mentioned above.

This is because the film addresses the conventions of this type of horror subgenre; its appearance in Spanish film, twenty years after its predecessors, makes it comic in its nostalgia. Father Ángel survives, and as the opening credits roll, he is shown arriving in Madrid, and the music, which had at first been church bells, becomes heavy metal grunge. As the spectator witnesses Father Ángel ignoring the pleas of a homeless woman, stealing money from a blind man, and pushing a mime down a flight of stairs, the likely reaction would again be a combination of horror and laughter. The use of a Catholic priest to do evil in a comical manner is a reinscription of this semantic of the horror genre into a different syntactical relationship with its themes and representations of religion and alternative culture.

Conquest by Muslims from Northern Africa in the eighth century, and a large medieval Jewish population, meant Spain was briefly a multifaith mecca.[28] The fourteenth to sixteenth centuries saw the emergence of the Counter-Reformation, a backlash against Protestant reform. This time also saw the Spanish Inquisition, which forced the vast majority of Jews and Muslims either to convert or to leave Spain on pain of death.[29] During the Fascist years, the Church had unprecedented power, with sole control of education and general morality, bringing the legal and education systems in line with Catholic moral codes and behaviours.[30] Those who supported the Republicans saw the Church and its clergy as a class enemy that legitimized an unjust government.

During the transition to democracy, the Church lost control over education and social services, and the crimes of the Church, such as rampant child abuse, were made public.[31] This is not to say that Spain is no longer a Catholic country, or that many Spaniards are no longer Catholics; but the influence of the Catholic Church began to decline rapidly in the late twentieth century. However, the tenets and rituals of Catholicism remain embedded in Spanish culture. Catholicism is a very theatrical religion, with specific rituals, performances, and sacred objects. Representations of Catholicism in films such as those aforementioned are often meant to invoke the experience of the fantastic. Father Ángel is convinced that a ritual must be performed, one that would go against a secular perspective that the blood of a virgin holds no magical powers. He is attempting to reconcile his Catholic beliefs with a crisis in a secular culture in a rather theatrical fashion. The theatricality of religion in the contemporary age also extends to its appropriation by secular culture: the album covers of the various heavy metal bands that Father Ángel finds are dominated by 'satanic' images, but are these signs of true Satanic worship, or merely a marketing ploy? The comedy arises not only from this seeming disregard for historical context, but also from his misinterpretation. Satanism becomes a superficial form of rebellion, a kind of satiric lifestyle option;

Fig. 1.2 Father Ángel gets ready to meet the Devil, *The Day of the Beast* (Anolis Entertainment, 2007)

for example, José María sings lines from *Jesus Christ Superstar* (Norman Jewison, 1973), another commercialization of a biblical story. In the same way, Cavan's television show is a neo-esperpentic distortion of ancient ritual Catholicism, adapted and commercialized for monetary gain.

In Spanish cinema of the Fascist regime, the Church was portrayed in a positive manner, such as in José Antonio Nieves Conde's *Balarrasa* (1951), in which a soldier becomes a priest after the Civil War, and Ramón Comas's *El padre Coplillas* (1968), about a singing priest raising money for charity. However, in 1979, Jesús Franco made a horror film, *The Sadist of Notre Dame* (*El sádico de Notre Dame*), in which a priest 'exorcizes' women by killing them. For Franco, the film was a reaction against what he saw as the lack of progress in Spanish politics and the control that the Catholic Church continued to have over the public's lives.[32] American horror films of the 1970s still showed the Catholic priest as something of a wizard, able to exorcize demons and read signs of impending doom. Andrew Greeley writes that when a priest presides over the sacrament, 'he stands in the role of Jesus the high priest and is touched therefore lightly but permanently by the transcendent'.[33] There is something of the fantastic in the role of the priest, who is seen as an extension of God, able to offer forgiveness and deliver restitution to his flock. The priest metaphorically turns wine and bread into the blood and bread of Christ during communion, and these acts of transubstantiation confirm the priest as existing in both the sacred (holy or transcendent) and profane (worldly) realms.

In *The Day of the Beast*, the priest is a hero, but a comedic one. The film is emphasizing that a new type of 'priest' exists on television in the role of Cavan, and the theologian/priest as represented by Father Ángel is no longer relatable for, nor can he relate to, the new Spain. This is a culturally-specific syntactical twist on the horror semantic character of the Catholic priest. He is hapless in his lack of understanding of the new urban life, and comic in his attempts to save a world whose signs and methods he does not understand. Father Ángel is a late-twentieth-century comic hero, entering a strange carnivalesque world for which he is ill prepared. He is what Robert Torrance would call 'the hero who commits the folly of stepping forth from the sheltered sphere… to confront reality with his uncompromising ideal [and thus] will be intrinsically and unavoidable comic'.[34] As a hero, Father Ángel is a leader, superior to other men, but not to the environment, in that what he does is subject to social criticism and the order of nature. This is in keeping with the Catholic priest as seen in American films; even Father Karras in *The Exorcist*, is a hero, sacrificing himself for the good of mankind, but still not above social criticism. Father Ángel follows a fairly standard outline of the hero's journey. He is given, or he gives himself, a task that will take him outside of his own realm, the sacred, and into the unknown. The world he is about to enter is the profane, especially as this city, Madrid, is in one shot referred to as the 'Gate to Europe… [symbol] of the avarice and corruption of recent times and the incomplete modernization of a struggling state'.[35] Father Ángel metaphorically annihilates himself through sin in order to achieve his goal, and his ignorance and ineptitude at being evil adds to the comedy. He reveals his plan to Cavan, and he admits to Mina that he is attempting to get some of her virgin blood: hardly the actions of a shrewd criminal mastermind. Whether or not Father Ángel defeats the actual antichrist or merely a criminal might be beside the point [See Figure 1.2]. His return to the world is not necessarily a triumphant one; while he believes he has saved the world, no one is aware of his accomplishment. As a Catholic priest, it is fitting that he does not receive any monetary compensation for his trouble. He walks away only with miniature boxing gloves, in which José María had kept his drug stash, as reminder and reward, for those who won the match and saved the world.

If Father Ángel is a hero, then every hero must have both his sidekick and his trickster. José María is his sidekick, or perhaps his court jester. He is not the classic choice as a helper to the hero: he has the appetite and thirst typical of the carnivalesque, with a love of abundance in food, sex and adventure. As Mikhail Bahktin notes, in Renaissance times the 'grotesque body [was] not separated from the rest of the world. It [was] unfinished, outgrow[ing] itself, transgress[ing] its own limit'.[36] José María is one of the marginalized of Spanish society, living in the cultural underground and considering himself a Satanist – not necessarily out of true belief, but out of rebellion against the establishment. This kind of anti-hero 'often employs gutter speech, tabooed expression, insulting and painfully vulgar signs, but he may also encrypt his wisdom or commentary in opacities difficult to decode'.[37] He is more interested in the contents of Cavan's home than the ritual, he abandons his post to look after his car, and he disregards his safety while climbing on the Schweppes sign. But in the end, he sacrifices himself to save Father Ángel.

Cavan is the trickster: a hero who does not want to change the world, but to play with it. Dean Miller writes that in Native American folklore, 'the energy of... the trickster-hero is drawn from or radiates from that other, powerfully energized and formative mythic realm, and his plans and acts display the closest conformance to patterns originally set by his mythic kinsman'.[38] Cavan receives his power from religious symbols and rituals that he manipulates for his own purpose. When Father Ángel and José María invade Cavan's apartment and tell him their plan, Cavan treats their request as a joke. He admits that the book he wrote on Satanic rituals is a fake and he has no belief that the devil exists. On the hero and popular culture, Roger Rollin writes that a mass audience gives the contemporary hero his or her status today: he or she is a celebrity. The celebrity is morally neutral, 'and thus to participate in his or her cult is to celebrate the superficial, to ritualize emptiness'.[39] At the end of the film, Cavan believes Father Ángel's story of the devil and tries to be a hero, but in the final scene he laments the lack of knowledge of their deed on the part of the public. Cavan only grudgingly accepts his fate as the unsung hero.

In Spain, one of the largest sources of celebrity in the 1980s was television. Unlike Spanish cinema, television was and is hugely popular. According to Paul Julian Smith, a top-rated drama or comedy can reach a larger audience in a single night than all Spanish film can reach in an entire year.[40] As of 2006, the average viewer watched four hours of television per day, and in the late 1990s, channels were dominated by locally produced shows. The quality of television (or lack thereof) lead to this era being referred to as the 'years of lead', when television programmes sounded a false alarm of social upheaval while focusing on the trivial.[41] In the early 1990s, much of television was dominated by reality and talk shows. Many critics felt these programmes were reductionist, showed contempt for privacy or respect, and were frequently untruthful and manipulative. Programmes such as *La máquina de la verdad* (Telecinco, 1992–94), hosted by Julián Lago (considered in the Spanish press as having no journalistic ethics and capable of doing anything to gain an audience), were seen as pushing far past the limits of public decency, particularly in efforts to gain the youth audience.

If Catholicism is a spectacular religion, it can find no better home than television, and Cavan's show manipulates this theatricality into trash television.

It is like a carnival sideshow, and claims to be of the occult, but this occult is a mixture of New Age, Paganism, and Catholicism (he performs a Catholic ritual exorcism on a young boy). Whereas in *The Exorcist*, where it is done behind closed doors, Cavan's show brings it out into the open. Cavan becomes a hero for saving this boy from the devil. He has, in effect, taken the place of the priest in contemporary Spanish society. Cavan is given his heroism, and his celebrity, from the outside, from the ordinary people, as opposed to traditional institutions. His show, 'Zona oscura', is presented as reality/talk show; programmes presented as such would have the spectator believe that what they are seeing is real, and at the same time that it is dramatized. Cavan becomes a priest for the new age, and a celebrity. As the trickster-hero, he plays with his audience's religious beliefs, steeped in Catholicism, and the 'new age' of the cult of television. He and Father Ángel are both unable to return to the worlds that they had left in order to vanquish the devil: Cavan to the world of celebrity, and Father Ángel to the world of theological study. Umberto Eco writes, 'the tragic seems to deal with "eternal" problems… while comedy seems to be more closely linked to specific social habits'.[42] The comedic end for these two heroes is linked to the social world they inhabit: each is a priest, a hero of their world; but in order to save that world, they had to sacrifice that which would maintain their heroic status.

Rather than just making comedic mockery of Spanish Catholicism, *The Day of the Beast* re-engages with it in an attack on contemporary politics and the social landscape, exploring the larger questions that pertain to contemporary political and social change, and to cinematic rebellion. Presented as a comedic fable of a hero's journey, the film wanders the streets of Spanish life as Father Ángel wanders the streets of Madrid, recording social change and the underbelly of culture, which had up to this point been ignored, and engaging with the fantastic as reflected at the edge of the millennium.

To date, de la Iglesia has made 13 feature films (including one documentary), five shorts, and a nine-episode television series. He has won numerous awards at film festivals around the world, though still only one Goya for his direction of *The Day of the Beast*. While his films have had varying degrees of box office success, his cult status among fantastic film fans both in Spain and around the world is unquestionable. His integration of older Spanish artistic forms with outside influences set a precedent for younger filmmakers. His extreme visions, both from a narrative and aesthetic perspective, helped launch the new wave of Spanish fantastic film, one that could reflect on Spanish culture and society, but more importantly, use the fantastic genres as a means of expression.

2

Heroes and Villains: *The Birthday* and *The Backwoods*

Once filmmakers such as Álex de la Iglesia had taken Spanish fantastic film in a new direction, a generation followed. These new filmmakers were not necessarily copying those before them; rather, they saw the potential of the fantastic mode and the possibility of making these kinds of films in Spain. Eugenio Mira and Koldo Serra are two such filmmakers. Both born in the mid-1970s, they were exposed to fantastic cinema from around the world as well as European auteur and arthouse films. For them, it was not only the works of Steven Spielberg and George Lucas, but also Joe Dante, Robert Zemekis, and the Amblin Entertainment adventure films that were inspirational. With their first feature films, *The Birthday* (Eugenio Mira, 2006) and *The Backwoods* by Serra, the filmmakers engaged with postmodern pastiche, reworking influences from American genres and fantastic iconographies – fantasy and comedy in the case of *The Birthday*, and the rural thriller in *The Backwoods* – and fashioning them with a style and narrative that arguably has stronger roots in more pessimistic European film. *The Birthday* engages with the neo-esperpento and narrative surrealism, while *The Backwoods* reworks the rural thriller in a contemporary Spanish context.

According to Marcel Durán, Spanish surrealism always had a predilection for the grotesque, a 'bizarre interpretation of the world, subjective landscapes and distorted mirrors'.[1] Of Max Estrella, the protagonist of Ramon del Valle-Inclán's play *Bohemian Lights*, Robert Lima writes that his life is a distorted existence that: 'moves steadily towards its tragic denouement while the grotesqueries of human existence become increasingly visible in the incidence of irony, cynicism, dissonance, satire, baseness, lewdness, opportunism, mockery and alienation'.[2] This is what happens to the main character in *The Birthday*. *The Birthday* offers the spectator a reassessment and examination of the idea of the hero. The main character is of a kind that would normally be used in a supporting role as comic relief, the butt of the jokes or the scapegoat. However, popular cinema has redefined the idea of the hero. Robert Torrance writes that the twentieth century, 'has been preeminently an era where the comic hero… has been almost the only authentic hero of any kind to emerge', after two world wars and great political and social upheaval.[3] Beginning with Charlie Chaplin's character of the Tramp, via later comedians as Jerry Lewis in the US and Cantiflas in Mexico, to more recent comedic actors such as Will Ferrell and Hitoshi Matsumoto, the comic hero has moved from the sidelines to the centre. All of these performers share a similar image: none are the handsome, virile hero of classical literature, and all rely on physical comedy and a sense of being out of place in their social environments to generate comedy. This is not to suggest that there are not contemporary dramatic heroes as well; merely that, through its rising prominence, the comic figure can be considered a hero as much as the dramatic one. This is seen in much of the American fantastic cinema of the 1980s, such as *Close Encounters of the Third Kind* (Steven Spielberg, 1977) and *The Goonies* (Richard Donner, 1985), as well as the teen films such as *The Breakfast Club* (John Hughes, 1985) and *Some Kind of Wonderful* (Howard Deutch, 1987). In these, the hero shifts from the more traditional, physically attractive man to the nerd or outsider, a character type recycled in *The Birthday*.

Rural thrillers have often been associated with or seen as developing from the American western, a genre in which the landscape is essential to the story.[4] The rural thriller extends from the urbanite's encounter with and reaction to the rural landscape and its inhabitants. The genre flourished in the 1970s in several American films, such as *Straw Dogs* (Sam Peckinpah, 1971), *I Spit on Your Grave* (Meir Zarchi, 1971), *Deliverance* (John Boorman, 1972), and *Last House on the Left* (Wes Craven, 1972). Films such as these depict people from urban centres entering the rural, and having an initial conflict with the locals that results in violence and/ or death. According to Sally Faulkner, much of Spanish nationalism is rooted in agrarian nostalgia, seen frequently in Francoist cinema of the 1940s and 1950s that idealized rural culture; this came from an ideology of self-sufficiency, noble peasantry, and the concept of the rural as a peaceful forest.[5] This began to change in the 1960s and 1970s, with films such as *The Hunt* (*La caza*, Carlos Saura, 1966) and *Poachers*, which articulated political dissent through the rural film. The Civil War and its continuing effect on Spanish culture was either symbolically restaged or recalled specifically in the rural setting.[6] The construction of what could be seen as the postnational space in film means there is often an emphasis on representing the general rural against the general urban, regardless of location or history, and the disruption and violence that can ensue. This is not to suggest that certain settings, such as that in *The Backwoods*, are not deliberate or significant; rather, that specific knowledge of the history of these spaces is less relevant than the wider implication of the rural space as such. Donald Melbye writes, while 'a landscape may remain constant… its figurative meanings are ever-changing according to the inherent mutability of human cultural presence'.[7] The folksy countryside becomes haunted by superstition and abuse in *The Backwoods*, moving the film in a somewhat different direction that usually found in American rural thrillers.

In Hollywood films, the hero and villain are more or less identifiable. While the hero might not always be in the right, or perform actions that could always be considered 'heroic', the line between doing what is necessary and doing what is right is clear, and usually the outcome is in the hero's favour. In films such as *The Goonies* and *Some Kind of Wonderful*, the outsider hero triumphs, even if that triumph doesn't always appear to be anticipated at the beginning of the film. In *Deliverance* and *Straw Dogs*, even though the 'heroes' can still be seen as invading a particular space to which they do not belong, they are clearly shown as forced into negative actions by circumstances by the more 'villainous' characters around them. In *The Birthday*, the hero, Norman, has his heroism thrust upon him, and while he does (eventually) act in a heroic fashion, the ambiguous ending leaves doubt as to whether he has triumphed. In *The Backwoods*, the line between the heroes and villains is blurred; both sides commit terrible and unnecessary acts and the conclusion raises doubts as to one side being victorious over the other.

Richard Dyer writes that genre pastiche signals imitation and 'mobilizes the qualities of and indicates a relationship with prior works'.[8] There is no denying *The Birthday*'s and *The Backwoods*'s respective American and genre cinema influences, nor would Mira or Serra attempt denial. But it is a relationship with prior works, as opposed to a direct imitation. The semantics are there: in the case of *The Birthday*, the romance between the outsider and the popular girl, the comedy of misunderstanding and fantastical events, the loser who becomes the hero; in *The Backwoods*, it is the outsiders in the unknown, rural space, resentment from the locals, and the violence which ensues. But it is through their syntax, the placement of the various influences, that shows a more European, and Spanish, approach to their different fantastic modes.

Both films were released in the last two months of 2006, and although neither was successful at the Spanish national box office, each grossing less than €300,000, both have become cult favourites among cinephiles. Both are first feature films by their respective directors, and are in English, an indicator not only of the influence of outside cinema, but also the influence of market forces and the desire, and perhaps necessity, to reach a wider audience.

The Birthday

Among the films in this book and Spanish fantastic film in general, *The Birthday* is arguably the hardest to classify in a particular genre. It is fantastical, as there are supernatural elements, but it is not classic fantasy; it is frightening at points, but it's not horror; it's a comedy born out of social dysfunction, but it is very dark. Indeed, of all the contemporary Spanish fantastic films that could call themselves neo-esperpento, *The Birthday* fulfils that label not only in style, but also in content. Yet its postmodern pastiche of influences creates a singular and unique product.

Mira and co-screenwriter Mikel Alvariño are children of the 1980s, a time when Spain was flooded with cultural products from around the world. In particular, it was flooded with American popular culture, blockbuster films from Hollywood, and the increased use of the young adult as a main character. And yet, *The Birthday* displays influences from American independent film and European art cinema, rather than traditional Hollywood fare. The American location and setting in the past are themselves neo-esperpentic devices, distorting the contemporary empirical reality and setting the film as a neo-esperpento fantasy.

Mira's short film 'Fade' (2000) had a successful run on the film festival circuit, and producer Ibon Cormenzana approached him about making a feature film. Mira and Alvariño discussed their various 80s film influences, as well as the influence of European auteurs such as Luis Berlanga and Ingmar Bergman. For Alvariño, 'these were stories about families, teenagers, told through the fantastic, and we wanted to do that too. In Spain, we grew up watching that American way of life, and it's so close to us. It's not too difficult to see ourselves in that world to tell a story'.[9]

It is 1987, and Norman Forrester is attending the birthday party of the father of his rich girlfriend, Alison, at her family's historical hotel in Baltimore. Norman tries to ingratiate himself to the family, embarrasses Alison, and tries to avoid a group of frat boys from his old school. Midway through the evening, he is informed by one of the hotel waiters that a religious cult intends to resurrect an ancient god that evening, and he needs Norman's help in order to stop the cult. Norman must then juggle his duty to his girlfriend with his forced role as hero.

Mira and Alvariño decided that the film would have certain rules: it would be set in a single location, the story would be told in real time, and it would have the point of view of a single character, who would be in every shot. On top of this, when writing the script, they tried to imitate American 1980s film dialogue, in Spanish, apparently even reciting the dialogue to each other in the dubbing style of

Spanish actors. To them, the story of the 'loser' who gets the most popular girl in school was one they had seen before, but the story always ended when the couple first got together; they wanted to show what would happen if that couple had been together for a while. Again, this is a far more European, somewhat pessimistic perspective than most American/Hollywood cinema would allow. For Alvariño, it was almost a comedic fantastic version of *Last Year in Marienbad* (*L'année dernière á Marienbad*, Alain Resnais, 1961), and this shows in its neo-esperpento qualities.

In Valle-Inclán's *Bohemian Lights*, the main character Max says that, 'the tragic sense of Spanish life can only be rendered through an aesthetic that is systematically deformed'.[10] The concave mirror through which *The Birthday* is viewed allows a slow degradation and deformation of a world the spectator thinks they know. In *Bohemian Lights*, Max wanders the streets of Madrid, which are full of maddening and exaggerated characters, as he tries to save his existence and perhaps that of his world as well. In *The Birthday*, Norman wanders around a hotel, which is full of maddening and exaggerated characters, trying to save his existence and that of his world as well. But whereas Valle-Inclán's play was a study in modernist surrealism, the film is a study in postmodern surrealism, generic homage, and the hero – or more accurately, the anti-hero.

The film follows a fantastic scenario, in that there is an ancient god being resurrected to wreak havoc on the world. A classically-formed narrative drives the story (in that the action is propelled by cause and effect), but the mise-en-scène and subjective perspective suggests an allegiance to art cinema traditions of authorial expression. The film begins as a comedy, but at the midway point turns into fantasy as well. While Norman has been in this carnivalesque world since the beginning of the film, his quest only starts at this point. Films can have a generic verisimilitude, and a broader social or cultural verisimilitude. The social verisimilitude of comedy can be recognized through the misfit or loser out of place in high society. The addition of a fantastic element is part of the syntactic distortion in generic verisimilitude that appeals to a spectator versed in both European art cinema and Hollywood fantastic films, and who is more able to adjust to a change in generic direction.

The Birthday opens with a title card that informs the viewer that they are about to watch 'THE MOST AMAZING <u>117</u> MINUTES IN THE LIFE OF NORMAN FORRESTER'. The first shot of the film gives a second title card, with the location (Baltimore MD, a city that can stand in as a generic representation of eastern America, as well as a nod to the American filmmakers that Mira loved), and a date (November 24th 1987, 8:17pm). Setting the story in an unlikely and unfamiliar city, in the past, gives the impression of a fantastic tale, especially as it is accompanied by a strange instrumental rendition of a pop song from the 1960s.[11] 'It's My Party' is likely familiar to the spectator as a sad song about an unfortunate birthday party, giving a hint that the party within the film will also end in disaster. Above this title card is the image of a 1920s art deco-styled elevator, an architectural mode reaching even further into the past. Indeed, this is nostalgia within nostalgia: the film was made in 2005, set in 1987, features a pop song from 1963, and interior design from the 1920s. There is constant reinforcement of intertextuality, not only between genres and films, but also between other cultural and artistic modes, and these differences reinforce the fantastic mode.

The elevator doors open, and Norman appears; he hesitates and looks around before exiting. All around him is black; the audience is not given the location of the elevator for several seconds. The mode of the fantastic is set by information given to the viewer through context (setting, time) and observation (a darkened space entered into by the main character). Norman begins walking into the corridor before lights reveal it as such, further giving an impression of the unknown, leaving the spectator more likely to be open to generic variations. Through the opening title cards and the opening shot of the solitary image in a sea of black, the visual and audio cues establish a fantastic mode that the spectator will carry with them even through what is the seeming realism of the opening scenes.

The film is told entirely from Norman's perspective; not only does the camera convey everything that Norman sees and hears, but he is in almost every shot. The camera (which for the majority of the film is a steadicam) is not just a window, but also that concave mirror which is distorting reality for Norman, and at the same time allowing the spectator to see the effect of that distortion on Norman. In one scene, Norman is seated at a dinner table with Alison, her father, and various family members. The camera circles in the middle of the table, focusing on the different characters before swinging back around to Norman. The camera does not linger on the person speaking, rather it acts as Norman's (and the spectator's) eyes and ears as he attempts to interpret and understand his position in the group. The grotesque is interested in the body in exaggerated form; the camera exaggerates the body through spinning in this strange circle, and in making the camera an extension of Norman's body and thus the spectator's.

As the film continues, the camera movement becomes more intent on close-ups and exaggerated movements to convey Norman's increasingly erratic emotional state and his perspective on the increasingly absurd narrative. The perception of the film is changed not only through grotesque characters and situations, but using the camera itself as a grotesque object. The camera is analogous to the concave

45

mirror of esperpento, first by including Norman in the majority of shots and then as the story progresses, having its movements imitate the increasing absurdity and confusion of the story.

In the scene when the ritual begins, the camera moves from steady to shaking, as though, in keeping with the carnival analogy, the film were a roller coaster, slowly cresting to the top of a hill, and then plummeting down. Norman discovers the cult's machine in the kitchen and there is an explosion. After this, the first part of the next scene is a single shot, filmed with the shaking camera, lasting several minutes. As it is shaking, the camera is no longer a neutral observer but part of the narrative that would invoke the distorted reality. This is evoked through conveying the story purportedly in real time exactly as it occurs to Norman and how he views it, and the camera goes from being a neutral observer to a part of the neo-esperpento. As the spectator experiences the fantastic in *The Birthday*, it must be as Norman is, reflected through a narrative that recounts everything that happens to him, and a camera that remains with and on Norman for the duration of the film.

Norman does not leave the hotel for the duration of the film, and enters every different type of space within the hotel: bedrooms, the kitchen, the furnace room, and the roof. Each space offers him a different physical and psychological circumstance [See Figure 2.1]. Most of the other characters, particularly those of the upper class, remain within a single space. These characters are both part of the fabric of the carnival, and subject to the actions and events within. The hotel is never seen from the outside, except in the form of a cake given to Alison's father. It is suggested that it is that model, and not the real hotel, inside which the characters are trapped. Much like in *The Shining* (Stanley Kubrick, 1980), the hotel seems to have a mind of its own; Alison's father tells the story of the purchase of the hotel, from the funds he and his brother received for taking part in drug experiments. It is because of these that the ancient god is manifesting through the brother. It is as if the hotel is part of the cult's conspiracy, keeping the frat boys on their floor until they are needed, and the party guests trapped in the ballroom. The elevator becomes the gate through which Norman is taken into the funhouse.

A carnival world is not one that is concerned with rules, though it would seem that Alison expects Norman to follow certain rules that he does not understand. According to Umberto Eco, Aristotle wrote that comic effects were realized through the violation of a rule, committed by someone with whom the spectator does not sympathize, allows the spectator to feel superior and laugh.[12] Norman's world is not that of a fancy hotel, so he is out of place. Myth and religion divide the world in a sacred realm and a profane realm, and myth can 'infuse certain specific times and locations in the profane world with sacred energy from the sacred world'.[13] The

Fig. 2.1 Norman walks the hall of the strange hotel, *The Birthday* (Atomic Films, 2008)

world that Norman enters from the elevator would seem to be the profane (or real) realm: he is in a hotel, among humans, in a realistic scenario, and yet he is both friend and stranger. There are two hierarchical orders of class represented: there are the party guests, most of whom are from the upper classes, and there are the working classes, represented by the hotel staff and the musicians. But as Mikhail Bahktin points out, the carnival of the Middle Ages was a 'temporary liberation from the prevailing truth and from the established order; [marking] the suspension of all hierarchical rank, privilege, norms and prohibitions'.[14] The upper classes lose control over the situation, and the lower classes invade and attempt to usurp power.

Norman himself is of the lower classes, as he admits to working at a minimum wage, dead-end job, but he has a girlfriend and friends of the upper classes, so he is able to move between the two. This movement continues in the carnival world, where as a member of the lower orders (some of whom are now attempting to take control), he can attempt to prevent disaster, and is accepted in this role by the upper classes, which have lost control. All of the characters are presented though Norman's eyes, and in many ways this makes them caricatures. As an outsider among the upper classes at the beginning of the film, Norman is socially awkward. He is unable to convince the doorman that he is invited to the party; he cannot communicate properly with either the waiters or Alison's uncle; nor can he communicate with Alison. But as the story unfolds, and Norman is the only one who sees all, he is the only one who can tell what is happening, and try and stop it.

The comedy in *The Birthday* arises from a mix of unusual narrative and the style of performance. The narrative situation is fantastic enough to be a departure from the norm and thus wreak havoc with convention. The sheer absurdity of the situation creates a comedic address to the spectator, both deflating and inflecting the terror. The presentation of performance comes from the fictional world built around the persona of Norman, and Corey Feldman, the actor who portrays him. Feldman had success as a child and teenage actor in such films as *The Goonies*, *Stand by Me* (Rob Reiner, 1986) and *The Lost Boys* (Joel Schumacher, 1987). In these films, he would typically play an outcast and/or loser who was witty, sarcastic, and wise beyond his years. There is an intertextuality between Feldman as performer and the character of Norman, as to a certain degree Norman is not a character typically associated with Feldman's previous work. The casting of Feldman becomes another neo-esperpentic twist: gone are the sarcasm and wit, but the outcast is still present. The intertextuality arising from his former teenage star persona then becomes the textuality of the character within the film, from loser to hero.

Norman is the hero of the film, but a most unlikely one. First, he is physically slight, speaks in a strange voice, and has facial and head tics. This is not the body of the male as seen in late-twentieth-century Spanish film, which usually translates into a handsome, strong, mature man. But John Hopewell identifies the Spanish film tradition of a particular type of hero: the '*desgraciado*, a social failure, a nobody'.[15] The foreign body of Feldman is adopted and adapted into this recognizable Spanish form through Norman, much as Norman is the foreign body within this upper class world. He is what Northrop Frye would categorize as the low mimetic hero, mainly found in comedy and realist fiction: not superior to the observer, and thus to whom the reader/spectator responds because of his common humanity.[16] He is also the ironic hero, considered inferior in power and intelligence. Dean Miller might refer to him as the Coward Knight, who emerges as an antitype to the heroic norm, and must be put through a test to become a hero.[17] Like the fool or court jester, his speech is plain, and he is usually physically slighter than the hero, hence the doubts as to his success. Norman's physical awkwardness immediately put him in a low status not only with respect to his fellow characters, but to the spectator, who would likely find little with which to empathize. It is only as the story progresses, and Norman faces the 'test' and must assert himself, that he begins to take on more traditional heroic qualities.

At the end of the film, it is not known if Norman achieves his goal. His quest to save the world does not begin until midway through the film, although it is arguable he has been on a less macrocosmic quest since the beginning, to meet Alison's family, impress them, and impart to her the depth of his feelings. The final shot of the film shows Norman with an axe, presumably about to kill Alison and thus complete his role as hero. In contrast to what might be considered the heteronormative Hollywood ending, in which Alison would survive and remain with Norman, the fate of both characters is unclear. The score, which for the last several minutes of the film had been melodramatic, reverts to the original version of 'It's My Party' for the credits, in recognition that the party was, indeed, Norman's, and the tragedy is his. Not only is there no happy ending, but there is no tragic ending either. This lack of resolution is another neo-esperpentic twist on the hero's journey, as it is left incomplete and unresolved.

The Birthday is a postmodern reinvention of the esperpento, incorporating an absurdist narrative centred on a character that is the opposite of the traditional hero. While the film sets itself firmly in the realm of the fantastic, this fantastic is a distortion of the reality more often seen in comedy, with a Spanish poor hero and an emphasis as much on character development as narrative progression. Its nostalgia and distortion of social and generic verisimilitude are a syntactic intertextualization typical of contemporary Spanish fantastic film.

The Backwoods

The Backwoods is set in Basque country in the late 1970s, and explores themes of the rural versus the urban, identity, landscape, and xenophobia. It uses the template of the American rural thriller to explore concepts of masculinity and violence in an international co-production (Spain/France/UK). The rural thriller and its semantics are adapted to the Spanish fantastic through specific locations, incorporation of culturally-specific dynamics, and estrangement in the unfamiliar environment. Melbye writes that landscape allegory can be understood through two parameters: through the diminishing emphasis on anthropocentric themes in pictorial representation, and/or contradictory relationship between realism and abstraction.[18] *The Backwoods* can be seen through the former, in that the 'foreigners' are progressively affected by the landscape, and the social and cultural customs therein, and the narrative undermines their anthropocentric vision of themselves as the centre of the universe.

The rural landscape offers isolation and an alien environment, where the spectator sees the main characters, typically associated with the contemporary, the non-violent, and the civilized, against the backdrop of an unfamiliar environment and its inhabitants. This antagonism begs the question of who is the Other, those of the city or those of the country. Maria Rovisco writes that rural thrillers 'draw attention to the textures and subtleties of locally bounded forms of social belonging in their connection, and often conflict, with a perceived national community'.[19] The rural characters in many of these types of thrillers are often characterized as rednecks or hillbillies, products of inbreeding, insularity, and/or sexual perversion.

These country folk are beyond the reaches of the law, instead keeping older customs and rituals which city folk find unfathomable or abhorrent. The portrayal of rural people in Spanish film has not conformed exactly to this description; their differences were either idealized (in films from the Francoist period) or viewed as a reaction to/result of trauma (in films from the transition and 1980s). By making the location and its historical implications more covert, *The Backwoods* can be interpreted as a postnational variation on the subgenre.

What it means to be a man in contemporary western society has changed dramatically over the past 50 years, particularly in relation to violence. According to Serra, *The Backwoods* takes inspiration from American rural thrillers of the 1970s such as *Straw Dogs* and *Deliverance* that also explored these issues. It confronts the idea of masculine violence in the rural, as urban men encounter the violent nature of the rural through its inhabitants, and are forced to become violent themselves. However, the specific time period and location bring an added historical dimension to the film, both political and cinematic: it is Basque country, in 1978. This is not the Spain popular with international tourists in the 1960s, and it is only a few years after the end of the Fascist regime. The outsiders represent the invading, unwelcome force of the modern world, and the locals are in a part of Spain isolated from the modernization of their country, living in a cultural and ritualistic bubble in which outside interference is not permitted. *The Backwoods* examines male violence and the rural versus urban divide by marrying the semantics of the rural thriller within a specific Spanish context, and at the same time the history and setting are metaphorical for the interpersonal violence between the characters. By drawing on both generic semantics from American rural thrillers, and Spanish syntax in setting and time period, the film articulates a postnational perspective.

Paul, a British man, has bought his family's old home in northern Spain, and goes there with his wife Isabel, and another couple, Norman and Lucy. They first stop at a bar, where their presence is not appreciated by some of the locals. The next day, Paul and Norman find an abandoned farmstead, and discover Nerea, a young girl who has been locked up, and they take her back to the cottage. The locals (three brothers and their cousin) arrive, claiming to be looking for their sister; Paul goes with them to look. The search party splits up, and two of the brothers, Lechón and Antonio, return to the cottage. Lechón attempts to rape Lucy, but Norman kills him. Meanwhile, Paco knows Paul took the child; Paul kills Paco's cousin, and Paco kills Paul. Norman, Lucy and Isabel take the girl and are given shelter in a nearby village, but Paco and Antonio find them. Norman kills Antonio, but Lucy stops him from killing Paco.

As Ángel Sala notes, the rural thriller had not been a popular genre in Spanish film until the 1970s.[20] Then, in films such as *Poachers, The Hunt*, and *Ana and the Wolves* (*Ana y los lobos*, Carlos Saura, 1973), violence was frequently metaphorical for the trauma of Fascism and the culture it created. With reference to *Pascual Duarte* (Ricardo Franco, 1976), Faulkner writes that its representation of violence in the rural landscape was in part a means 'to debunk the Francoist myth of nature and, by implication, attack the entire ideology of the regime'.[21] Peter Evans writes that these films stress male introspection on masculinity, as in *Poachers*, or use the child or woman as a metaphor for questioning male power and violence, as in *Ana and the Wolves*.[22] That kind of brutalization continues with the resurgence of recent Spanish rural thrillers such as *The Backwoods, Night of the Sunflowers* (*La noche de los girasols*, Jorge Sánchez-Cabezudo, 2006) and *King of the Hill* (*El rey de la montaña*, Gonzalo López-Gallego, 2007).

Serra states that, in the past 30 years, violence has been a perpetual aspect of Basque society, but the area remains largely unknown to international spectators. Indeed, when the film secured international financing, there was a suggestion from some of the non-Spanish producers that it be relocated to either Ireland or Canada, landscapes with which an international audience might be more familiar. However, Serra felt more comfortable in his native land, being familiar with its people and customs, and understanding the association of the rural location with violence.[23] While the casting of UK film stars Gary Oldman and Paddy Considine, and European stars Virginie Ledoyen and Aitana Sánchez-Gijón, is both a feature of the co-production arrangements and a postnational strategy designed to attract an international audience, keeping the original setting suggests an implication of the Basque location in the film's violence.

Like much of the Spanish countryside, the Basque country is subject to presentation and interpretation in film as an 'ancestral landscape of millenary trees and virginal beauty'.[24] However, several Basque filmmakers have not been afraid to show that violence was in many ways endemic to the way of life. Arguably, since the 1990s, the filmmaker most associated with his Basque heritage is Julio Medem. His films exposed the underbelly of Basque identity, rooted as he sees it as much in violence as in the pastoral. *Cows* (*Vacas*, 1992) explores three generations of a Basque family in the early twentieth century and the inherent rural male chauvinism; and *Earth* (*Tierra*, 1996) explores a landscape 'deprived of nostalgia for tradition and of affection for the localism of landscape'.[25] Other Basque directors, such as Juanma Bajo Ulloa in *Dead Mother*, and Daniel Calparsoro, in *Passages* (*Pasajes*, 1996), were also not afraid to dispel myths of the bucolic (though not all of their films were set in rural locations). *The Backwoods* is also exploring the social and cultural isolation that can bring out the violence endemic to a society.

According to Paddy Woodworth, the Basques have been somewhat type-cast as Europe's 'aboriginal' peoples, and all things Basque have been seen as 'ancient and original'.[26] Lying in the northeast corner of Spain, the region has always enjoyed a certain geographical isolation. The Basque language is Spain's only non-Indo-European tongue, with no clear relationship to either French or Castilian. Basque nationalism emerged in the late nineteenth century as a reaction against modernism, and Basque nationalists sided with the Republicans during the Spanish Civil War. Like other minority regions in Spain, the Basque language and culture were repressed under the Fascist government. The Spanish constitution of 1978 recognized the Basque country as a distinct region with a certain degree of autonomy. However, the radical group Euskadi Ta Askatasuna (ETA), formed in the late 1960s, fought for more than 30 years to have the area become a completely separate country, frequently employing violent means. The Basque people, for the most part, have always seen themselves as separate from Spain, due to their geographical isolation and unique language. The film presents the Basque country of 1978 as isolated and separate, making it the Appalachians of Spain, populated by those with their own ways and cultures that resist interference.

Spain has been no stranger to the invasion of British tourists, beginning in the 1950s, though tourists tend to go to the south for the warm weather and beaches. This trend was not lost on Spanish filmmakers. In Narciso Ibáñez Serrador's *Who Can Kill a Child?* (*¿Quién puede matar a un niño?*, 1976), British tourists go to an island off the south coast of Spain, only to find the children have killed all the adults. This film deals with themes of the invading outsider, the negative aspects of tourism, and the retaliation of children upon adults for the violent world in which they exist. As with the characters in Serrador's film, Paul is the invading tourist, imposing his values on the locals by breaking into the barn and taking Nerea. But he also presents himself as 'practically a local', due to his grandmother. While one local in the bar accepts this and enquires after Paul's family roots, the brothers laugh it off, suggesting the rejection of the outsider, not only by virtue of his British heritage, but also his urbanity. In this scene, the camera is frequently placed at the seated locals' eye level, looking up at Paul and Norman; while this angle is normally associated with the power of those in the frame, in this case it suggests a separation and lack of welcome. This is also emphasized by the lack of women in the bar.

The feminist movement of the 1960s and 1970s is said to have 'stripped away many of men's asylums', such as those where they might commit violent acts with impunity, and disputed the ideology of the self-made man 'who wielded authority and accrued advantages'.[27] This movement also gave rise to the idea of the 'sensitive man', who eschewed previous forms of masculinity that were based on violence and power and rejected machismo, instead opening himself to vulnerability and embraced open communication. Films such as *Straw Dogs* and *Deliverance* show this sensitive man confronted by a rural environment in which men reject this sensitivity and remain primitive. Both films suggest that a certain level of violence is justified, not only in self-defence, but also for the male, indispensable in expressing his character. *The Backwoods*, being made in the early twenty-first century, takes a different approach: while Norman's initial violence might have been justified by the attempted rape of his wife, its continuation beyond punishment of Lechón is rejected in the final scenes. Meanwhile, Paul, whose only true 'crime' was to rescue Nerea, and who only becomes violent in self-defence, is killed. This later act might speak more to a critique of interference of the urban in the rural.

These urban people have not only invaded the rural, but a specific rural culture. In the bar, the locals make it clear that they do not see Paul as one of them, despite his familial connection. And yet, when Paul and Norman are hunting, Paul espouses a connection with not only the land, but also the sport, having learnt how to hunt from his grandfather, who learned from the locals. Paul pushes his own 'postnational' status, being both British and Spanish. Paul tells Norman that he must stop thinking (i.e. being 'urban') in order to be a hunter. After he kills a rabbit, the same prey of choice as in *The Hunt*, he comments that there are thousands of prey in the world. He is the one with the connection to the land, and speaks the language, but cannot connect himself with the culture. He claims to understand the way these rural people think, and yet he is murdered. In *The Hunt*, the enjoyment of rabbit hunting is associated with the economic/political class that supported the Fascist government; in *The Backwoods*, this is changed to the invading outsider.

In *The Backwoods*, the villains are both the British and the locals. The British represent not only the urban, but money that would transform a traditional way of life. It is indicated that Paul and Norman could afford to live in Spain independently. How the locals make a living is unknown, but their socioeconomic class is indicated as low, especially through the possibility of inbreeding as represented by the dimwitted brother and deformed sister. Not only the British, but also the wider representation of capitalism and tourism threatens their rural landscape. Melbye defines the experience of place as 'a complex network of impulses derived from intertwining emotional and intellectual capabilities'.[28] These impulses are displayed in the scenes between Paul and Paco in the forest: both men claim a connection to the land, and an understanding of its secrets. Yet when Paul sets off with

Fig. 2.2 The urban man among the rural men, *The Backwoods* (Momentum Pictures, 2008)

them, he tells his friends that he knows how to handle 'these people', indicating a separation of emotion from intellect, or at least an idea that he, Paul, is superior due to his intellect [See Figure 2.2]. When Paul tells the brothers that his dog is also missing, Paco replies that city dogs often become disoriented in the country-side; this is as much a remark about Paul as it is about the dog. Paul invades their space when he breaks into the barn and takes the girl, and he becomes disoriented after Miguel attacks him. When Paul kills Miguel in self-defense, the camera follows the action in extreme close-up, as if to indicate that Paul alone is responsible for this action, and Serra uses different shots to separate these actions from the surrounding landscape, as if it is an affront to it. The murder of Paul is not shown; instead, there is a wide shot of the forest and the sound of the gunshot, as if it is the land that is killing him, as revenge for his intrusion.

The first shot of the film is of guns, the second is of a dog: both these images can be associated with hunting. The third shot shows two cars crossing a wide space, as if they are bringing this hunting, and its subsequent violence, to a pastoral setting. Norman and Lucy make strained conversation, and when Lucy seems to be ignoring Norman, he turns on the radio to hear the song 'There is a War'.[29] There is a deliber-ate coordination in the editing of sound and image: Lucy turns down the volume at the line 'a war between the man and the woman'. The dialogue briefly stops at 'there is a war between the ones who say there is a war and the ones who say that there isn't', and at the same time as the image freezes in black and white on Norman. The next line, 'why don't you come on back to the war, that's right, get in it', plays over a black and white frame of Lucy, as though this is their real conversation. The song then moves from diegetic to non-diegetic, and the final lines, 'There is a war between the left and right, a war between the black and white, a war between the odd and the even', are heard over the credit that give the location and date of the film. The music then returns to the diegesis, and cuts off before the end of the song. Those final, non-diegetic lines provide clues for interpreting the story, and the conflict between the individual characters, as well as the culture and social clash. This is one of only two songs in the film (the other also being a Leonard Cohen song, 'Lover Lover Lover' [1974]), and its implication is quite clear, in that Norman and the others are about to enter a war (in this case, urban vs. rural) in which the violence perpetuates itself to disastrous ends. While the song lyrics may be indicating a political or class war, the 'war' in the car is a personal one. These historical metaphors within the song are being used to represent the personal and gendered war between Norman and Lucy.

In rural thrillers, there is often an early confrontation scene between the invaders and the locals, which will signal the initial reasons for the violence. The scene in the bar suggests that the locals don't feel the British capable of such masculinity as the rural place requires, especially in a place where violence is ubiquitous. In his normal environment, Norman would not shoot Lechón, but call the police; but in this landscape, his violence is acceptable. Arguably, there is not as much violence in *The Backwoods* as in its international cinematic predecessors: there are four killings and one attempted rape, but only three of the killings are seen, and two of them happen with a single gunshot. It is almost a naturalization of violence within this landscape. If this is viewed from its specific location, it could be understood through a violence that is seen as ubiquitous in the area's history. If viewed from a generic perspective, then there are signs of a change in that naturalization: at the end of the film, Norman is not allowed to bring his gun into the villager's house, and that villager uses his gun only to force Norman toward the police, suggesting the move away from the violence of the rural.

It is a dichotomy of language that extends to the presentation and experience of the landscape, especially by the outsiders. In an early scene, Paul and Norman are hunting in the woods, while Lucy and Isabel are swimming in a pond in another part of the woods. They are shown in a picturesque setting, skinny-dipping in a pond that evokes a pastoral perfection, yet at the same time perpetuates an idea a woman's body as object, as the camera shoots them from a distance, as if someone was spying on them. The women are effectively fixed within the landscape, as though they are a part of it, again emphasizing them as objects. Meanwhile, Paul and Norman are moving through the space, where the sun doesn't easily penetrate the woods. Paul claims a connection with the land, while Norman is reluctant to even be holding a gun. They are only seen attempting to shoot an animal at one point, and it is unsuccessful. It is on this hunt that they discover the girl locked away. Their transgressive acts upon the landscape and those who 'naturally' exist there are punished by the landscape, through the fallen tree and the pouring rain the following day, which hamper the outsiders' attempt at getting help. The pastoral beauty of landscape, as shown in the swimming scene featuring two women, is contrasted against the harsh treatment of Nerea. The war is personal, between these people, as opposed to larger political ideals. While historically Basque country resists invasion of outsiders through violence, here the Basque landscape and its violent associations are metaphoric for interpersonal conflict, between the couples and between the outsiders and the locals. This landscape resists and rejects them not as Basque country against an outside force, but the rural landscape against any outsider, especially an urban one.

While it is an homage to the American rural thriller of the 1970s, *The Backwoods* situates itself within its Spanish setting and contemporary perspective. Exploring issues of the rural, masculinity, violence and landscape, the film both recalls Spanish films that explore violence in the rural, and is distanced from them by its use of more postnational generic semantics. The film uses the specific politics of Spanish history both in its own representations and as a metaphor for interpersonal politics within the rural thriller.

The Birthday and *The Backwoods* do not hide their intertextual references; in fact, arguably, they depend on them to a certain degree, and on the spectator's ability to recognize such references. The esperpento is about the comic, the distortion of the real that as such provokes laughter at horror; *The Birthday*, through semantics of location, setting, and mise-en-scène keep one foot in the real, while through syntax, puts its other foot through the concave mirror of the neo-esperpento. *The Backwoods* takes its cue from American rural thrillers, with themes of antagonism, masculine violence, and the landscape as unknowable and uninviting, using English not only to reach an international audience, but also to emphasize differences in cultural identity. *The Birthday* and *The Backwoods* are meeting points between the influence of international fantastic film and influences from Spanish film and culture; at this point, the postnational Spanish fantastic is found. The films are metaphoric mirrors of Spanish culture that give new meanings to the fantastic film and the Spanish postnational film.

3

Alejandro Amenábar: The Drop-Out Auteur: *Open Your Eyes* and *The Others*

Only a few years after Álex de la Iglesia was challenging the cinematic status quo, Alejandro Amenábar would do the same, though in a very different manner. He too was reaching out to his own generation, who rarely saw themselves on screen; his young audience might not have been quite as marginalized, but still felt alienated. Where de la Iglesia's work was excessive and extreme, Amenábar's worked in subtler ways, though was no less indebted to outside influences.

Amenábar is arguably the most well-known Spanish director apart from Pedro Almodóvar. Walking a fine line between commercial and auteur cinema, Amenábar adapts generic semantics to appeal to both the auteur and genre cinema spectator. Vicente Rodríguez Ortega writes that 'Amenábar... knows too well the conventions of generic categories to merely repeat them but is perhaps too calculating to let his oeuvre supersede them and break the illusionist drive that runs across most of commercial cinema worldwide'.[1] While two of his six feature films fall into more standard genre categories, (*The Sea Inside* [*Mar adentro*, 2004] is a biopic, and *Agora* [2009], a historical drama), his leanings have generally taken a fantastic bent, with an emphasis on horror (*Thesis*, *The Others*, *Regression* [2015]) and science fiction (*Open Your Eyes* [*Abre los ojos*], 1997). Despite his lack of citation of major influences from Spanish cinema, Amenábar's involvement in almost all aspects of production, and his perhaps unconscious use of Spanish philosophies, mark him as a European filmmaker.

Born in Chile in 1972 to a Chilean father and Spanish mother, Amenábar was only a year old when his family moved to Spain. As a child, he rarely watched television, and instead spent his creative time reading and writing stories. It was not until he was a teenager when, having made friends with a neighbour, he began to visit their house and watch movies on VHS. It did not take long for a passion for cinema to take hold, and at 17 he bought his first camera. In

1990, he began studying in the information sciences department at Universidad Complutense in Madrid, as at the time it was the best substitute for a film school (the national film school would not open for another five years). It was here that he met his frequent collaborator, Mateo Gil. However, Amenábar found himself bored by many of his classes and did not get on well with several professors, and so dropped out.

Amenábar made three short films, 'La Cabeza' (1991), 'Himenóptero' (1992) and 'Luna' (1995), before making *Thesis*, which was released in 1996. Starring Ana Torrent (of *The Spirit of the Beehive*) and Eduardo Noriega in his first major role, its exploration of on-screen violence and voyeurism, much like in de la Iglesia's work, drew attention to the disconnection between the dominant national cinema and the interests of mainstream audiences. It received positive reviews after it played at Berlinale, and Spanish critics gave Amenábar the nickname 'Orsoncito', little Orson Welles, after the filmmaker whom he often cites as a major influence.[2] By the time *Open Your Eyes* was released in late 1997, he was already being called an auteur. His first English-language film, *The Others*, was the top-grossing film at the Spanish box office in 2001, eventually making over $200 million worldwide, and remains his most financially successful film. It was also the first English-language film to win a Goya for Best Picture. That he should follow up with *The Sea Inside*, a biopic about real-life crusader for euthanasia, Ramon Sampedro (played by Javier Bardem), would seem a strange departure for someone who had made his name in the fantastic genres, but the film won the Academy Award for Best Foreign Language Film in 2005. While *The Sea Inside* was successful both in Spain and worldwide, *Agora*, about ancient Egyptian philosopher Hypatia (Rachel Weisz), grossed less than $1 million in the US, though did gross more than €20 million in Spain. His most recent film, *Regression*, is a return to Amenábar's horror roots, and earned more than €8 million in Spain.

In finding a balance between European auteur cinema and popular genre film, Amenábar's work both breaks new ground, and recycles and adapts traditional semantics into a new syntactic form. *Open Your Eyes* is one of the first contemporary puzzle films, in which vital information as to the physical state of the main character is kept secret both from that character and the audience. This is applied to the setting of contemporary Madrid and contemporary characters, reflecting on the identity of Spain in the mid-1990s and the entanglements of love, money, and sex. Amenábar uses a similar puzzle device in *The Others*, but in this case, reshapes the traditional gothic horror film, which relies upon mood and tone to induce fear in the spectator. While *Open Your Eyes* is set in Madrid and is, at least consciously, reflective of its culture and society, it could take place in any number of western cities. *The Others* takes its cues from classic gothic horror, which has almost no tradition in Spain, either in film or literature.

Open Your Eyes is an example of what Elliot Panek would refer to as the psychological puzzle film, possessing 'narratives in which the orientation of events in the plot to diegetic reality is not immediately clear'.[3] The spectator (and frequently the characters) must try to untangle the events and actions, which can be tangled due to a non-linear plot or withheld information. Some examples of other puzzle films are *Dark City* (Alex Proyas, 1998), *The Sixth Sense* (M. Night Shyamalan, 1999), *Memento* (Christopher Nolan, 2000), and *Donnie Darko* (Richard Kelly, 2001). In *Open Your Eyes*, the puzzle manifests through withheld information; the main character is caught in a sequence of lack of knowledge, unstable reality, and time loops, while the spectator only has as much knowledge as the character. Much of a puzzle film's narrative centres around the hold of causality; this hold can often be loosened by the use of the dream/virtual state. By placing the spectator in the same position as the character, the puzzle film is asking the spectator to enter into the same puzzle-solving as the character. Ruth Perlmutter identifies several devices used to create psychic disturbances, both inter-and-extra textual; the ones most relevant to these films are non-sequential order of events, fragmented plot lines, and application of Freudian dream mechanisms.[4]

Carmen Rabalska identifies a Hispanic philosophy of dualism, a constant pairing of idealism and realism, mysticism and the mundane, the holy and the profane; this fusion of disparate style and content leads to the grotesque.[5] This grotesque manifests both in the main character's monstrous appearance, and the constant shift between the 'dream' and 'reality'. The puzzle comes not only from parsing out the real from the dream, but how the main character understands their literal and metaphorical placement within the story.

The Others is presented as a gothic melodrama. However, it also qualifies as postmodern for a spectator familiar with gothic melodrama. The gothic mobilizes associations with the sublime, which has both religious and familial connotations in the film. Jean-François Lyotard wrote that the postmodern sublime 'puts forward the unpresentable in presentation itself'.[6] Philip Shaw writes that the contemporary age finds that 'the sense which the highest of the high is nothing more than an illusion brought about through our misperception of reality'.[7] Representing the unpresentable in presentation itself for a contemporary audience means that the film re-engages with the fantastic mode, finding a new means of representing the gothic melodrama in the context of postmodern culture and postnational film. The gothic examination, then, is an attempt to present the pain and pleasure of the sublime through fantastic representation. It is the effect of the gothic sublime that is crucial, the effect of excess represented through the fantastic elements of a gothic film. Vijay Mishra writes that what 'the postmodern inherits is the sublime mediated by the gothic's rendition of the absolutely great, the unpresentable, as the self's own dissolution with and confrontation of death'.[8] *The Others* is Amenábar's attempt to reinvent the gothic horror film, and articulate the sublime for a postmodern audience.

With his second and third feature films, Amenábar solidified his status as an auteur, through a use of popular genre semantics mixed with what would become some of his signature syntax: old-school mystery and lo-fi effects together creating atmospheric puzzle stories.

Open Your Eyes

Thesis grossed €2.6 million at the Spanish box office in 1996, no small feat for a low-budget Spanish film. *Thesis*'s story of a university student's investigation into snuff films, and her seduction by a handsome and dangerous man, helped propel Amenábar, co-writer Gil and star Noriega to rising fame. Given that Amenábar was only 24 years old at the time, it also created more than a little pressure for his next film to be equally as good and financially successful.

Gil, Amenábar and other friends were conversing over drinks one night, when the subject of cryogenics came up. Amenábar claimed he was going to be frozen at death so that he could have a second life. As a child, he, his mother and brother were involved in a serious car accident, which gave him nightmares for years; and later, he once hitchhiked home from school, where he was picked up by an aggressive and intimidating driver. These stories and memories, and the idea of making a cheap science fiction film, were the catalysts for *Open Your Eyes*. Due to the success of *Thesis*, Sogecine, a financially solvent national film company, became a backer, which gave them a larger budget. Again collaborating with Gil, Noriega, and actor Fele Martínez, the film (released in December 1997) grossed almost €6.5 million at the Spanish box office, the biggest take in Spanish cinema at that time. A small release in 1999 by Artisan in the US saw it earn a little under $400,000, which is a good amount considering it was a small foreign language film with no stars, as supporting actress Penélope Cruz was not yet well-known in the US. It was well received enough to catch the attention of Tom Cruise, who would back an English-language remake of the film, *Vanilla Sky* (Cameron Crowe, 2001), in which Cruz repeated her role.

Amenábar has said that *Open Your Eyes* is 'the story of a man who wants to live in heaven and ends up in hell'.[9] Part science fiction, part paranoia thriller, with tropes of eroticism and from German expressionism, it is one of the progenitors of the puzzle mode. It examined the moral values of a then-hedonistic Spanish youth culture of affluent middle-class kids who were unaffected by historical trauma and depoliticized. Paul Julian Smith writes that the film 'internalizes the two factors most characteristic of recent Spanish cinema: innovation within a genre framework and localization of culture'.[10] Amenábar and Gil originally centred the story around a beggar who sells his body for science experiments, and turns out to have been living in a dream. That eventually changed to a story of a rich young man, enabling them to explore questions of beauty, identity, perception, and the reliability of memory in a culture on the verge of the millennium, fragile to the point of possible collapse.

Open Your Eyes begins with César, masked and recounting recent events to a psychiatrist, Antonio, in the prison where he is awaiting trial for murder. In his acccount, César meets Sofía at a party, and they spend the night together talking. When he leaves, he discovers Nuria, a former sexual conquest, has followed him, and he allows her to take him to her place. But instead Nuria drives her car off a bridge, killing herself and disfiguring César. César is unable to cope with his deformity, and loses Sofía. Then, after a drunken bender, Sofía finds him on the street and declares her love. Miraculously, doctors are able to restore his face. But soon, Nuria is there, claiming to be Sofía. Everyone insists the girl who looks like Nuria is Sofía. Later, breaking into Sofía's apartment, César finds photographs that show Nuria as Sofía. Sofía returns, looking as César remembers her, but later she changes again. César murders her, and his face returns to its monstrous state. He and Antonio find the company Life Extension, and discover that César had killed himself decades earlier and had himself cryogenically frozen until his face could be restored. He also signed a clause that would allow a virtual reality programme to create a life for him in the twentieth century.

The first words heard in the film are its title. A female voice, speaking softly, repeats, 'open your eyes'. Chris Perriam writes that the film's title 'heavily implies that we are meant to be attentive to the play of appearances, alert to the risk of poor vision, false images and lack of insight'.[11] The camera shows César's perspective: we see the pillow on which his face had been placed; then the camera shifts to above César's body, his face in the pillow. His face is first shown in his bathroom mirror, as he perceives himself. The spectator's attention is drawn to César as he dresses and leaves. As he drives through the streets, he notices that they are empty, even though it is late morning. César stops his car and runs down the empty street, shouting for the missing populace. The screen fades to black, and the sequence repeats itself, except this time there is a different voice-over, and the previous scene was a dream that César is recounting to Antonio. There is still the sound of the alarm, César waking, looking at his reflection, dressing, and driving into the city. Only this time, the streets are crowded and full of everyday activity.

This Madrid of the mid-1990s, shown through the opening credits, was affluent, culturally relevant, and hopeful for the future. César represents this Madrid, though this representation turns out to be an exposure of the superficial and vain mood at the time. Amenábar presents a series of images along the Gran Via, Madrid's central thoroughfare, filled with shops and tourists: a film crew, a homeless man, a woman selling goods to the drivers, even a shot of Sofía doing her street mime performance. César has been established as a handsome man of independent means. To be in a city where no one can recognize this, as in his dream, is a nightmare to him. César had lived a life of leisure, enjoying food, friends and sex, and so the repeated sequence shows a city where he is seen in that capacity.

At the same time, there are images of those things that César does not see: the poor people; the girl who will be the cause of love and grief; and a film crew that may be, unknown to him, filming this dream. Here is an additional moment of syntactical change from traditional esperpento: Ramón del Valle-Inclán's Madrid of the 1920s was one of self-interest and political corruption, and so he deformed that reality in his self-reflexive plays.[12] Similarly, Amenábar's Madrid of the 1990s as seen in *Open Your Eyes* is distortion of reality through a neo-esperpento lens, but in a more postmodern context, represented as self-interested and decadent, and the opening sequence reflects this by putting clues of self-reflexivity through the presence of poor people, Sofía, and the film crew.

According to Thomas Elsaesser, puzzle films may share several common traits:

1. The protagonist participates in or is witness to events whose meaning escapes him, with suspension of cause and effect. (César does not understand how his face keeps reverting to its monstrous state.)
2. The protagonist seems deluded or mistaken about the difference between reality and imagination. (César confuses Sofía and Nuria.)
3. The protagonist has a friend who turns out to be imagined. (Antonio.)
4. The protagonist asks, who am I and what is my reality? (César begins to ask this as soon as the women change.)
5. The protagonist is unable to distinguish or be aware of the different worlds until the end. (César is unaware of the virtual reality until the final scene.)
6. The protagonist is persuaded that the self-delusion is brought on by trauma. (César believes the strange events are a result of the trauma of his accident.)[13]

There are clues that might lead the spectator to solve the puzzle: César sees information about Life Extension at least twice; when he first wakes up from his drunken stupor in the street, he sees Nuria's face; and he recounts his dreams of signing a strange paper. That César keeps reverting between a prison cell and his nightmare existence suggests the imposition of a syntactic parallel to the Golden Age Spanish play *Life is a Dream*, by Pedro Calderón de la Barca (1635). In the play, Segismundo, the son of the King, is placed in a prison soon after he is born, as his father, following an astrological prediction, believes his son will eventually overthrow him. To test this, once Segismundo is an adult, the King drugs him and brings him to the palace, telling him that his life in prison was a dream and he is actually a prince. However, Segismundo becomes a tyrant, and the King returns him to prison, where he is told that his life as a prince was a dream. In an update of this, César is first the prince and then the prisoner. Like Segismundo, César cannot decide between the dream and reality. And like Segismundo, when returned to the 'perfect' life, César becomes a tyrant through murder. Once the solution to the puzzle is revealed, César is given a choice of whether to return to the dream, where he is a prince, or face an unknown reality. The dream state of the play works against the idea of an order that can be forced upon the world, particularly of an ideology of power that would control forces best left to chaos. In an update of this, *Open Your Eyes* seeks to undermine a late-twentieth-century propensity to believe in a stable reality, especially one based on superficiality and control over one's destiny.

In this postmodern metropolis, there appears to be no direct access to unmediated reality. That is to say, not only is the perspective always subjective to César, but all scenes are recreated through a flashback from his point of view, and exist within a virtual reality. This virtual reality is constructed as opposed to perceived. Perriam calls the film a 'critique of cinema's marketing of good looks and society's consumption of this dream', especially in relation to Noriega's physical appearance and growing stature as a movie star.[14] The people on the streets are reminders of the superficiality not only of César's life, but also of the film image, and as shadows of reality (as at this point it is part of César's virtual state). But without others to perceive his body, and without other bodies to perceive, it is as if César doesn't exist. Again, this marks a return to the dream state of the film within the film: the cinematic apparatus of the virtual reality machine is creating the illusion based on César's memories, with his body at the centre, a body which, in effect, does not exist in the dream state.

The first view of César is via a mirror; the film shows a close-up of César looking at himself. His expression is one of boredom; that César is handsome is not in doubt, but the first scenes of the film show a man who is so assured in his beauty that he is almost oblivious to it. Disfiguration of the face and its effect on identity is a trope seen in horror films such as *The Phantom of the Opera* (Arthur Lubin, 1943) and *Eyes Without a Face*. César's face is his social signifier: without it, he is nothing, not even with his money. The close-up, a cinematic device that allows a face to be seen in all its detail large on the screen, shows what Bela Balázs would call the language of the face. He writes that this language 'cannot be suppressed or controlled', seeing facial expression as a subjective manifestation revealed by the close-up that becomes a soliloquy, allowing the spectator to see into the soul of a character.[15] After he is disfigured, César abandons his prosthetic mask quickly, as if it is absurd to try to hide when the mask is such an obvious lie that cannot hide his monstrosity. As Mikhail Bakhtin writes, 'my own exterior is not part of the actual, concrete horizon of my seeing except for those rare cases... when I contemplate my own reflection'.[16] What is seen is not the true exterior, however, but the reflection of the exterior.

After the accident, César's face is disfigured to the point where he refuses to look at his own reflection. In a repeat of the first scene, when César now goes to the bathroom, he does not contemplate his face with boredom, but with anger. When his hand slams on the mirror to hide his appearance, it is not just to hide it from himself, but from the close-up, which would reveal the difference from his handsome face in such detail that not only can César not bear to contemplate it, he wishes no one else to do so either. In the previous scene, a dream, he describes his face as being that of the phantom of the opera. But his deformities bring him closer to Dorian Grey: the mirror is now the painting, reflecting his face on which all his previous sins are on display.

Henri Bergson writes that the body, and our image of our body, occupies the centre of our perception: 'Here is a system of images which I term my perception of the universe, and which may be entirely altered by a very slight change in a certain privileged image – my body'.[17] As a walking painting of his sins, César now looks on his universe with horror and anger, as he believes that, where it once worshipped him, the world now judges him negatively because of his appearance. Doctors give him a mask to hide his deformity; the mask is devoid of expression, almost similar to the handsome face César first contemplated in the mirror. In one scene in a dance club, César wears the mask on the back of the head, and the camera keeps this image in the centre of the frame, strongly backlit, so only the outlines of the mask on one side and the face on the other can be seen [See Figure 3.1]. This focuses on the duality of César: the reality and the dream, though the lack of light on the two faces suggests the puzzle, as it is hard to tell which is which for a few seconds. Returning to the

Fig. 3.1 The two faces of César, *Open Your Eyes* (Lionsgate, 2007)

dualism of Spanish philosophy, is one holy and the other profane? Perhaps the handsome represents the holy and the grotesque the profane, or César is a contemporary Dorian Grey, in which case the grotesque is the holy, as it reflects César's true nature.

With any puzzle film, the thought always turns to who is controlling the puzzle. Jean-Louis Baudry writes on the ideological nature of the cinematic apparatus, pointing out that it may seem as though the camera operates only an intermediary position in the process from raw material to finished product. Is this the case? Baudry writes that, 'it is the apparatus that creates the illusion, and not the degree of fidelity with the Real'.[18] The institution that is creating this virtual state has appropriated his memories; but then again, it is César's mind that is confusing the images of the women. Is he a posthuman subject because of this virtual state? He is living a purely mental existence, his life manufactured for him. For Katherine Hayles, the posthuman subject privileges informational patterns over material instantiation, just as César refuses to belief that Nuria is Sofía, despite material evidence.[19] In the posthuman, there are no differences between bodily existence and computer simulation; information becomes paramount, and through this, 'the dialectic of pattern/randomness tends toward ascendancy over the dialectic of presence/absence'.[20] In effect, while the film's puzzle is solved once the true nature of César's physical state is learned, the answer would suggest that the posthuman state is impossible, at least to the extent that the human mind and psyche are too complex for virtual reality. The film begins and ends with a renaissance perspective shot (the basis of cinematic illusion): in the beginning, with César running through the 'painting' of the Gran Via, still in its emptiness, and in the end, with César looking out over the cityscape, again still in its emptiness, a painting in which he has no place. The 'real' setting of Madrid becomes virtual, or fake, much as César's life before the accident. In order to recover the real, to resolve the puzzle, he must die.

Open Your Eyes combines suspense and science-fiction, exploring the division between dreams and reality, beauty and the monstrous, the human and the post-human. While it has postmodern leanings in its focus on the visual as a represen-tation disconnected from reality, it combines cultural references to the Spanish grotesque with influences from popular thriller and science fiction cinema, as well as being one of the first contemporary puzzle films. The puzzle film, arguably a film mode without a national origin, plays a part in the construction of the post-national spectator, who engages with the mode without national prejudice.

The Others

The Others began as a small-scale film project for the European market. Having originally written the script in Spanish and set it in Chile, Amenábar intended the film to explore the repressions of his childhood, the impact of religious dogma on family life, and the education of children. After the remake of *Open Your Eyes*, the project caught the eye of Cruise/Wager Productions, as well as US production and distribution company Miramax. Relocated to the UK and a familiar historical period, *The Others* features Australian and British actors, and stars Nicole Kidman at the height of her fame and box-office power, although she worked for less than her usual fee. Sogecine once again provided financing, so that the film could still be made in Spain with a Spanish crew. It was something of a risk, given that Amenábar was still relatively unknown outside of Spain, but its positive reception and gross of almost $60 million in the US in four weeks proved that gothic melo-drama was still a favourite with audiences.

Amenábar's choice of gothic melodrama follows his postmodern approach to narrative and style that rearticulated horror (in *Thesis*) and science-fiction (in *Open Your Eyes*). Ernesto Acevedo-Muñoz sees *The Others* as 'an essentially Spanish narrative [made] into an elastic generic form whose national context is even underscored by the non-specificity of its setting'.[21] To him, the film is an allegory of Spanish Civil War trauma and the 1970s democratic transition, work-ing with themes of isolation, Catholicism, repression, and motherhood. While the themes are consistent with other Spanish films of different genres, the alle-gorical interpretation is inferred rather than implied. This is not to suggest this interpretation is misguided. But rather, the film is exploring themes that are not necessarily solely associable to Spanish culture or history.

Set at the end of World War II, *The Others* tells the story of Grace, who lives on Jersey (a dependency of the UK, occupied by the Nazis 1940–45) with her two children, Anne and Nicholas. Three servants, Bertha, Edmund and Lydia, appear looking for work. Grace hires them, as her other servants have disappeared. The children claim to see ghosts of a family and an old woman. Grace accuses them of lying, but then she begins to hear strange noises, and it would appear that the servants are not disclosing everything about themselves. When she goes to get the village priest, Grace finds her husband (who had been a soldier in the war) returning. He stays at the house briefly, during which time Anne tells him a secret that makes him leave again. The next morning, Grace awakes to find her husband gone and all the curtains removed, putting the children in danger. She accuses the servants and insists they leave. Later that night, Grace and the children discover that not only are the servants ghosts, but they are as well; Grace killed her children and then herself in a fit of madness, and the 'ghosts' are actually the living family now occupying the house.

The gothic has remained popular since its inception in the late eighteenth century. The combination of imperiled heroines, dastardly villains, haunted houses, and supernatural events was a mainstay of novels in the nineteenth century, such as *The Castle of Otranto* (Horace Walpole, 1764) and *The Mysteries of Udolpho* (Ann Radcliffe, 1794). Fred Botting writes that the gothic 'signified the lack of reason, morality and beauty of feudal beliefs, customs and works'.[22] As science began to overtake religion as a way of interpreting the world, the gothic became popular as a means of exploring metaphysical spiritualism within an increasingly secular society. According to Andrew Smith, in gothic texts, 'ghosts are… ciphers for models of subjectivity which refer to culturally specific notions of psychological trauma'.[23] This kind of trauma, related to the break between reason and the supernatural, is explored in *The Others* through the indulgence of strong emotionalism, moral polarization and schematization, extreme states of being, inflated and extravagant expression, dark plotting, and suspense.

Ángel Sala notes that in the mid-twentieth century, Spanish fantastic cinema often intersected with genres such as film noir.[24] Thus, there was a gothic noir horror represented by films such as *El ojo de cristal* (Antonio Santillán, 1955) and *La melodía misteriosa* (Juan Fortuny, 1955). Narciso Ibáñez Serrador's *The House that Screamed* is often cited as a gothic film, and many of Jesús Franco's early films, such as *The Awful Dr Orlof*, use the gothic mode. In the 1980s, horror films were viewed as non-Spanish; their melodramatic undertones and use of 'cheap thrills' were not considered fit to represent a national cinema. This changed in the 1990s, in no small part due to filmmakers such as Amenábar. Having already found a new (younger) audience, Amenábar 'managed to capitalize on the mainstream appeal of genre films... where this tradition was notoriously underexploited in the mainstream arena'.[25] *The Others* combines what is essentially a story of death and redemption with a ghost story in the gothic melodramatic. The film does not deny the presence of the uncanny, but it does question the role of Catholicism as the answer to the uncanny. As fits with Amenábar's noted distaste for violence and gore, the horror is created through tone and mood, by use of sound editing, music, and narrative.

Early gothic novels explored the cross-contamination of reality and fantasy, and the return of the past to haunt the present. The genre began with British authors exploring the ordered and civilized English society coming to fruition after the Enlightenment, and infusing it with its superstitious and pagan past in the form of ghosts and haunting. *The Others* displays many of the gothic tropes seen in films such as *Rebecca* (Alfred Hitchcock, 1940), *The Spiral Staircase* (Robert Siodmak, 1945) and *The Innocents*: an isolated setting, female characters on the verge of insanity, spectres, apparitions from the past, and a deep interest in the psyche of the main character(s). Melodrama included what has been defined as a feminist gothic cycle due to the films' female mode of address and use of gothic motifs such as the haunted house and ghosts.

Both melodramas and gothic films use dramatic music to heighten emotional effect; in *The Others*, the score (written by Amenábar) leans more towards horror, as when Anne claims that Victor is in her and Nicholas' room, or when Grace tries to find the source of the noise in an unused room. The music heightens the emotional fear felt by the family, as well as acting as a cue to the spectator of important and frightening events. In one scene, Anne tells Nicholas that the boy Victor keeps opening their curtains. At first, the score uses soft woodwind instruments, as if imitating the sounds of fairies or children's voices. As the camera moves between shots of Nicholas' face and the window, string instruments are introduced, which imitate the sound of a creaking floor. Then, when Anne tells Victor that she's going to tell her mother about him, the score moves to deeper, lower notes, as if helping to introduce the adult world and, with it, another level of gothic and melodrama. Christine Gledhill writes that melodrama takes place in lived experience, but it acknowledges the limitations of language in expressing heightened emotion.[26] Music in both melodrama and horror represents emotion that exceeds words.

While various clues are given that would hint at Grace's and the other character's state of death, this becomes subterfuge to keep the characters (and the spectator) guessing. Rodríguez Ortega refers to the narrative as an instance of Christian Metz's plausible text: we can believe in the real because that is what we are presented with.[27] When Grace and her children discover the truth about the servants, it is through empirical discovery: the children find the servants' graves, and Grace finds the photograph of the servants in their state of death. For the majority of the film, the spectator shares the perspective of the family, and therefore shares their belief that they are ones who are being haunted.

Aviva Briefel writes, '[d]ying is not only a corporeal failure, but also a cognitive act: those who overlook their deaths are not really dead'.[28] The film focuses its narration on prolonging the unravelling of the cognitive process of knowing and understanding demise. Grace and the children are not aware that they are dead; in this state comes the sublime, which pushes all of them, especially Grace, to the point of madness. Mishra writes, 'The experience of the sublime pushes the imagination to crisis point, to a point of exhaustion and chaos', which echoes Immanuel Kant's sentiment of the sublime as an outrage to the imagination.[29] Grace cannot imagine that she and her children are dead, which speaks to her inability to remember murdering them. In one scene, when Grace investigates noises on the second floor, Anne tells her that there are other people in the house. Grace goes into a room, where at first she is frightened by a mannequin, then finds a mirror: the camera is beside Grace, filming both her and what she sees in the reflection, as a door closes seemingly by itself [See Figure 3.2]. This is accompanied by non-diegetic music that crosses between melodramatic and horror extremes, as if the combination of the two is the state of sublimity. That is to say, the use of shots that indicate an unseen presence in combination with the melodramatic score connect with extreme feelings that indicate the sublime. Again, the melodramatic music serves as a bridge for the lack of language to connect Anne's words with Grace's physical experience; it is the bridge of the sublime that indicates to the audience Grace's inner emotional state in the moment of fear.

The film begins with a voice-over narration by Grace: 'Now children, are you sitting comfortably? Then I'll begin', which sounds like the beginning of a fairy tale.[30] Mishra sees the sublime as a moment of entry into the dream-text; the opening narration sets the film and its story into a dream-state akin to the sublime. Lyotard writes that the aesthetics of the sublime are a 'kind of cleavage with the subject between what can be conceived and what can be imagined or presented', and so language turns to storytelling.[31] Dani Cavallaro further writes that storytelling 'is a means of structuring and publicly articulating human fears and its principle aim… is to provide arenas where in an otherwise intractable Beyond may be grappled with'.[32] The pictures accompanying the voice-over are also suggestive of

Fig. 3.2 Grace thinks she sees a ghost, *The Others* (Dimension Home Video, 2003)

the fairy tale; but the voice is recounting the story of creation from the Bible, as though it should be treated as a fairy tale. These pictures are illustrations of scenes within the film, up to the point at which Grace first sees the face of the psychic lady, her first visual confrontation with the uncanny. Each is asking the audience to follow the story as if it were a child's book, the illustrations as a map to the book and to the discovery of the uncanny that exists beside the real.

The aesthetic of the film conveys the cognitive darkness in which Grace is kept. The house is kept in darkness due to the children's alleged photosensitivity; darkness is also associated with the dream state, and the formlessness of that which evokes the sublime. The film presents clues to her current state, such as doors left open, footsteps with no bodies, and a fog that cannot be traversed. These are also clues for Grace to follow that will lead her from the pain of sublimity to the pleasure of cognition. The pain of the sublime comes from the trauma of killing her children. In order to preserve her sanity when she is unable to process the murders into her life narrative, Grace forgets and turns to storytelling to make sense of her current situation. The horror surfaces as representations of the traumatic memory, and when Grace remembers, the pleasure of the sublime returns.

The house is the only space that Grace and her children can occupy after death as, in their status as mother and children, it is the only place that will allow them some type of existence. The rise of capitalism in the eighteenth century coincided with the separation of public and private life; the private life, centred on the home, was the woman's domain. The rise of the gothic novel coincided with changes in social conceptions of the domestic space, and the space of women. Women may have been subordinate to their husbands, but the home was their domain and as such was meant to be ordered and civilized. As husband and father, Charles is able to return briefly, but leaves once he learns of Grace's crime. In melodramas, fathers/husbands were frequently absent, due to war, business, or alienation from the domestic sphere.[33] In this case, his alienation is either the result of his death in another location, or his inability to reconcile with his wife's murderous act.

In *The Others*, the intruders are, until the end, heard as opposed to seen. The first time Grace is confronted with a visual representation of the truth (the psychic in place of her daughter), that which would give her the knowledge to move past the pain of the sublime, to the pleasure of cognition, she reacts violently, and the image disappears, leaving her to remain in the state of pain. If a mark of post-modernism is the heavy use of irony as a mode of expression, Amenábar may be moving beyond postmodernism, as there is nothing ironic in the sublime. The film reinforces the transcendental significance of the sublime, as it is through the atmosphere of heightened feeling that Grace comes to know and understand her state. Irony would suggest that the sounds Grace hears are a product of her imagination; but they are real. The sublime state does not allow for irony. Sublimity leads Grace to the other side in her realization of her crime against her children.

The story that Grace tells her children in the opening scene is from the book of Genesis in the Bible, specifically the story of God's creation of the world. It is told from a Catholic perspective, in simplistic words so the children can understand it. The gothic novel has often been cited as very anti-Catholic. The gothic raises the status of 'the Other' to a narrative principle, in whatever forms it takes. That Grace is a devout Catholic, whose beliefs are overturned by her status as ghost, would seem to uphold an anti-Catholic sentiment within the film. When Anne is reading the Bible on the stairs as punishment for lying about the noises in the house, it is the beginning of the story of Abraham almost killing his son: another clue left for Grace, and a comment on the negative side of religious fervour. According to Maria Purves, anti-Catholic sentiment found in early gothic novels was connected to a Protestant distrust of and distaste for the symbols and rituals of Catholicism, which were viewed as backward, bordering on barbaric.[34] Grace had stopped the story of the creation of the earth just before God separated night and day; indeed, all is in darkness in Grace's story. That the film ends with the children able to go into the light begs the question of what story Grace will now tell.

Cavallaro writes, 'through the discourse of haunting, the gothic vision posits both the ghost and the persecuted subject as existentially incomplete'.[35] Grace is both the persecuted subject and the ghost; thereby leaving her at a stalemate. The gothic clichés – dark shadows, eerie voices, and strange noises – are used to highlight Grace's crisis of faith. Ismael Ibáñez Rosales writes that the reconstruction of Grace's identity is presented as an 'inner struggle between her predetermined Catholic beliefs and her unconscious refusal to accept her newly acquired condition'.[36] The only ghosts (other than the Holy Ghost) allowed in Catholicism are demons, which must be exorcized. Grace never considers herself or the children demons, even when the living family is attempting to banish them from the house. The Spanish themes of Catholicism and its accompanying repression are in question. In the beginning, Grace uses the repression of Catholicism to keep her children in the dark, literally and figuratively. By default, it would seem that Grace must renounce her faith once she discovers the truth. It is to Bertha that the family now looks for guidance, as if in place of a male god, there is now a female earth mother, harkening back to a more primordial religion in which the living and the dead exist side by side. This would seem to be turning its back on both traditional gothic convention, in which science and reason give a natural explanation to supernatural events, though it does support the Catholic idea of limbo, a place where those who have not been baptized linger instead of going to heaven (though it is likely that Grace and her children would have been baptized).

The Others is both a reworking of the traditional gothic story, with its focus on religion versus enlightenment, and a postmodern pastiche of the genre. Its popularity and success cannot be separated from the popularity of its director and star, nor from its variation on the gothic melodrama and its contemporary, secular viewpoint on representing the supernatural. By placing the film in a historical setting, *The Others* acknowledges the roots of the gothic and melodrama genres, while at the same time combining and developing them into a contemporary form for a postnational film.

Amenábar has found critical and financial success both in Spain and internationally, with both fantastic and non-fantastic films. His approach to production, with involvement in nearly all production aspects of his films, is reflective of not only of a European auteur, but also of a fantastic genre filmmaker, whose knowledge of the semiotics is essential to creating a new syntax. The popularity of his films, both nationally and internationally, marks him as one of the first of Spain's contemporary postnational fantastic filmmakers, appealing to both genre and non-genres audiences.

4

The Haunting of Houses: *The Abandoned* and *The Orphanage*

Haunted houses are popular tropes in fantastic cinema, and films such as *The House That Screamed* and *The Others* set a precedent for this trope in Spanish films. *The Abandoned*, directed and co-written by Nacho Cerdà, and *The Orphanage*, directed by Juan Antonio Bayona and written by Sergio Gutiérrez Sánchez, were first features for each director. Both feature films centre on a haunted house, a female protagonist, and violence against children. However, while *The Abandoned*, an English-language film, is more experimental in form, *The Orphanage*, a Spanish-language film, is a more classical gothic melodrama.

The Abandoned earned almost €400,000 at the Spanish box office, making it a moderate success there, and a respectable success in the US with slightly more than $1 million. *The Orphanage* was a huge success, grossing over $7 million in the US (only *Pan's Labyrinth* and Almodóvar films had been more successful), and it was the top film of the Spanish box office in its year of release, grossing more than €37 million. This speaks both to the fantastic film fan base and perhaps more to successful marketing campaigns. Both films played to critical acclaim at TIFF. *The Abandoned* was distributed in the US by After Dark Films, who have had success marketing cult cinema. *The Orphanage* had Guillermo del Toro as a producer; it was released only a year after *Pan's Labyrinth*, and del Toro's name was enough to sell a certain kind of film to a wide audience.

Cerdà's short films were made just when the contemporary Spanish fantastic boom was beginning in the mid-1990s. For Cerdà, horror was a genre to be taken seriously, and films such as *The Abandoned* should not be set alongside what he viewed as lighter horror-comedic fare. His second short film, 'Aftermath', won the Audience Award for Best International Short Film in 1997 at Fantasia. However, it was also viewed by some audiences in Europe as being obscene and pornographic in its gory depictions of an autopsy. Cerdà has tried to distance himself from the 'gore' label, feeling that the depiction was realistic as opposed to indulgent. He views this short and his others, 'The Awakening' (1990) and 'Genesis' (1998), as a trilogy, and it is available as such on DVD. In each of these films, he approaches the subject of death and its consequences on mind, body and spirit; this theme would recur in *The Abandoned*. Despite the critical and audience success of his shorts, it was several years before his first feature was made.

Bayona attended film school in Barcelona, and also had success with his first short films, 'Mis vacaciones' (1999) and 'El hombre Esponja' (2002). 'Mis vacaciones' won awards at films festivals in Spain and France. Both of these shorts focused on children and childhood memories, influenced by his own childhood and his love of comics. As a teenager, he interviewed del Toro about his film *Cronos* (1993) at the Sitges festival, and they remained in touch, as Bayona kept del Toro informed about his film career. It was del Toro's patronage of *The Orphanage* that was arguably the launching pad for its success. Bayona has gone on to make *The Impossible* (2012), starring Ewan McGregor and Naomi Watts, a drama based on the true story of a Spanish family caught in the tsunami disaster in South East Asia in 2004, and *A Monster Calls* (2016), with Sigourney Weaver and Liam Neeson. A return to the fantastic genre and children, it tells the story of a boy who copes with his mother's terminal illness through an imaginary friend. Both of these films are in English, and *The Impossible* broke all box office records in Spain, as well as earning nearly $20 million in the US.

Both first films have a specific setting: a haunted house. Gaston Bachelard describes the house as 'our first universe', and argued that the memories of a house are fixed within it, securing and strengthening them.[1] For Piera Scuri, the house reflects the personalities, desires, and fears of its inhabitants, and therefore 'if one's spatial identity is distorted, the completion of one's personal identity is threatened'.[2] According to Barry Curtis, Sigmund Freud conceived of the human psyche as a building or labyrinth, a series of rooms and corridors through which it finds symbols and memories to interpret identity; to come, or return, to this building is akin to returning to the scene of a crime.[3] Each film presents a home (or connected buildings within a small geographical space) in which the characters' interpretation of empirical reality is disabled, and the uncanny is a constant presence. Writing in German, Freud used the word 'unheimlich', which literally means 'unhomely' as opposed to uncanny. Taking this literal definition, the feeling of the uncanny is especially acute in a place that is unhomely; a place that was once known as home, and in which the characters find themselves unfamiliar.

According to Freud, the uncanny is a type of fear or doubt arising from a lack of certainty around defining a perceived object or situation. This uncanny feeling is caused either by the uncertainty over whether an inanimate object is now animate, or by the perception of something that was once known and had been, until this point, forgotten.[4] For Freud, this is a return to a more animistic view of the universe, one in which mysticism allows the subject to believe that something beyond the realm of scientific reasoning is the cause of the uncanny feeling. Using Freud's uncanny for the interpretation of literary texts, Tzvetan Todorov sees the fantastic as the representation of the uncanny: that hesitation, in the interpretation of things or events. For Todorov, a story can be considered fantastic-uncanny if, at the end, a rational explanation is revealed; if there were a supernatural explanation, the story would be fantastic-marvellous.[5] As their conclusions support the existence of the supernatural, both *The Abandoned* and *The Orphanage* are fantastic-marvellous. But each takes a different approach: while *The Orphanage* follows a classical gothic narrative, updated for the twenty-first century, *The Abandoned* adapts more a more surrealist tone in form and content.

Tom Gunning sees the uncanny as a product of a contemporary culture in which there are fewer folkloric/mythic beliefs, and so the uncanny becomes an unwelcome sensation.[6] Anthony Vidler expands on this, writing that:

> The uncanny... might be characterized as the quintessential bourgeois kind of fear: one carefully bounded by the limits of real material security and the pleasure afforded by a terror that was... kept well under control, [and] best experienced in the private sphere of the home.[7]

While one is a house being made into a home, and one is a long-abandoned house that will likely only be a home for ghosts, both homes in the films examine this bourgeois fear of the limits of materiality and its effects on identity.

IMDB lists over 700 films from countries around the world as involving haunted houses, and most of them have 'horror' as at least one of their listed genres, though not all may be frightening or involve the supernatural.[8] Some, such as *Let's Scare Jessica to Death* (John D. Hancock, 1971) and *Intruders* have psychological/human condition conclusions as opposed to the supernatural, and *Casper* (Brad Silberling, 1995) and *The Haunted Mansion* (Rob Minkoff, 2003) are family-oriented comedies with mild horror. Some haunted house films such as *Black Christmas* (Rob Clark, 1974) and *House* (*Hausu*, Nobuhiko Obayashi, 1977) are set in sororities or among a group of friends, rather than with a nuclear family. But the concept of the 'unhomely' and its trope of the haunted house crosses cultural boundaries, and those boundaries mean that many haunted house films can either have strong or weak connection to the national cultures of their creators.

Arguably, neither *The Abandoned* or *The Orphanage* are identifiable as 'Spanish'; issues of domestic harmony (or lack thereof) and family ties can be found in any number of national cinemas, and the inclusion of the fantastic element within such themes, indeed with a fantastic element used a direct means of exploring these themes, is also not exclusive to any one nation or culture. These films present a new type of postnational cinema, using genres and modes and their accompanying techniques to explore themes often left to more realist cinema.

The Abandoned

From a production perspective, *The Abandoned* has many transnational elements. Cerdà is from Catalonia, a region of Spain that many (particularly those from it) do not consider culturally the same as its governing nation. Its other two co-writers are not Spanish (Karim Hussein is Canadian, and Richard Stanley is South African), it is set in Russia, filmed in Bulgaria, and the main spoken language is English. Ángel Sala writes that *The Abandoned* is in many ways typical of Catalan cinema in its auteurist expression, but it was also important to the production company Filmax.[9] The year before, Filmax had integrated its previously separate horror label, Fantastic Factory, into the parent company, and was continuing its pursuit of Spanish-led international features.[10] Previous films by Spanish directors such as Jaume Balagueró (*Darkness*) and Paco Plaza (*Romasanta*) had given the company a reputation for English-language cinema that was sellable in the international market. *The Abandoned* was part of the now-regular production of films made for the international market, revealing influences from such a wide range of cinematic trends that it could only be called postnational.

Marie has come to Russia to find a lawyer who knows of the farm belonging to her birth family. She goes to the countryside to visit it, but upon arrival, the man who drives her to the farm (isolated on an island surrounded by a deep river) disappears, and Marie nearly drowns. A man who claims to be her twin brother, Nicolai, saves her; he grew up in Russia, and was informed by the same lawyer about the farm. They are visited by what appear to be corporeal ghosts of themselves in a state of death. Nicolai claims that his trouble began when he saw the doppelgänger of Marie two days before, when he began his journey to the farm. Escape from the house and island seems impossible; even when Marie appears to cross the river by boat, she is returned to the house. Eventually, Nicolai is eaten by wild boars, and Marie drowns in a final escape attempt.

Cerdà's short films 'Aftermath' and 'Genesis' gained cult fame for their twist on traditional horror semantics, the brutality of their narratives, and their surreal tone. While *The Abandoned* is identifiable as a horror film through its semantics of the isolated location, haunted house, and danger from the doppelgängers, it twists those semantics into a different syntax with surrealist qualities, through a non-linear narrative and an exposition that reveals the cause of supernatural events in a confused order.

Writing on fantastic literature, Todorov surmised that the uncanny occurs during the point of hesitation, when the character and/or reader does not know if events are real or supernatural in origin. Rosemary Jackson notes that the fantastic mode inverts 'elements of this world, re-combining its constitutive features in new relations to produce something strange, unfamiliar… absolutely "other" and different'.[11] As a fantastic film, *The Abandoned* inverts realistic elements, and enacts hesitation through the possibility of the supernatural, in a story of family trauma. *The Abandoned* adopts a certain syntax of surrealism in its use of non-linear time, working in conjunction with horror. The possible interpretations of the various fantastic elements lead away from the strictly metaphorical/master narrative to an unstable relationship between signifier and signified that is representative of postnational genre cinema.

Todorov writes that the fantastic 'is uniquely linked to the sentiments of the characters and not to a material event defying reason'.[12] The material event that brings Marie to the farmhouse at first seems to have a rational explanation: she is attempting to discover her origins. Marie's motivation is to discover the truth about her past. The story is in the realm of Todorov's fantastic-marvellous: the supernatural explains the events, and the audience must accept the supernatural as part of the real. Several elements are presented in the film that support an approach that seeks to create a hesitation, a sense of unhomeliness through dissonant elements. It is in part a haunted house story, except that the ghosts are corporeal. The credits use a Cyrillic typeface that is antithetical to the English language spoken through the film. The colour template changes depending on the timeframe of a particular scene, as opposed to location. In the opening scenes with Marie, the camera never focuses directly on her face, preferring to show her from a low angle, or with her back to the camera, as if to create a disconnection between her and surroundings. The horror mood is developed in the opening sequence and through the dialogue between Marie and the other characters, and through the surrealist mode expressed in shocking imagery pieced together in a non-linear narrative by virtue of the time loop. The mode of representation puts the film into an oneiric state, a dream state, akin to the surrealist mode, whose beginning and end points are difficult to define.

Duncan Wheeler notes that films with depictions of domestic violence were scarce in Spain prior to the past 15 years.[13] Before 1999, even if such violence was portrayed sympathetically towards the woman, in films such as *Club Virginia Orchestra* (*Orquesta Club Virginia*, Manuel Iborra, 1992), and *Gimlet* (José Luis Acosta, 1995), it was represented as naturalized within the social structure. Only recently have films such as *Only Me* (*Sólo mía*, Javier Balaguer, 2001) and *Take My Eyes* (*Te doy mis ojos*, Icíar Bollaín, 2003) addressed and represented the issue directly. Certainly, violence against women is not culturally specific or limited to Spain, but in a country that, until the mid-twentieth century had laws that deprived women of autonomy, such depictions are not uncommon and wife-beating practices are all too familiar. Some scenes in *The Abandoned* present violence as socially naturalized, but with the addition of violence through a fantastic lens, it becomes denaturalized. Near the end of the film, Marie is caught in a time loop, wherein she follows past images of her father taking her and her brother as infants to the barn to shoot them. The adult Marie witnesses her mother shooting her father before she (Marie) is returned to the present. The violence between Marie's parents is consistent with that portrayed in films such as those mentioned above, but here it is presented through the time loop, suggesting such violence resonates beyond not only its point in time, but for those who did not experience it directly, necessitating representation in the fantastic mode. The violence enacted on Marie and Nicolai is not metaphorical of that of the past, but metonymically contiguous with it.

The doppelgängers and the scenes from the past embedded in the present, represented as moving photographs, are presented as uncanny through the time loop. It is as though the house itself has been the site of a film, recording the violence within, and that the pro-filmic violence has no closure given the absence of the siblings. Marie and Nicolai are brought to the past through photographs and documents. They are haunted and attacked by corporeal beings as opposed to spectres [See Figure 4.1]. The doppelgänger of their father comments that there is still one missing family member, Marie's daughter, whose face is never seen, suggesting that, because of the lack of a photograph, she is not (or at least not yet) a part of this 'picture'. The daughter's final speech indicates that she will not go to Russia, though this narration is heard over shots of her family's house and land. This suggests a continuing connection between her and the space of the haunting, but the lack of a facial identity and a disembodied voice lead to a lack of cohesion between the character and the space, other than through filmic (uncanny) means. It could mean that the film of the house is still running, waiting for its conclusion with the daughter's arrival.

Fig. 4.1 The doppelgängers hunt down Marie and Nikolai, *The Abandoned* (Momentum Pictures, 2008)

While the film might adhere to a spatial continuity (in that most of it takes place within a small area), it abandons a linear continuity. There is no 'flashback' sequence in the film per se; any moment in which the past is either remembered or visualized is contiguous with the present moment, and is frequently prompted by an encounter with the doppelgänger, representing the future. While the narrative seems to follow Marie through a linear time frame, the past and the future both crowd in upon this time. Her body in the space of linear time is not a given, as she is confronted by her past in the form of ghosts and memories, and the future, in the form of her doppelgänger. The given violence of the past and the presumed violence of the future give the present and future bodies of Marie a volume in the haunted space, allowing both to exist. Near the end of the film, as Marie is attempting to flee, she is transported back to the lawyer's office, and sees her own past self approaching the building. This is shown with the same colour filters as the original scene, suggesting that she is somehow there, though not necessarily in corporeal form.

In his book on the time-image and its relevance to post-World War II cinema, Gilles Deleuze proposes that within film, time is a labyrinth within which any corner may yield something from the past, present, or future.[14] *The Abandoned* is a subjective narrative, in that the story is told from Marie's perspective and experience. Deleuze writes that there is 'no present which is not haunted by a past and a future, by a past which is not reducible to a former present, by a future which does not consist of a present to come'.[15] This is the time-image of cinema: the past, present and future together, where 'people and thing occupy a place in time which is incommensurable with the one they have in space'.[16] As is the case for Marie and Nicolai, surrealist film often represents a dislocation and displacement of things and people from their own time and space.[17]

While there are changes in colouration of scenes in order to indicate a change in time frame, Marie remains the same in each scene, as if she were the only constant. This might belie Deleuze's theory somewhat, but this version of Marie, the one the story follows, allows for a fixed point through which the past and future that invade the space can be understood. In a fantastic narrative, linear time either has no place, or does not need to be adhered to. Fantastic narratives do not work with clocks, and Bliss Cua Lim argues that these narratives frequently have 'multiple times that never quite dissolve into the code of modern time consciousness'.[18] The supernatural allows for an acceptance of multiple timelines, or time displacement; indeed, that is a common signature of a supernatural or fantastic narrative. A haunting refuses a linear progression; the ghost of the father is stuck at the time of his murder, and the doppelgängers at the time of their deaths. Such is the fictional symmetry common in ghost and haunting stories. This kind of temporal alterity, forced from a time frame outside of the strict narrative, is centred upon the structure of the house, which 'mediates between geological time and human time'.[19] Slippage between the contemporary and the timeless encounter occurs in the space of the abandoned house, an uncanny temporality that emphasizes the haunting and the lack of a linear construct in the narrative. Lim further writes that 'fantastic narratives… have a propensity toward temporal critique, a tendency to reveal that homogeneous time translates disparate, non-coinciding temporalities into its own secular code'.[20] This happens quite literally through the fantastic genre/surrealist mode of *The Abandoned*, as the secular code of homogeneous time is broken when the three timelines coincide.

According to Otto Rank's study of the double, folklore reads that if one sees one's doppelgänger, one will die within a year.[21] It becomes one's fate as soon as one attempts to be rid of it or, in the case of Marie, tries to escape it. The double is indeed terrifying and forces the subject to destroy it, in effect killing him/herself. Marie's doppelgänger might be classified as that which is outside language and beyond signification; it is a monster, inexplicable and unrepresentable, and therefore is represented as herself. As Marie and Nicolai confront their doubles, they recognize different means of death; this is especially significant for Marie, who sees the wet clothes of her double, and knows that she herself cannot swim. When Nicolai shoots his doppelgänger, he is shot. The question in *The Abandoned* is, who is replacing whom? This is an example of literal representations of metonymy in film: the doppelgängers are not metaphors for their respective characters, they are them; and as a piece of the metonymic puzzle, they work in conjunction with the horror element of the supernatural, and the more realist dramatic element of family trauma.

In the lawyer's office, Marie is shown a photograph of her mother; later, Nicolai recognizes the image in the photograph as his mother. Nicolas Royle sees the photograph, and film, as a thing of uncanniness in itself.[22] In the house, Marie is confronted by the doppelgänger, a moving photograph that shows her in her future state of death. When Marie is in the barn witnessing the events of the past, Nicolai is in the house, where he sees a doppelgänger of his mother. She leads him into the hallway, where pigs appear from another room. The doppelgänger then becomes Nicolai's father; the next time Nicolai is shown, his body is discovered by Marie, being eaten by the pigs (which almost happened when he was a baby, as seen previously). The moments with Nicolai are shown in slow motion, and are edited between Marie's scenes where she is briefly transported to the past, in the lawyer's office, with the lawyer now speaking as her father. In writing on family photographs and the effects of mourning, Marianne Hirsch writes that 'the referent haunts the picture like a ghost: it is a revenant, a return of the lost and dead other'.[23] This photograph of the mother, and the apparent living photographs of the doppelgängers, are not just a literal return of the dead or a flashback, but the living trauma of violence that manifests corporeally.

Avery Gordon relates haunting to trauma, stating that haunting often registers 'the harm inflicted or the loss sustained by a social violence done in the past or in the present'.[24] In *The Abandoned*, the violence of the past and the violence of the present are metonymical to each other. This is further emphasized when Marie drowns while attempting to escape, and one of the final shots shows her doppelgänger returning to the house, as though the time loop might begin again. The camera itself seems to be physically pushing Marie through the labyrinth of the house and island, and taking her in this circle of replacement and signification of herself in the doppelgänger. Marie's identity is constantly called into question. In an early scene in her hotel room, the camera never quite focuses on her face; it is either out of focus, or shows her in slight profile as she looks in the bathroom mirror, and speaks on the phone with her daughter. When the camera does show Marie's full face, it is more often than not acting as the projector of her image onto herself. When she does break the mirror in her family home, it is out of outrage of seeing her own (rather than her doppelgänger's) reflection. She is continually pushed towards her destiny and demise.

As a film that examines domestic abuse, overtly through representation and covertly through the fantastic, *The Abandoned* offers a metonymic examination via the syntax of the uncanny. While the uncanny and horror are often paired in film, the inclusion of surrealist elements of time disjunction and corporeal manifestations of the dead suggest an attempt to find a different mode of interpretation and presentation of the fantastic. The combination of international creative influences, folklore, temporal flux, remote locale, and promotion as international cinema both adheres to a European auteur cinema and the growing trend of postnational cinema in Spain.

The Orphanage

For his article on *The Orphanage* in *Sight & Sound*, Charles Gant chose the title, 'Tell no one it's subtitled,' in reference to the marketing of the film outside Spain.[25] The article also notes that the film's marketing inside Spain, and how that marketing emphasized its connection to del Toro, one of its producers. This was to capitalize on the success of *Pan's Labyrinth*, seeking to entice audiences who might enjoy what was being advertised as a similar film, without alienating audiences who might not attend a non-English-language film. Gant notes that distributors chose to focus the trailer on the ghost story, did not include any dialogue scenes and gave no indication of its country of origin. Indeed, if the film were set in another western country, and spoken in another language, it is arguable that nothing significant about the story would need to be changed. Paul Julian Smith sees *The Orphanage* as engaging 'in the repetition and recognition of preceding generic archetypes'.[26] In his review of the film, Spanish critic Jordi Costa Villa referred to the film as the work of a strategist as opposed to an auteur; meaning that it contains known and predictable horror tropes, of which Bayona was fully aware, specifically to make it sellable to an international audience. The film topped the box office in Spain in the year of its release (the first Spanish film to do so since *The Others*), and won several Goya awards, including Best Production Design and Best Script.

Laura, Carlos, and their adopted son Simón move to a former orphanage, where Laura had lived until she was adopted. An old woman, Benigna, comes to Laura inquiring about Simón; she is discovered sneaking around the grounds later that night. In the following days, Laura finds Simón drawing pictures of his invisible friends, who are wearing uniforms such as those Laura and the other orphans had worn thirty years before. At a party, Simón dresses in the same costume wearing a mask; he and Laura fight, and he disappears. Laura discovers that Benigna used to work at the orphanage with her son, who had a facial deformity and wore a mask. He was shunned by the other children, who abandoned him in a seaside cave, where he drowned. Benigna then killed the other children as revenge and burned their bodies in the oven. Laura discovers the basement where the disfigured boy used to hide, and where Simón hid after their fight. She had accidentally trapped him in the basement where he then died. She kills herself, joining the ghosts of her son and the other children.

The Orphanage offers several of the standard semantics of the gothic film: an old house, dark corners and hidden rooms, ghosts, death, and family tragedy. The film is set in the twenty-first century, yet connects to the past through the haunting, and moves to a more contemporary space while still adhering to the essentials of the mode. The social world of the film is contemporary, as is the family: Laura and Carlos are modern parents, there is equality in their relationship, and they are philanthropists both through their son's adoption and the establishment of the orphanage. Religion is never mentioned; instead, there is a clear distinction between the natural and the supernatural.

Science is only put aside once it has been exhausted; instead of a priest, a psychic is called. Séances are a common feature in gothic novels, but this is updated to a twenty-first-century setting through the use of cameras and other recording equipment. This equipment is meant to verify the psychic's claims, to provide a scientific basis for the supernatural. When Laura first approaches the psychic group, she attends a lecture of the Paranormal Sciences, on a discussion of the double. The lecturer cites Carl Jung's theory of the living and the dead meeting in the subconscious, and the figure of the doppelgänger as the herald of death. Laura equates this with her sighting of what she believes was Tomás' ghost on the day of Simón's disappearance. She later learns that is was Simón in costume, but this does not detract from the fact that it was in this costume that he was trapped and subsequently died. If the gothic in its earlier forms was an examination of the debate between ancient beliefs and scientific knowledge, the contemporary interpretation of the genre, as it is used here, suggests the joining of these forces, an acceptance of the supernatural within that which can be determined through scientific means.

The narrative is told almost entirely from Laura's perspective, and in each scene, she encounters other characters or objects that are clues to solve the mystery, first to the house, then to the disappearance of her son. These clues are given to Laura, as if the film were created for her as a puzzle of scenes to reach the end. It is after the first treasure hunt that Simón tells Laura that he does not believe she is his mother. There is then a brief scene when Laura and Carlos tell Simón the truth about his adoption and illness; Simón has reached the end of his puzzle, and in the following scene he disappears. Later in the film, Laura also follows a series of clues that lead her to the basement, where she discovers Simón's body, and the resolution of the puzzle for her, leading to her death.

Jaume Balaguero's film *The Nameless* (*Los sin nombre*, 1999, discussed in the next chapter) focuses on a mother whose child had gone missing; in Elio Quiroga's *The Haunting* (*No-Do*, 2009), a mother talks to the ghost of her dead daughter, who is visible to the spectator, but not to the other characters. While representations of trauma resulting from the loss of a child are certainly not unique to Spanish film, Smith points out that at the time *The Orphanage* was made, the loss, abandonment and trafficking of children featured heavily in Spanish news.[27] Unlike Grace in *The Others*, Laura does not have repressed memories of Simón's death, as she does not realize that she was its inadvertent cause. In interpreting Freud's writing on repetition and trauma, Cavallaro that it 'relates… to a compulsory tendency to re-enact traumatic experiences, largely repressed, in an attempt to bind their energies and reach a state of balance or even entropy'.[28] Laura's re-enactment of the game is traumatic in that it brings back the memory of her lost son, but in its re-enactment she finds the clues to his disappearance and death. It also recreates the traumatic experience of her removal from the orphanage; traumatic, in that she returns to the house because she views it as her home, and in her death, keeps it as her permanent home.

While the narrative is more or less subjective, the camera frequently appears as if it were the eyes of the ghosts that are following Laura's progress in the game. When Laura hides the file on Simón in the kitchen, the camera (or the ghosts) watches in a corner from the adjacent room, which will lead to the treasure hunt that ends at the same kitchen drawer. When Laura opens the front door to find a trail of seashells, the camera becomes Tomás' ghost now returning to the house. The camera is not only following the game, but participating in it as well. At specific points during the film, to give an indication that the ghosts of the children are about to enter the scene, there is a shot of the merry-go-round moving without means of propulsion. The camera is positioned at a low angle, as if taking the child's perspective looking up at the house, waiting either for Laura to come out and play, or to approach the house for the same reason. When Laura begins her experiment in reverting the house to its previous state, it is not the call of the bell that makes the ghosts appear, but playing a game, the same game as at the beginning of the film, right before Laura left the orphanage. Their universe is now one of constant play, and in Simón's death they find another playmate. The ghosts must play the game until Laura can understand and participate. The gothic iconography of the film and the horror-styled music score (composed by Fernando Velázquez) are fully-fledged representations of the sublime. Devendra Varma writes of nineteenth-century gothic that its 'quest was not merely after horror… but after other-worldly gratifications'.[29] In this rearticulation of the gothic, Laura's

Fig. 4.2 Laura tries to summon the ghosts, *The Orphanage* (Optimum Releasing, 2008)

state of sublimity becomes a quest to find the answer to the disappearance of her child. When she reaches the abyss of sublimity, in the realization of her accidental killing of her son, her only route to pleasure is death, the other-worldly gratification that will reunite her with Simón.

Curtis writes that the 'project of architecture is to create structures, spaces and surfaces in which the past can dwell, while at the same time deploying the aesthetic and functional imperatives of the present'.[30] That past is the memories accrued in the structure, in which the residents exist in their present state. In the haunted house, the past not only dwells, but also is alive. Laura returns to the orphanage because of her happy memories, and her wish to recreate the environment that she and the other orphans had. Curtis further writes that what 'haunts [a house] is the symptom of a loss – something excessive and unresolved that requires an intervention in the present'.[31] Laura intervenes in the present to resolve the past; but to do so she must recreate the past. It is as though the house itself cannot resolve the violence of the children's deaths without a recreation in its walls. The house itself is not evil; it was a house of refuge for children, and the murder of those children means that their ghosts continue to inhabit the space, until Laura can return and solve the puzzle.

Because the murder happened in the past, Laura must set up the house to look as it did when she was a child, to create a continuity of time and event [See Figure 4.2]. When the ghosts still do not appear, she touches the house itself to awaken them. At this point, rather than editing between one shot of Laura and another of the approach of the ghosts, the camera moves between the two with no edits, and the camera is unsteady, as if the house is now the eyes watching Laura, guiding her to the ghosts and the clues to solve the mystery. The end of the film sees the house seemingly abandoned, but as the camera pulls away from Carlos in the penultimate shot, it would seem to reverting to its past state again, and ready to accept Carlos as part of its new state.

The house is the centre of the domestic world. The gothic frequently features women in the home at the centre of narratives, more often than not as a connection between the real and the supernatural. Curtis writes that, '[h]aunted houses are characteristically confronted and explored by young women, as if they have a particular responsibility for resolving problems of habitations gone wrong and bring a courageous capacity for entering into a relationship with the troubled past'.[32] Laura is connected to the house in three ways: as a woman in her 'natural' place; as the mother of Simón and mother-figure to the other children; and as a former resident. Thus, only she, as former resident and mother, is in touch with both the real and the supernatural. When Laura turns to the supernatural for guidance, the house opens to her to give her the final clues. As the unconscious of the house,[33] the cellar keeps the darkest secret. To discover Simón is also to discover this secret, and the house only reveals this for the price of Laura returning to the house as companion and mother to the ghosts. Smith writes that the conclusion opens 'a space for reflection on the moral dangers of confusing fantasy and reality'.[34] The house is that space, both literally and metaphorically, as the space where parents engage with children in both fantasy and reality.

While Carlos allows the psychic to visit the home, he leaves Laura alone for her re-enactment; as the father in the gothic genre, he represents unwelcome rationality. Indeed, while the film frequently shows Laura in close-up, it rarely shows Carlos in anything closer than a medium shot until the final scene, when he is visiting the house after Laura's suicide. This last scene then shows Carlos in similar close-ups and camera movements, such as a slow sweep towards him, as Laura was shown when she was playing her game of discovery. Carlos finds a necklace; the next shot shows the doors opening, seemingly of their own volition; and the next shot is a close-up of Carlos, slowly smiling. This suggests that the game of discovery is about to begin again, and by extension would suggest the eventual inclusion of Carlos in the ghostly family. In the contemporary setting, the father is now also part of the domestic sphere, and also able to cross the supernatural boundary. This somewhat open-ended conclusion also rejects a classical narrative, which would have been definitive, ending when Carlos places a rose on Laura and Simon's grave. Instead, like *The Others*, *The Orphanage* suggests a continuation of the haunting.

Christine Gledhill writes of female melodrama that 'its central protagonists become objects of pathos because [they are] constructed as victims of forces that lie beyond their control and understanding'.[35] Victimized in her own home by the ghosts and Benigna, Laura becomes an object of pathos, centring her in an ideological conundrum. That is to say, as the mother in a gothic melodrama, her responsibility is to the domestic. She failed the orphanage when she left it, and she failed her son when she caused his death. Once she understands these forces, she must make way for the consequences and enact her own death. The house, the centre of a woman's existence, gives her this opportunity.

Laura escaped the death that fell upon her fellow orphans by the accident of her adoption. But the narrative, through the presence of the ghosts and the death of Simón, suggests that she must return to it, and the children, because that is where she belongs. Laura tells Simon the story of *Peter Pan and Wendy* (J.M. Barrie, 1904); like Wendy, Laura did not remain in Never-Never Land, but grew up and had a family of her own. Unlike Wendy, she chooses to return. Laura is, in some ways, an unnatural mother, because of her adoption of a child rather than natural birth, and role as surrogate mother to the ghostly children. When she changes the orphanage to resemble its past state, she sees it as it was when she was a child; she even believes that Simón is still alive. Her mind regresses to the happiest place she has known: in the orphanage, surrounded by children. On one hand, she never grew up; on the other, all children need a mother, even ghost children. She dresses not as one of the orphans, but as a matron of the house. Laura cannot become a child again; she dies as a mother, so will she live in this afterlife with the ghosts as their mother, bound to them by childhood connection, yet in an alternate role. Davies sees the restoration of the normative family as coming at a price: 'the suicide of Laura… can be seen as the acceptance of guilt and the need for punishment' so that the restoration can occur.[36] Laura's suicide, then, becomes a capitulation to the sublime, the only prospect of pleasure beyond the pain, and her restoration to motherhood.

The Orphanage rearticulates the modes of gothic and melodrama into a new form, in which the usual meanings of tropes are overturned. If postmodern society adopts the simulacra, where copies and repetitions have no original (thereby liberating them from myths of an ultimate real), then the film seeks to find new meaning in the signs and symbols which it presents, those which reflect, through various new meanings, the difficulty in articulating the sublime. First there is the house: in the gothic film, it is the centre of a haunting, usually evil. But the evil of this house comes from a living person (Benigna), and the ghosts of the children are the (relatively) innocent victims. The house in melodrama is the centre of the domestic and private sphere; but a home for orphans is both public and private, even though a nuclear family is at its heart. Laura is both archaic and contemporary: she is a traditional mother, more attached to her son than to her husband, more attached to her home than the outside world, and through her death permanently located within the domestic sphere. But she also has narrative agency, and works as a detective (traditionally a male trope) would to solve the puzzle.

The ending of the film is neither conclusive, nor necessarily definitively happy or sad. Laura and Simón are dead, victims of despair and circumstance respectively, but there is a suggestion that Carlos might join them in their ghostly world. Both parents pass through a sublimity of pain to reach pleasure. This is shown, unironically, in Laura's reception of the ghostly world she will now inhabit, and Carlos' smile at the gravesite of his family. Claire Colebrook writes that postmodernism consists of pastiche, simulation and cynicism, and an all-encompassing irony where nothing really means what it says.[37] While *The Orphanage* offers pastiche and simulation, irony depends on tone. Irony is tied to intention, and there is no suggestion that the film intends irony in its use of gothic and melodrama. Even the intertextual reference to *Peter Pan* is not meant ironically; it doesn't mean something else, but rather indicates a reflection of the *Peter Pan* story in *The Orphanage*, through Laura's death and journey to the fantastic realm.

The Orphanage rearticulates the gothic and melodrama through its contemporary setting and portrayal of the sublime, family, trauma, and motherhood. It is a film that in many ways hides its Spanish origins for the sake of the international audience. It is indicative of much of contemporary Spanish fantastic film that privileges the international audience over the national.

The Abandoned and *The Orphanage* show how, even when two films are from the same country, their representation of fantastic genre tropes can be widely divergent. Each has a main female character confronting a trauma; each is set in and around a haunted house; and each has ghosts. One adopts a surrealist mode, the other a traditional mode. Other than language in *The Orphanage*, neither can be readily identified as a Spanish film, and both relied on marketing that de-emphasized any particular national cultural perspective. *The Abandoned* and *The Orphanage* utilize the fantastic to explore themes of trauma and family strife as part of the new wave of postnational film.

5

Jaume Balagueró: The Horror Aficionado: *The Nameless* and *Darkness*

Like the filmmakers in the previous chapter, Jaume Balagueró is from Catalonia, and has become one of the key figures in contemporary Spanish fantastic film. He gained cult status with two short films, 'Alicia' (1994) and 'Días sin luz' (1995), the former of which won an award for Best Short at Sitges festival. He has directed five features solo, *The Nameless, Darkness, Fragile* (2005), *Sleep Tight* (*Mientras duermes*, 2012) and *[REC]4: Apocalypse* (*[REC]4: Apocalipsis*, 2014), and two with Paco Plaza, *[REC]* (2007) and *[REC]2* (2009). These films show a fascination with and adaptation of classic horror semantics, most specifically with the nature of evil, either in the form of cults, monsters, or individuals. Like Cerdà's, Balagueró's use of horror tends toward the more serious, and is more concerned with how reality is reflected in horror, and vice versa.

Raised in and around Barcelona, Balagueró had a love of horror and fantastic film from childhood. His influences range from Steven Spielberg and James Cameron to Lucio Fulci and Dario Argento. He studied communications and photography at a local university, graduating in 1991. Afterwards, he worked as a radio host and film critic, as well as editing a popular horror fanzine, *Zineshock*, influenced in part by the underground scene in London, which he had visited. He wrote scripts for two shorts film that were never made, and he considers 'Alicia' his first film, feeling that his vocation was really to be a director. The film was made with friends he worked with at the fanzine, and with help from the Alternative Cinema Factory in Barcelona. Like his first feature-length films, 'Alicia' explores themes of perversion, evil and cults. Balagueró wanted to include images of religion and sadomasochism, something that would both disturb and frighten the audience.

His second short, 'Dias sin luz', dealt with similar ideas, in part influenced by a radio programme on which Balagueró interviewed Domina Zara, a sadomasochist with whom he developed a friendship. Both films reflect a European, pessimistic outlook, and Balagueró's interest in existential philosophy and darkness. Arguably, he is more well known in Spain than in the international community, except among hard-core horror fans. But his steady output, and the quality and success of that output, both financially and among critics, identify him as one of the most consistent and reliable directors of horror film in Spain. Made in both Spanish and English, the consistent quality of his work speaks not only to his talent as a filmmaker, but to his attention to genre semantics and how they work with audiences, and the postnational nature of fantastic film.

The horror genre is named as such from its desire to draw an emotional response from, and frighten, the spectator. *The Nameless* and *Darkness* both centre on religious cults that sacrifice children, and the nature of evil; in the former, the evil of humans, and in the latter, both human and supernatural horror. *The Nameless* is in Spanish, but is based on a novel by UK horror writer Ramsay Campbell, with the story transplanted to Spain. *Darkness* is an English-language film with an international cast, marketed to the international spectator. Each film uses the semantics common to horror film to reach the spectator across cultural lines, using what Noël Carroll calls the complex discovery plot, common to horror films.

Through a structural and cognitive analysis, Carroll writes that the 'point of the horror genre… is to exhibit, disclose and manifest that which is, putatively in principle, unknown and unknowable'.[1] Horror film seeks to represent that which is unknown, and to frighten through this representation. The core of what Carroll calls erotetic narration, is that scenes that appear early in the order of exposition, are related to later scenes, allowing the spectator to follow and decipher a story's clues.[2] In the case of horror films, this is the question of whether the object of fear will be discovered, and how the extent of knowledge possessed by character and spectator adds to the horror. Carroll writes that horror films generally follow a complex discovery plot: onset, discovery, confirmation and confrontation.[3] The object of fear arrives attended by disturbing events; the object is discovered by the main character(s); an investigation confirms the object; and the main character(s) confronts the object. There are variations within this: discovery may happen at the same time as onset or confirmation, or more time might be spent on one section than another. While each film adapts the representation of its main object of fear – evil in *The Nameless*, through the acts of the cult, whereas *Darkness* represents the dark almost as a character – each plays with spectator expectations of and reactions to fear.

According to Tzvestan Todorov's criteria, both films begin as fantastic, but *The Nameless* ends with the uncanny, in that there is a rational (yet terrible) explanation, and *Darkness* ends with the marvellous, in that the supernatural is real. Both films also feature cults, missing children, and traumatized families. Like haunted houses, cults and children are popular horror film tropes, seen in other films such as *Rosemary's Baby* (Roman Polanski, 1968), *The Wicker Man* (Robin Hardy, 1973), and *Martyrs* (Pascal Laugier, 2008). There is usual a religious connection, and in both *The Nameless* and *Darkness*, the cults are connected to Christianity, though not Catholicism (the dominant religion of Spain) per se. Films such as *Rosemary's Baby*, *The Wicker Man* and *Martyrs* all feature groups who hide their true beliefs from the public eye, while kidnapping, injuring and/or killing innocent people in order to bring about events such as a good harvest, the reincarnation of Satan, or an understanding of death. Children have always been prominent in Spanish film of any genre, particularly those that relate a story of trauma. The cults in *The Nameless* and *Darkness* are both attempting to discover or unleash pure evil. As children are seen as the opposite of this, cast as innocent and pure, they are often the main characters in horror films featuring cults. And as children and cults appear in horror films from several nations, Balagueró is using these stories to engage with postnational horror.

While both films are set in Spain and filmed in and around Barcelona, there is no mention of the country or city in either film. The setting in *The Nameless* is meant to be the modern metropolis, but it is unnecessary to know its specific location, as Barcelona could stand in for any western city. In *Darkness*, it is significant that the family is living in a foreign country, but again, the specificity of Spain is more or less irrelevant. In order to fulfill a postnational mandate, their narratives and references must go beyond the Spanish context. This means turning to an intertext of horror, combining genre semantics such as the haunted spaces, religious cults, and the dysfunctional family within an internationally relatable cultural context of language and casting. As the first features in Balagueró's oeuvre, *The Nameless* and *Darkness* are examples of the kind of fantastic film that could be successful both in the national and international markets.

The Nameless

While Balagueró's fanzine generally covered more gory horror and trash cinema, his films show a dedication to more of a thriller mode. His noted influences such as Argento and David Cronenberg show his interest in body horror, which certainly appears in *The Nameless*, but he also looks to the core elements of horror in order to engage his audience. Andrew Willis writes that *The Nameless* 'accepts the boundaries of the psychological horror film and attempts to offer depth in order to say something about the human condition'.[4] In other words, Balagueró looks for the most basic fears to exploit, while at the same time combining horrific images of bodily harm with deeper human psychological trauma.

The Nameless eschews any cultural specificity in favour of the kind of horror film that could be understood and appreciated by genre fans around the world. Like Amenábar, Balagueró balances auteurist and commercial cinema, making films that contain his signature themes of bodily harm and family strife in combination with aesthetics representing the effect of the past on the present. His first short, 'Alicia', was about the kidnapping of a teenage girl by a cult who wanted to sacrifice her to an ogre; his second, 'Días sin luz', was about the trauma of a young boy abandoned by his family. In *The Nameless*, Balagueró has combined his twin interests in embodied and psychological trauma.

The body of a girl is found in an abandoned warehouse, mutilated almost beyond recognition. The only clues as to her identity are a bracelet with her name, Ángela, and the fact that one of her legs is shorter than the other. Detective Bruno Massera tells the girl's parents that, even with only this to go on, it must be their daughter. Years later, her mother Claudia (now separated from her husband) cannot get over the loss. She struggles with drug addiction, and spends her nights watching home movies of Ángela. One morning, she receives a phone call from a girl claiming to be her daughter; the caller says she was kidnapped by a cult, and her mother can find her at an abandoned hospital near where they used to take holidays. At the hospital, Claudia finds clues that suggest Ángela is still alive. She contacts Messara, recently retired, and convinces him to help her investigate. They find out about a cult group, The Nameless, which began with a man, Santini, who was imprisoned and tortured by the Nazis; during this time, he began this cult whose purpose is purification through doing harm, particularly to children, in order to discover pure evil. They discover that the body thought to be Ángela was another girl, used to distract the police. The group tortures and kills Massera, and Claudia discovers her husband is part of the group and used Claudia to conceive a child that could be raised in evil.

In using the complex discovery plot, *The Nameless* follows not only the semantics of horror film, but also of suspense film. Like fantastic films, suspense films tend to emphasize a labyrinthine structure or convoluted plot, partial knowledge or vision, and they often include maze-like spaces. For Carroll, the key component of emotional suspense is a cognitive state of uncertainty.[5] In writing on suspense literature, Richard Gerrig notes that 'suspense occurs when readers, using only their own resources, cannot determine which… outcome will be [obtained]'.[6] One could easily substitute the word 'suspense' with 'uncanny' or 'fantastic' in this context. The difference in the usage is that one does not usually think of the supernatural when watching a suspense film. Lothar Mikos positions suspense as a pleasurable flirtation with fear, characterized by a loss of control, awareness of danger, and the thrill of observation.[7] Again, the main difference between suspense and the fantastic is the use of the possibility of the supernatural as the agent of the fear.

Balagueró focuses on the psychological effects of trauma, as well as the investigation of the source of the horror. While the cult featured in the film is given a religious origin, and there is some mention of a connection with the Nazis' well-documented interest in the occult, neither are explored in depth. This is the window dressing that Balagueró uses to represent a more pure horror to his audience; he strips away the fabric as much as he can to reveal what horror film is about in essence: the root of human evil.

The opening scenes of the film present the complex discovery plot as both horror and suspense. Massera arrives at the scene of the crime; Balagueró shows him arriving in the rain, with set decoration and sounds effects typical of suspense/detective films (police cars and radios), and exposition about the crime [See Figure 5.1]. This is intercut with flashes of what appear to be bodily torture, aged photos of harmed children, and even an image of a young girl sped up so that she appears to move in a way reminiscent of a dream state. The setting is an abandoned warehouse, akin to both horror and suspense; but the breathing mask that Massera wears gives him the appearance of a monster, adding a horror semantic element. The discovery of the body, and the coroner's description of what happened to the body, go far beyond what most suspense or detective stories would allow, save perhaps recent US television shows *Hannibal* (NBC, 2013–15) and *True Detective* (HBO, 2014–).

This onset phase of the complex discovery plot has a different syntax than most horror films (similar to suspense/detective films); usually, in a horror film, the story would lead to a climax of the body's discovery, i.e. the story would present what happened to the unknown girl. Instead, Balagueró shifts the syntax to the discovery of what happened to Ángela after the body's discovery, in that the ends are known before the means. The film keeps to a cause-and-effect narrative common in most films (horror and other genres), in that the scenes are relegated to action that aids in either necessary character building or information leading to discovery and investigation. When the discovery is made – when Claudia receives a phone call from Ángela – rather than show Claudia's full face in the frame, the camera shoots the side of her face, obscuring much of it behind the telephone. This moment of discovery, then, is made as much from the perspective of Ángela as it is from Claudia, and by extension the spectator. By placing the telephone at the centre of the frame, the spectator is put in the position of independent investigator, somewhat detached from Claudia's emotional reaction. This is not to suggest

Fig. 5.1 The scene of the gruesome crime, *The Nameless* (Dogwoof Pictures, 2006)

that the spectator does not feel sympathy for Claudia, but rather, at this point, the spectator must remain neutral. This shifts when in the following scene, Claudia goes to the abandoned hotel and finds items related to Ángela; the final shot shows Claudia's full face, allowing the spectator to become fully invested in her and her investigation to follow. When the third part of the film begins, with the final stages of discovery and confirmation, the musical score is reminiscent of those composed for Alfred Hitchcock films by Bernard Herrmann, emphasizing the suspense that keeps the spectator somewhat apart from a stronger empathy to the characters. The concluding scenes return to a more horror-styled score that leads to greater emotional inclusion. The usual semantics of horror and suspense are brought together, working both with and against each other, in a new syntactical arrangement that thwarts audience expectation.

As stated, *The Nameless* is a combination of body horror and family drama that combines horror with suspense. It is uncanny, but there is a real-world explanation for the events: human evil. Even though the story is about bodily harm and torture, only two scenes and a few of the brief images show violence: the autopsy of the girl's body early in the film; Claudia's drug dealer Tony's mutilated body; and the torture and murder of Quiroga, a photographer assisting Claudia. These images serve more for their effect on the characters as opposed to the importance of the actions themselves, although they also further the narrative. Instead of relying on gory effects and violent imagery, Balagueró focuses on the psychological effects of said violence. The liberation of the soul through extreme pain, which is the focus of the cult, is described and shown briefly in photographs, as opposed to enacted in the film. When Claudia meets Santini, the founder of the cult, his description of what he suffered in the concentration camps, and his subsequent creation of the cult's doctrine, is done purely through dialogue, as though what Claudia (and by extension the spectator) will picture in their minds would be far more graphic and horrifying that any imagery Balagueró could put on screen. When we learn of Massera's own psychological trauma due to the death of his pregnant wife, it is from brief images of her, then a nightmare he has of her in the hospital, with no explanation as to the cause of her death. Again, the horror is more talked about than visually represented, emphasizing the psychological trauma as far more affecting than visual representation.

In an article on *The Nameless*, Julio Ángel Olivares Merino described what he termed the 'Balagueró effect': this includes fast editing of images together with no immediately coherent transition, abrupt cuts, and constant movement between images of reality, dreams, the past and the present.[8] The 'ghost within' comes through technology: home movies on VHS that Claudia watches repeatedly; the telephone calls from Ángela; and Massera's search for information on the cult via microfiche archives. The source novel was published in 1981, and while the film was made in 1999 and does not necessarily attempt to adhere to the book's time setting, Balagueró still features these analogue means of investigation and remembrance (in 1999, widespread internet use was still uncommon and mobile phones still fairly rare among the general public). Unlike digital, these are not clean technologies. While the connection to the past through technology gives an effect of distance, it is also a connection, but that connection is rough, somewhat untraceable, and prone to elusiveness and mistakes. The sound effects that accompany the images, which sound like distorted scratches and screams, add to this impression of noise. Claudia's fractured memory and mental state are traced through the worn VHS tape, and reflected in her nightmares. These nightmares (which Massera also experiences) are presented, as with the opening scene, as flashes of images, frightening in their incoherence. Balagueró is aiming not to recreate a nightmare, but a waking person's memory of that nightmare, when only these flashes of images remain. The incoherence of these past/nightmare images is placed alongside the investigation of the cult, when information is uncovered in pieces that only form a coherent whole at the climax. And while the investigation builds one piece upon the next, the nightmare/past image flashes serve as part of the investigation as well, as part of memory that might serve to help form that cohesive whole.

The modern city setting of *The Nameless* is not only unidentified; it is also grey and colourless. As in David Fincher's *Se7en* (1995), the particular city is irrelevant. It is worth noting that, in the case of *The Nameless*, a city as popular with tourists and architecturally beautiful as Barcelona has been rendered faceless and, as in the title of the film, nameless. In the story, the cult is said to have originated in the UK, which is likely in keeping with the source material. But its transplantation to Spain is relevant only from a production perspective. The lack of colour, mostly grey and brown tones for two-thirds of the film, is another syntactic device: while the film maintains an objective perspective, the main characters, Claudia and Massera, suffer from depression due to the loss of loved ones. They see no colour because there is no colour in their lives. This is perhaps a somewhat simplistic interpretation, but its simplicity conveys how a minor change can affect the spectator's experience. Colour begins to return when Claudia and Massera meet Quiroga, who will be key to uncovering the truth about the cult. Subsequently Massera meets a colleague at an amusement park; in this place for children, yellows and greens are brightly shot, as if to emphasize that the truth to Ángela's disappearance is coming closer, and she might return to her state as Claudia's child. The most important colour, of course, is red. At first, it only appears in one of Claudia's home movies: her red headband is the only bright colour, pointing out that it is through her 'blood'/maternity that the cult will fulfil its mission. Later, red is prominent in the club Tony where he is picked up by the cult members, and then later when his mutilated body is put on display for Claudia. Colour is at first a sign of mourning, then a sign of hope, then a sign of psychological torture. In the nameless city, lack of colour reflects the lack of life, and by extension the human evil that lies beneath.

As the central character, Claudia's role as mother is the main focus. She is shown to have suffered serious depression after the alleged kidnapping and death of her daughter, and taken to drug addiction. Unlike many fantastic films, in which being a mother is all or nearly all of a woman's role (as seen in *The Others* and *The Orphanage*), Claudia is also shown as successful in her job, editing a book of intimate body photography, and as a sexual being through her affair with Tony. Tony may be an unsavoury character, and her affair with him might be a negative reaction stemming from her depression, but it still gives Claudia a more-well rounded psychology. Sadness over the loss of a child is not only a mother's prerogative; Massera is also shown as suffering from the loss of his wife and unborn child, which manifests in his early retirement from the police force. Both he and Claudia find (or attempt to find) solace and redemption through their investigation. Massera is killed, though his death is not explicitly shown, as though how he dies is less important than the fact of his death, which leaves Claudia as a final girl, surviving the men, even with her sexual past. But even she is not redeemed; her reaction to the suicide of Ángela in front of her is not shown, as if this final, terrible act is all the necessary information, and to show what lies beyond would be too horrific even for Balagueró.

As Balagueró's first feature film, *The Nameless* sets up much of what would become his signature: fast editing; description as opposed to display of violence; cults and children. Balagueró would return to evil of the human kind in his later film *Sleep Tight*, but *The Nameless* set a standard for his blend of body horror and examination of the affects of horror on the human psyche. His next film would turn to a more literal manifestation of the fantastic.

Darkness

After the success of *The Nameless*, Spanish production company Filmax got behind Balagueró's next film, as part of their campaign to make more English-language horror films. They brought American studio Miramax on board as co-producers and distributors in English-speaking nations via pre-sales, which gave the film a budget of $11 million. It was successful at the Spanish box office in 2002, grossing over €4 million. Although it was not released in the US until 2004, it was also a success there, earning over $22 million in three months. Antonio Lázaro-Reboll writes that the marketing of the film relied heavily upon the name of Filmax, as a producer and distributor of quality commercial genre films, and Balagueró's growing status as a horror filmmaker. Filmax was aware of Balagueró's popularity and reputation among horror film fans, as well as his positive critical reception in a broad range of periodicals from *Screen International*, a trade journal, to *Dirigido por*, a specialist film magazine, both of which labelled his films as showing the marks of an auteur.

As Ángel Sala notes, *Darkness*, with its melodramatic style and focus on the family and madness, references horror classics such as *The Shining* and *The Amityville Horror* (Stuart Rosenberg, 1979). The legibility of motifs such as fear of the dark, family, and madness across national traditions places the film in a postnational position. With a cast from New Zealand, Sweden, the UK, Spain, and Italy, a Spanish director and crew, Spanish and American producers, it is, from a production and financial perspective, a transnational film. In addition, *Darkness* uses several horror semantic staples that are legible across cultures and therefore are not nation-specific.

The film opens with a young Spanish boy telling a strange story to a police officer, about running away from a house; at the same time, shots show a group of children trapped in a house, children whose fate is unknown. An American family – father Mark, mother Maria, teenage daughter Regina and young son

Paul – moves into a home in the countryside, where Mark spent his early child-hood. Mark's father, Albert, has helped with the arrangements. The house has elec-trical problems, with the lights constantly blinking; at the same time, Paul senses a presence in the house. While taking Paul to school, Mark has a strange attack, and it is discovered that he has had a type of schizophrenia in the past. Paul tells Regina that he sees the ghosts of children in the house, and Regina begins to inves-tigate. Regina and her friend Carlos find the house's architect, who tells them it was designed in the shape of a temple to re-enact occult rituals. Regina traces the cult to her grandfather Albert, who admits that there was an attempt to open a portal to hell, with children being killed by their parents. Regina returns to the house, to find her father collapsed and her mother attempting to perform a trache-otomy. Regina takes over, but accidentally kills her father, completing the ritual. The house then opens to hell, with Regina, Maria and Paul trapped inside.

One of the greatest assets any horror filmmaker has is his/her use of the dark as a tool for invoking fear both in characters and spectator. If removed from its horror context, *Darkness* is a family melodrama; the addition of semantic tropes of the supernatural and a religious cult make it a horror film. The film uses motifs and imagery common to horror films that focus on the dysfunctional family unit and the supernatural, such as *The Amityville Horror*, *The Shining* and *Poltergeist*. But its use of an international cast, in addition to these common motifs also make it an attempt to find an internationally recognizable version of the horror film and project this to the international spectator.

In *Darkness*, the religious cult seeks to create a gateway to hell through the murder of eight children. The fact that the cult is a sect of Catholicism reinforces its European location (though not necessarily specific to Spain), and refers back to horror films that feature Catholicism in connection with the supernatural. According to Carroll Fry, films with cults 'adapt some of the traditional gothic atmosphere of darkness, storms and haunted space', frequently adding the rel-evant cultural signifiers such as Biblical origins, Satanic practices, and urban leg-ends, to contextualize a particular cult, and the time and location of the story.[9] But the specific beliefs/rituals of the cult are representative of the fear being explored by the film; for example, the cult in *The Wicker Man* represents a fear of open sexuality and matriarchal society. In *Darkness*, the actions/events created by the cult draw out representations of the unstable family: Albert could not kill Mark because he did not love him, and Mark left the country with his mother. Upon his return home, the ensuing tension of the melodrama is represented through the return of Mark's mental illness, driven by supernatural forces. The resolu-tion of the narrative – the entrapment of the remaining family members in the home – represents the idea that an unstable family is doomed. This is in contrast to films such as *The Amityville Horror* and *Poltergeist*, in which the family escapes more or less intact. *Darkness* breaks from the conventional Hollywood ending in its arguably more European pessimism. It also includes the haunted house and nearly constant bad weather or scenes set at night, which reinforces the feeling of primal fear.

The narrative of *Darkness* focuses on the mental illness of the main character. Madness has frequently been represented in multiple ways in film, from *Psycho* (Alfred Hitchcock, 1968) to *A Woman Under the Influence* (John Cassavetes, 1974) to *The Fisher King* (Terry Gilliam, 1992), all of them depicting the state of insanity albeit across different genres. Michael Fleming writes that, '[f]or the film artist madness is principally a subject whose depiction probes the darkest and most hidden side of our being'.[10] As a medium of observation, film allows directors to literally and metaphorically represent madness, not just in the narrative but also in the aesthetic style, through, for example, unusual camera shots or angles, sound or special effects. Horror films frequently use the supernatural as a trope to disturb or displace reality. The mad characters are the centre of a seemingly supernatural object/event, adding both credence to and understanding of their mental condition. Examples of this type of film are *Repulsion* (Roman Polanski, 1965) and *Don't Look Now* (Nicholas Roeg, 1973), both of which involve a main character whose belief that the supernatural is causing events leads to their descent into madness. *Darkness* represents madness through the use of the fantastic. Jason Horsley writes that in 'western society… all minds are assumed to belong to a common, consensus "reality", and any deviance from this consensus is seen as sickness, psychosis, revolt'.[11] The horror genre allows the spectator to access both the mad character's perspective and the perspective of those who either support or deny the existence of the object of fear.

In *Darkness*, Mark suffers from a form of schizophrenia, a recognized mental illness. Jacqueline Noll Zimmerman writes that the representation of:

> people who suffer from schizophrenia… and other serious mental illnesses [is that they] often exhibit an otherness. They do not fit into the norm, either in their speech patterns, their facial expressions, the way they dress, or a combination of features and aspect.[12]

Mark's madness is represented through the possibility of violent behaviour, through his destruction of parts of the house, through various close-ups on his hands when violently cutting vegetables, and the reflection of his face in a macabre picture he finds and insists on displaying. These moments are seen from Maria's perspective in one instance, as if positioning them in a realist context, and also through Regina, who accepts the supernatural, placing them in a fantastic context. As an intertextual film, *Darkness* is drawing on previous representations of the mad person's distorted view of reality, such as in *The Shining*, especially in relation to the danger of violence within the family unit. Mark's first 'attack' occurs eight minutes into the film, accompanied by a radio report on the upcoming solar eclipse, as though the spectator is meant to associate the two events, leading to a suspicion that his illness is supernatural as opposed to being medically based. Patrick Fuery writes of portrayals of madness in film that, 'it is as if the mad sign, the sign twisted and exalted, performs a type of eidetic reduction, where things are seen in terms of their essence'.[13] In one scene, Mark breaks through a wall in the house to discover a secret room; in the macabre photograph, the faces of the three people in the photograph look dead (i.e. a certain amount of sunken decomposition). These visual and narrative images are representations of madness reduced to its essence, easily understood by the spectator.

Fuery further writes that an 'essential feature of madness (which is also the representation of madness) is this capacity to resist interpretation through seemingly endless generations of meanings'.[14] As *Darkness* makes intertextual references to horror films that focus on madness and the dysfunctional family, the spectator is asked to examine and even accept all representations of madness as possibilities. Such representations are metonymic; the meaning is not in the madness, but its representation, with the semantics (the mad character, the dysfunctional family, the supernatural elements such as the haunted house) working contiguously with the syntax (the cause of the madness) in order to form a cohesive whole that expresses horror. The meaning of Mark's madness shifts depending on perspective (his, Maria's, their children). Like the representation of the occult, it is a means to an end. From Maria's point of view, Mark has a legitimate mental illness, and from Regina's, he is affected by the supernatural forces in the house. Regina, as a teenager, is more willing to believe in the supernatural, whereas Maria, as an adult, is not.

Frequently, a nuclear family and their house are at the heart of a horror film. Anthony Vidler writes that:

> The house [provides] an especially favoured site for uncanny disturbances: its apparent domesticity, its residue of family history and nostalgia, its role as the last and most intimate shelter of private comfort sharpened by contrast of the terror of invasion by alien spirits.[15]

Seven minutes into the film, Balagueró shows the hallway seen at the beginning, so the spectator is aware that this is the same house, and knows before the characters that this house is likely haunted. Barbara Creed notes that children and women are more closely associated with the supernatural, that they sense it sooner than adults and men, and are more likely be represented as believing in its existence.[16] This is seen in Danny in *The Shining*, and Carol Anne in *Poltergeist*, both of whom are protected by their mothers. Regina, as a female teenager, straddles both worlds. She is frequently shown arguing with her mother over whether Mark's illness is caused by the biological or the supernatural. Paul, as the only true child, is the first person to be not only aware of the supernatural, but also influenced and affected by it, reminiscent of films such as *The Innocents* and others previously mentioned. Mark might be an adult, but his mental illness renders him an incomplete adult; he is susceptible to the supernatural, but unaware of it. As the madman, he must die in order to break down the wall between the real and supernatural. Maria is the only true adult in the film (excluding Albert as orchestrator of the supernatural); but she, and the children, remain trapped in the house.

The private comfort of the home, an intimate space meant to be filled with familial love and understanding, becomes an unnatural home for its opposite, hell. Although different cultures might have different familial social structures, the essence of the home is easily translatable. The fracturing of the family under the supernatural is shown in that they only appear as a family in one or two scenes, and the dissolution of the family relationship is easily achieved in the final scenes. The house itself, shot with very little natural light, never becomes a family home. Although it is love (through Regina's accidental killing of her father while trying to save him) that allows the supernatural to take over, it is this connection between love and evil that is one of the fundamental semantics of the horror genre. At the end of *Poltergeist*, it is love that rescues the daughter from the ghosts and brings her back into the real world; in *The Others*, it is love that makes Grace realize she is a ghost. *Darkness* is more readily connected to *The Abandoned*, in which the supernatural evil triumphs. In all these examples, which are centred on family, the horror in part comes from the connection between love and evil.

All horror films have a monster, the object of fear, whether it is a human being or a supernatural creature. In the case of *Darkness*, there are a few monsters. First, there are the ghosts of the murdered children, who are fixated on Paul and even assault him. There is Albert, the overreacher whose experiment, once botched, will now succeed. There is the house itself, waiting to become hell. Even Mark could even be considered a monster due to his madness. In Carroll's complex discovery plot, the monster first comes into the story to unleash disaster; one or more of the characters discover this monster; the character(s) confirm the monster's existence;

Fig. 5.2 Regina investigates, *Darkness* (The Film Factory, 2005)

and finally, the character(s) confront the monster. Many of these monsters are red herrings, and the complex discovery plot follows these red herrings. The onset comes first with the ghosts (one of the most common horror motifs); then Mark in his madness, at which point the combination of these two leads Regina to discovery and confirmation, through her investigation [See Figure 5.2]. This confirmation leads to the confrontation with the real monster: darkness. Each monster then serves a purpose.

The ghosts, as children, represent the dark side of the innocence of childhood; these monsters are never fully shown, but instead they are framed in split-second shots with little facial or bodily recognition, as if to indicate to the audience that this monster is a ruse. Children, whether alive or as ghosts, have been the source of evil in horror films such as *Village of the Damned* (Wolf Rilla, 1960) and *Who Can Kill a Child?* Mark straddles the real and the supernatural; medical evidence suggests schizophrenia as the cause of his behaviour, yet Regina believes he is being manipulated by the house, as shown by his obsession with the old photograph. When it is revealed that he is the child from the opening sequence, his madness is represented as justified.

Fear is common to all humans and animals, and manifests in similar ways, such as hair standing on end, cold perspiration, and screaming.[17] And as stated, fear of the dark is one of the oldest fears. Balagueró makes a deliberate effort to keep the interior house dark (both the walls and furnishings are in dark tones), in an almost constant state of low lighting until the final scenes. Acknowledging that a certain level of lighting is needed to show a scene, the scenes are lit to keep as much detail as possible in a smoky shadow, especially inside the house, in the kitchen (when Mark and Maria argue) and in the hall by the stairwell (where Mark hangs the old photograph). Horror films presenting various images of fear in the form of monsters, ghosts, haunted houses, etc., have taught spectators to look for clues as to the origin of the fear experience, and to accept certain symbols as representing certain types of fear. In a contemporary culture attuned to the classical plot and style of horror films, a red herring might not be unexpected, but the film breaks down the fear experience into its various components, such as invasion from the outside, invasion from the inside, the supernatural, or religious cults, and asks the spectator to question if they all come down to the same fear. In the final scene of the film, when Carlos, Regina and Paul drive (or think they are driving) away, the camera never shows their faces directly, nor in full light exposure; Regina tells Paul that the incident is over, but Paul replies that they are still in the house, just as the car goes into a tunnel. This suggests an extension of this fear experience beyond the confines of the film, and beyond the confines of the history of the narrative of such experiences.

Darkness is a representation of the primal and family horror story, in semantic narrative and syntactic form. By invoking semantics from a variety of horror films, it also presents itself as both an implicit and explicit text, through representations of madness, the family, and the haunted house. These various elements are standards in horror film semantics, but have been brought into one film for the purpose of creating the intertext that will appeal to an international audience. It is a postnational film, using semantics and syntax that can be understood by the international horror film spectator.

The Nameless and *Darkness* cemented Balagueró's reputation as an auteur of horror cinema. Both films return to the roots of horror, using semantics commonly recognized, and both rational (human) and supernatural explanations respectively. By returning to these roots, the films self-consciously reflect on horror's genre mechanisms while exploiting its pleasures for the postnational spectator. Both films have a Spanish connection in their setting, yet that Spanish connection is only important from a production perspective, proving that fantastic genre film can cross cultural lines regardless of where it is made. This does not mean that any relation to Spanish culture that is presented is insignificant; rather that, its significance lies in how it relates the fantastic mode as intertext for the postnational.

6

The Spanish Fantastic Woman:
Sexykiller and *Hierro*

Whether she is a victim, a damsel in distress, the final girl, or, in rarer cases, the hero, a woman's perceived vulnerability seemingly makes her an appropriate choice for a character beset by danger, supernatural forces, or monsters. *Sexykiller* and *Hierro*, two films very different in story and style, feature lead female characters in unconventional roles. While the former film is a bombastic pastiche that challenges the horror tropes of slasher films, the latter blends European art cinema with a classic thriller/fantastic scenario.

Both films are in Spanish and are solely Spanish productions, but each is aimed at a different market, both national and international. *Sexykiller* was produced in part by Warner Brothers Spain, and aimed at the teen and young adult market with its young star, its soundtrack of popular music, and its teen sex comedy/ slasher genre appeal. While it played at several film festivals, winning at Audience Award at the Brussels International Festival of Fantastic Film, it only had a theatrical release in Spain, grossing a little under €300,000. Roxbury Pictures, a small independent production company, produced *Hierro*. It premiered in Critics Week at the Cannes Film Festival in 2009, and also played at several festivals; its star, Elena Anaya, won awards for Best Actress at Fantasporto and Sitges festivals. It had theatrical release in Spain, but also in Finland, Mexico, Peru, Poland, Portugal, Russia, and the UK. Like *Sexykiller*, it grossed a little under €300,000 at the Spanish box office. It was marketed at a more serious arthouse cinema crowd, and not necessarily as a fantastic film.

While both films understand and present certain tropes of women as expected in their respective subgenres, each also challenges those tropes and presents alternatives, both in the semantics and syntax. *Sexykiller* exposes the influence of the slasher film, while at the same time adhering to Spanish roots of dark comedy. *Hierro* looks to European arthouse cinema, as well as incorporating tropes of the rural thriller similar to *The Backwoods*. A female protagonist in a slasher film is not unusual, nor is having the slasher be female (though it is not common); but having that female be both the protagonist *and* the slasher gives rise to an exploration of the common semantics of horror film, as well as semantics of teen sex and comedy films, and how they can be recycled together into a new syntax. In the rural thriller, a female protagonist is uncommon, though like horror films, not necessarily unheard of. Usually she is a victim of extreme violence and much of the action centres around her revenge, such as in *Last House on the Left* or *I Spit on Your Grave*. In *Hierro*, while there is trauma, the main character is not a victim per se, and so the focus of the narrative on both her personal movement through that trauma, as well as her actions of investigation and violence, again add a different syntax to the common semantics of the subgenre.

Like melodramas, horror films often have female protagonists, often with narrative agency, as in *Carrie* (Brian de Palma, 1976), *Halloween* (John Carpenter, 1978), or *The Silence of the Lambs* (Jonathan Demme, 1991). For David Greven, these types of horror films are the 'concealed woman's film', as opposed to the unconcealed woman's film of melodrama.[1] Greven views this 'concealment' as for the benefit of male viewers, who are presumed not to be interested in films with a female protagonist with whom they are meant to identity. *Sexykiller* challenges ideas and representations of the woman protagonist in horror films through the main woman character as both hero *and* villain, one who is readily identifiable as a woman, but who defies the stereotype of the woman victim (even if that victim has narrative agency). Greven writes that many modern horror films have female protagonists 'whose resistance to the limitations of gender identity [becomes] the chief source of narrative drama'.[2] As will be discussed, *Sexykiller* challenges gender stereotyping in the slasher film with a resolutely feminine protagonist who is also a murderer. Greven further writes that the 'woman avengers of modern horror frequently destroy not normative men but the freaks and geeks, the mother-obsessed, arrested-development males who frequent slasher films in particular'.[3] While the exploration of gender identity might not be the character's (or the film's) modus operandi, gender's textual significance is another indication of the film's recycling of fantastic genre tropes and its position as a postnational film.

Violence against women is not uncommon in social realist films. The oppositional cinema of the 1970s explored the repression of women and their role in society, for example in the work of Carlos Saura in the films *Ana and the Wolves* and *Raise Ravens* (*Cría Cuervos*, 1976). Women frequently take the lead roles in Almodóvar's work, and they are more well-rounded, complicated characters whose problems were treated seriously even through a comedic lens. Female filmmakers such as Pilar Miró and Isabel Coixet have also made films with women characters that assumed narrative agency. Duncan Wheeler notes that, prior to 1999, there were three modes for the portrayal of women and violence in Spanish cinema: the comic, the passionate, and the allegorical.[4] These modes often combined in low-brow comedies of the 1990s, such as *Mutant Action*, *Airbag* and *Torrente*, where the violence is often trivialized, or made to seem natural and unavoidable. Violence perpetrated by women in films such as *Dying of Laughter* (*Muertos de risa*, Álex de la Iglesia, 1999) and *Blinkers* (*Salir pitando*, Álvaro Fernández Armero, 2007) is treated almost entirely as a joke.[5]

Rural thrillers rarely have a woman protagonist but, like *Sexykiller*, *Hierro* is an extension of melodrama, in this case drawing on both arthouse cinema and the gothic through the female protagonist as mother, although unlike in *The Others* and *The Orphanage*, there is little or no indication of a fantastic-marvellous conclusion. The protagonist of *Hierro* might be more closely related to Ripley in *Aliens* (James Cameron, 1986) or Sarah Connor in *Terminator 2: Judgment Day* (James Cameron, 1991). Both of these films feature female protagonists as mothers, but are also action films, in which the mother must actively fight to protect and save her offspring. *Hierro* features less action, but still focuses on the role of motherhood for the protagonist. This contemporary mother is more comparable to the ancient or archaic mother, one whose grief over the loss of a child is matched only by her capacity for action to retrieve or save the child. *Hierro* combines the rural thriller with the arthouse film, two genres or modes that are normally antithetical, the former containing an action-driven plot and the latter being more contemplative and character-driven.

While operating in different modes and aesthetic styles, *Sexykiller* and *Hierro* both offer new representations of female protagonists in Spanish fantastic film. Both infuse genres associated with American cinema, with European syntax of the neo-esperpento and the art cinema mode, respectively.

Sexykiller

Sexykiller opens in a female locker room, showing close-ups of girls in towels, chatting about boys and sex, while rubbing lotion on their bodies. When one girl is left alone, a boy enters in the killer costume from the *Scream* film series. Looking for naked girls, he spies someone in the same costume. That person turns out to be the lone girl, Bárbara, who, after a chase, cuts off the boy's head. What began as a teenage sex comedy becomes a teenage horror comedy. In *Sexykiller*, the comedic coding of the situation, stylized performances and generic hybridity mark the film as decidedly ironic in presentation and intended reception, particularly for a new generation of spectators adept at recognizing semantics from Spanish and international horror films. *Sexykiller* exposes the influence of the slasher film, while at the same time adhering to Spanish roots of dark comedy. The use of direct address and different generic modes and media draw attention to its self-reflexivity. Bárbara, who is a hybrid of action heroine, psychotic killer and final girl, embodies the neo-esperpento: she exists in the concave mirror of filmic representation, a new kind of Spanish heroine for the new Spanish fantastic film.

Directors Dario Argento and Alfred Hitchcock both espoused a similar theory about horror films: if you want to get the audience's attention, be sure to include beautiful women in your cast, and then torture and/or kill them.[6] Although these directors came from different eras, they knew that beautiful women in danger created an image appreciated by audiences. Certainly in horror films, there is no shortage of nubile women who either end up tortured, raped, or dead. *Sexykiller* is neo-esperpento in that it shows a distorted reality, representing an inversion of power through explicit reference to social taboos that are usually repressed. The film is distorting and parodying not only the horror, exploitation and action genres, but also the representation of women in such films.

Set in the present day on a university campus, the film introduces the spectator to Bárbara as she recounts her story. A bright medical student, she seems to be the quintessential modern woman in that she is pursuing a career, and yet still worships fashion, likes boys, and hopes to marry a plastic surgeon and have a family. She is also a serial killer. She describes her various killings and their almost-afterthought motivations, and her growing romance with pathologist Tomás, whom she believes is also a serial killer. As the police search for a male killer, Tomás and his friend Alex develop a machine that can view the last images a dead person has seen, in the hopes of finding the killer. Unfortunately, this machine also turns the dead into zombies, and Bárbara and Tomás must fight them off. While Tomás saves Bárbara's life and she learns he is not a killer, she finds she must kill him too, leaving her the last person alive.

In the 1970s, US horror films began to explore metaphors for the moral panic over sexual experimentation among young people, and several made a point of killing off sexually active teenagers, thereby seeming to condemn the social group and its practices.[7] Films such as *Texas Chainsaw Massacre* (Tobe Hooper, 1974), *Halloween* and *Friday the 13th* (Sean S. Cunningham, 1980) featured a psychotic killer who preyed upon teenagers, allowing only one girl to survive the slaughter. Much 1970s US horror and exploitation film was inspired by European horror cinema of the 1950s and 1960s, in particular films from Italy and Spain, such as the giallo films by Argento and Mario Bava.[8] In twisting this form, Miguel Martí and screenwriter Paco Cabezas create a parody of the slasher film, making a female serial killer who is the antagonist of her progenitors. It is a coded performance: she is no less psychotic or violent than the killers featured in previous slasher films, or less arbitrary in her reasoning of action or choice of victim. But because the killer is a woman who directly addresses the audience, the spectator is invited to laugh as much as gasp at her murderous success. This in itself is a distortion of both the semantics and syntax of the slasher film: although the spectator may know who a killer is, it is rare to know, let alone hear in detail, the killer's reasoning. This kind of unmotivated horror is also an inversion and parody of contemporary horror films such as *Se7en* and *American Psycho* (Mary Harron, 2000), in which male serial killers are only to be feared.

The film is coded through the use of generic tropes from outside the milieu of the fantastic. Early in the film, Bárbara receives a dog; she calls him Jason, which is a nod to the knowing spectator aware that this is the name of the serial killer in the *Friday the 13th* series. When she emerges from her room in her metallic killer costume, carrying a transparent purse with the head of one of her victims, it is in marked and comic contrast to the dog. In other words, in a traditional horror film, this could be a frightening image when seen with knowledge of Bárbara's murders, but the presence of the dog, and the conversation she has in the hallway with other female students, invokes laughter. Fast editing between Bárbara and the girls, combined with sharp sound effects of the opening and closing of a knife and the girls' conversation about condoms, draws attention to the comedic inference. A familiar device of suspense or thriller films is the recitation of narrative through flashback; Bárbara does this with one of her victims, recounting her tales of murder for most of the film [See Figure 6.1].

The film also includes musical sequences: when Bárbara is describing her relationship with her mother and her dreams of adulthood, it becomes a musical number reminiscent of pop videos seen on channels such as MTV, with the characters wearing bright costumes and wigs. The colours are reminiscent of Almodóvar films such as *Women on the Verge of a Nervous Breakdown* (*Mujeres al borde de un ataque de nervous*, 1988) and *All About My Mother* (*Todo sobre mi madre*, 1999), and the music reminiscent of the recent comeback of the Spanish musical with works such as *The Other Side of the Bed* (*El otro lado de la cama*, Emilio Martínez Lázaro, 2002) and *20 Centimeters* (*20 centímetros*, Ramón Salazar, 2005). When one of Bárbara's victims, Ángel, is stumbling around

Fig. 6.1 Bárbara tells her story, *Sexykiller* (Mediapro, 2009)

her room with his hands tied and a plastic bag around his head, this horrific moment of death is juxtaposed with music reminiscent of a screwball comedy or accompaniment to a silent comedy film, as though Ángel's physical predicament is presented not only for narrative information, but also for comic effect. However, it is quite real, setting a tone of comedy and horror. When another victim is chased through the woods, split-screen is used to show Bárbara and her victim at the same time in different locations. Both this and the accompanying music mimic exploitation films, as well as American crime television shows of the 1970s such as *Mission Impossible* and *Charlie's Angels* (ABC, 1976–81).

As stated, most of the film is in flashback. And as the spectator is reminded frequently, Bárbara is telling the story to a man who is pinned down to his car by a knife that she has stabbed through his hand. The first scene in which Bárbara beats and traps this man, with fast editing and sound effects reminiscent of animation films, sets the comic tone for the subsequent scenes of retelling. It is a deliberate manipulation, self-consciously played by the film to engage its audience, and becomes comic as opposed to frightening. This mixture of generic semantics and its self-conscious syntax is embodied within the character of Bárbara, representative of the self-reflexivity of the film and the esperpentic distorted reality.

It would seem that the film is the epitome of postmodern parody: a film where the semantics of past films are being recycled and regenerated into a new form through a shift in syntax. For Linda Hutcheon, this is representative of a broad refusal of the master narrative, an attempt to redefine parody and repetition through ironic signification of difference.[9] In the case of *Sexykiller*, the parodic form is the meaning, its irony found in the intertexuality of generic modes and spectator expectations of those modes. By presenting itself both as a parody of slasher films, and as a neo-esperpento film, it works in the mode of what Hutcheon calls the ex-centric, focusing on those who have, until recently, been marginalized by the dominant form of filmic representation in Spain and are attempting to find a new language of expression.[10] In this case, it is a postmodern one, which is self-reflexive and parodic in the expression of its discourse. That is to say, the narrative of the film is recognizable as homage to the slasher film, yet it is distorting that subgenre in order to reflect its own parodic nature as well as its originating culture.

Sexykiller portrays a woman who is coded as the desirable female: her clothes are provocative, she takes great care with her appearance, and she displays an obsession with a physical ideal of beauty. And while Bárbara fits within this stereotype, her murders deliberately distort this representation. Following Laura Mulvey, Linda Williams writes that:

> [The] male look at women in cinema involves two forms of mastery over the threat of castration posed by her 'lack' of a penis: a sadistic voyeurism which punishes or endangers the woman through the agency of an active and powerful male character, and the fetishistic overvaluation, which masters the threat of castration by investing the woman's body with an excess of aesthetic perfection.[11]

In contradiction to this classical feminist critique, we might gaze at Bárbara as the passive object, but she also assumes narrative agency. The gaze of the spectator (which is traditionally male by default) is being challenged through the presentation of Bárbara as both object and subject. Through her narrative agency, the sadistic voyeurism of the male gaze is reversed into one of masochistic voyeurism: Bárbara kills several of the characters that are aligned with the spectator's gaze, such as Ángel and Alex. Her excesses extend into her killing, and the threat of castration comes not only through her murders, but her agency and direct address. In other words, she has control of the gaze. As a serial killer, she would seem to use any and all 'phallic' weapons at her disposal for her killings: knives, hooks, brooms and, at one point, the heel of her stiletto – perhaps the ultimate phallic symbol.

The film also encourages the spectator's gaze toward Bárbara through its use of direct address and flashbacks. Early in the film, as Bárbara is preparing for a costume party while looking in a mirror, she quotes lines from the film *Taxi Driver* (Martin Scorsese, 1976), imitating the character Travis Bickle as he rehearses what he would say and do if confronted. A few minutes later, Bárbara addresses the camera and the spectator, drawing attention to the film, and to her status as a serial killer. Within the flashbacks, not only does Bárbara address the camera, but Martí also incorporates fantasy sequences into these instances of direct address. When she is about to kill Ángel, she addresses the camera and, in the style of an infomercial, discusses the supplies necessary for a killing, accompanied by title graphics as one might see on a television shopping channel. When sitting in a class, she reads the magazine 'Cosmokiller' and using fashion magazine iconography, describes various killing methods. These instructions also include the amount of calories one could burn while committing these crimes, drawing attention to the language of the magazine. The song 'Barbie Girl' underscores this moment, reminding the audience of Bárbara's previous dream and this impossible ideal of femininity.[12] At one point her professor asks her to whom she is speaking and she replies 'to the camera', although it is invisible to him. The intermedial modes of address also force the self-reflexivity of the gaze through which we understand the genre of the slasher film. It also distorts, in esperpento style, the 'reality' of the effect of that gaze upon the female form. It forces the spectator to understand the male gaze through the eyes of one who looks back in comic fashion.

But Bárbara is not just a killer, or a femme fatale. She is also an action hero. Yvonne Tasker notes that the female in the action film is often played for comedy, shown as a hysterical figure that needs to be protected, in contrast to the more serious male hero.[13] In the traditional action film, the male is both the figure that advances the narrative and the spectacle of the narrative, a role that in other types of films is usually relegated to the female. Marc O'Day writes, '[r]epresentations of the action heroine as a figure in the landscape allay their active masculine connotations by stressing the heroine's sexuality and availability in conventional female terms'.[14] Characters such as Ripley in *Alien*, the Bride in *Kill Bill: Vol. 1* (Quentin Tarantino, 2003), and Nikita in *Nikita* (*La Femme Nikita*, Luc Besson, 1990) have been the subject of the narrative as opposed to the object of the gaze, whereas Bárbara is both. The film combines this action heroine with the serial killer. Bárbara becomes the monstrous feminine as both object of the gaze and through embodying the phallic symbols by virtue of her murders. Unlike most portrayals of female serial killers in film, Bárbara needs little motivation or impetus, and she emasculates the men sexually and physically. In her first kill, she dresses in the *Scream* killer costume to match the man who dares to enter the girls' locker room, thereby emasculating him at his own game. When Ángel hits her after sex, she ties him up while he is still in his underwear, wraps a plastic bag around his head and pushes him out the window – another act of emasculation.

Only the police detective proves a difficult kill. We are not shown how Bárbara overpowers him, as though the fact that she does is the only necessary information. But she must use a gun to finish him off, whereas her past weapons have been less traditional. The police detective is portrayed by Ángel de Andrade, who played the abusive husband in Almodóvar's *What Have I Done to Deserve This?* (*¿Qué he hecho yo para merecer esto!*, 1984), and other hyper-straight, *machista* roles. This marks his detective character as at once the opposite of Bárbara in her femininity, and yet similar, as he also commits murder. Once again this is a distortion of the slasher genre semantics, as the police in these films are usually supportive of the victim, though largely ineffectual. In this case, the police are still ineffectual in discovering Bárbara as the killer, but the detective is definitely not the good guy.

In the final scene of the film, the detective, now a zombie, is about to kill Bárbara, but Tomás saves her. For a moment, this seems to be a rather stereotypical romantic ending, with the two lovers reunited. Tomás appears to be the one male who would survive, redeemed by warning of the zombie invasion and rescuing of Bárbara. This rescue might indicate that Tomás is the hero, and as a consequence that he, and his vision of the future (marriage, children), will prevail. But Bárbara refuses this rescue by the male. She must kill Tomás, who is less possessed of masculine traits than she.

She then becomes the final girl, a common trope in slasher films. As Carol Clover notes, both male and female spectators are meant to identify with the final girl. 'The gender of the Final Girl is… compromised from the outset by her masculine interests, her inevitable sexual reluctance… her apartness from other girls'.[15] As Bárbara is not only the final girl, but also the killer, she does not conform completely to this description. Her interest in serial killing could be described as a masculine trait and she is noted in the first scene as being apart from other girls. But sexual prowess is one of her weapons and she would never be described as naive. The final girl is usually 'the only character to be developed in full psychological detail'.[16] Bárbara then is both killer and final girl. The final shot shows Bárbara walking off in the light of the full moon, carrying the now-dead Tomás in her arms. Whether she will continue her killing spree or marry her plastic surgeon is uncertain. What is certain is that *Sexykiller* is a significant departure from traditional Spanish film, traditional slasher films, and at the same time part of the new wave of Spanish fantastic films.

Sexykiller is highly self-conscious and ironic, linking Spanish *esperpento* and genre semantics from action, horror, and sex comedy films. It plays with the generic conventions of the slasher film, parodying them through the introduction of semantics from action, film noir and thriller genres, and altering the syntax through intertextual and intermedial use of different forms of media representation. *Sexykiller* is representative of Spanish postnational fantastic films that are self-reflexive genre hybrids born of their originating culture and the influence of international fantastic cinema.

Hierro

Hierro is a rural thriller that features a character who goes to a place with which she is not familiar, and must solve a mystery involving a child, placing her at odds with the locals. Set on the smallest of the Canary Islands in the present day, it explores themes of the rural versus the urban, identity, landscape, and xenophobia. But *Hierro* also incorporates the mode of art cinema alongside the thriller to investigate female identity and motherhood. The rural thriller and its semantics are adapted to the Spanish fantastic through specific locations, incorporation of culturally-specific dynamics, and estrangement in the unfamiliar environment.

Hierro begins with Julia and her son, Mateo, in a car, driving quickly at night along a dark highway. The car veers off the road, and when Julia wakes the next morning, she finds Mateo has disappeared. The next scene shows the main character, María, at her job in an aquarium, and with her son Diego. María and Diego are going on holiday to El Hierro, via a ferry. On the ferry, Diego disappears. The crew searches the ship, but Diego is not found. Months later, the police on El Hierro tell María they have found a body matching her son's description, and she flies to the island. María claims it is not her son; as the police thought the identification would be positive, they did not ask a judge to come and supervise a blood test, and one cannot arrive for a few days, forcing María to remain. María learns about the other missing child, Mateo, and believes Diego has been kidnapped. María begins her own investigation. She goes to the camper of a German woman, and finds Diego locked up. She and Tania fight, but María manages to escape with Diego, and for an unknown reason evades the police while she attempts to escape with her son. She takes Diego to the ferry, which leaves the island; but María, injured, falls asleep on the ferry and when she wakes, Diego is gone. When she finds him talking to a ferry employee, she realizes it is Mateo, whom in her desperation she saw as Diego. In fact, the body in the morgue was Diego.

Hierro presents an effect of the landscape on character, but with an emphasis on the landscape as an individual subject. There is a similar presentation of the urban, sophisticated citizen versus the rural hillbilly as seen in *The Backwoods*. The syntax comes from the peripheral location of the Canary Islands, their landscape, and the combination of the art mode and the rural thriller genre. This combination makes the local postnational, with narrative frameworks of a character entering a space unknown to them and the spectator, so as to facilitate introduction into the landscape and how it is represented in postnational cinema.

Islands can be seen either as places of splendid isolation or frightening desertion. Of islands as landscape, Peter Conrad writes that they 'test our psychological fortitude. The modern equivalent of a spiritual trial is internal and invisible, but it can be made real if it happens on an actual island and is documented in film'.[17] *Hierro* presents such a trial in the genre of the rural thriller. The film presents a woman who is searching for her missing son, setting her at odds with the local community, while at the same time she is exploring her own grief and loneliness. While her search is narrated through thriller genre conventions, her spiritual journey evokes the art cinema mode. That is to say, there are elements of the fantastic both through the rural thriller, in the action of the search, and elements of art cinema in the representation of her grief. María's violent acts are juxtaposed against the exploration of a mother's grief and the image of the mother as gentle and kind. El Hierro provides a unique and atypical Spanish setting, even farther on the outskirts than the Basque country, with less politically-specific overtones, but nonetheless a mysterious quality. This is not to suggest that the Canary Islands have been unaffected by their governing country; rather that, as the islands are on the periphery (closer to Africa than Europe), the isolation of El Hierro within the island group makes it a unique setting.

Art cinema, as it is commonly known, is better defined as a mode than a genre, and is associated with European cinematic modernism of the mid-twentieth century, descending from German expressionism, French impressionism and literary modernism.[18] In classical Hollywood cinema, the narrative motivates representation; that is to say, the action carries the story, and each scene is designed to convey goal-oriented characters through the plot to its conclusion. David Bordwell writes that this can be seen through '180° continuity, cross-cutting, montage, particular camera distances and length, [which] all function to advance the narrative'.[19] Writing in 1979 about the late 1950s and early 1960s, Bordwell observes that, in art cinema, the links between cause-and-effect narration and events in the film are less fixed, there is frequently a lack of defined desires and goals in the characters, and the focus is on reaction as opposed to action.[20]

Continuing this study by looking at the films of the 1960s and 1970s, Stephen Neale writes that art cinema 'tend[s] to be marked by a stress on visual style... by a suppression of action in the Hollywood sense, by a consequent stress on character rather than plot and by an interiorization of dramatic conflict'.[21] In order to counteract the dominance of Hollywood cinema, many European countries offered grants and subsidies to national film production, placing an emphasis on so-called auteur cinema, which produced films that were clearly in opposition to more mainstream fare.[22] The dominance of Hollywood cinema during the economic crisis of Europe after was seen as a national problem; therefore, 'the production, distribution and exhibition of films [took] place within pre-defined national boundaries, cultures, governments and economies'.[23] Arguably it still does, with government-mandated policies to protect national cinema. Rosalind Galt and Karl Schoonover characterize contemporary art cinema as comprising feature films 'that can include foreign production, overt engagement of the aesthetic, unrestrained formalism, and a mode of narration that is pleasurable but loosened from classical structures and distanced from its representations'.[24] *Hierro* more or less conforms to this description: it is a Spanish-financed production with an almost entirely Spanish cast and crew; is concerned with the aesthetic; and is not completely engaged with classical film structures or representations. Like *The Backwoods*, it is not made solely for the arthouse circuit, or as a mainstream film. It situates itself as both a contemporary genre film in its use of thriller semantics, and as art cinema, with scenes concentrated on examining María's psychological state and inner turmoil.

András Bálint Kovács writes that postmodern cinema uses chance in film narrative in order to demonstrate that an accident is not a disaster, but the 'manifestation of an alternative reality', with things ending up as they should.[25] This is in contrast to art cinema, in which the goal is to 'impress upon the viewer the dramatic effect of accidents' and the randomness of existence.[26] *Hierro* conforms to the latter, as it is the dramatic effect of Diego's accident that becomes the driving force behind the narrative. Mark Betz writes that the heyday of art cinema frequently featured films with women at the centre; these characters were treated as positive agents, liberated and central to the narrative.[27] *Hierro* finds a match between the character study of art cinema and the action of the thriller genre, with a woman as narrative agent.

The first 15 minutes establish the plot: these scenes show María and her life with Diego, their trip on the ferry, and Diego's disappearance. Each scene moves the narrative from cause to effect. The next 15 minutes are in a more reflective mode commonly associated with art cinema. While some scenes show María's life since the disappearance, most are devoted to her psychological state, including hallucinations and dream sequences. One of these scenes, in fact, serves both the purpose of showing María's aquaphobia, and at the same time including a moment of hallucination, in which María imagines a swimming pool as the sea, and herself surrounded by water. It is causally unnecessary, as all that would be needed to show her phobia would be the last moment, when she backs away from the pool;

Fig. 6.2 María is left alone on the beach, *Hierro* (Optimum Releasing, 2010)

but the inclusion of the hallucination sequence denotes a deeper understanding of character beyond agency. In another scene on the island, María goes to a local beach [See Figure 6.2]. Non-diegetic music suggests contemplation, and the accompanying shots show María as she makes her first attempts at swimming again. There is nothing in this part of the scene that furthers the story; it is in the mode of character study, in connection with the previously mentioned scene. Midway through the scene, as María lies on the sunny beach, a cloud passes over her head; the music changes to a foreboding tone, as she sees a child she thinks is Diego, faints, and upon waking, discovers the camper. This half of the scene exists to further the plot. This is an indication to the spectator that the art mode and the thriller genre are working in tandem.

Conrad writes that islands are by definition eccentric, as the centre of the particular nation or culture is usually elsewhere.[28] Such is the case with El Hierro, both being far from Spain and far from the centre of the island group. In films set in such isolation, there is the question of whether there is a spiritual or antagonistic relationship between the character(s) and the landscape. For María, El Hierro is a symbolic desert island; once she begins her hunt for Diego, she is alone in its isolation, and the camera constantly pictures her against the unforgiving terrain. Water, once her favourite place, becomes her enemy. Ian Copestake writes, '[h]istorically, the sea was viewed both literally and metaphorically as an anathema to mankind due to its hostility and uninhabitability, and also because symbolically it embodied chaotic emotions that man should strive to define himself in opposition to'.[29] Maria's life revolved around water through her work at an aquarium. When the camera first shows Diego, he is sitting in an observation tunnel at the aquarium, as though his emergence from the womb continues in his connection to his mother in this womb-like space. A montage scene meant to indicate their strong bond is set in a communal bath. Of course, womb imagery and water is hard to escape or deny, but the water imagery goes beyond this simple metaphor. María first defines herself in conjunction with the water, and then in opposition to it: in her attempt to take Diego/Mateo off the island, the island, surrounded by water, is her enemy. As the landscape works against her, she must fight her phobia to take Diego/Mateo away; but the ferry, operating on water, works against her in her attempted escape.

María (and other characters) are constantly placed in connection and antagonism to the landscape; specifically, the camera moves in order to convey the smallness of the characters in comparison to the island. Director Gabe Ibáñez notes that while there was some colour correction in postproduction, the colour palette, light quality, and natural and varying landscapes of the island were used, which he felt marked a difference from what is typically seen in Spanish film.[30] In the opening scene, the overturned car is a dull red against the grey beach, and Julia's cries are insignificant as the camera zooms out to emphasize her isolation. When María drives to the beach, rather than there being a simple shot conveying the journey, the camera moves above the car and snakes with it through the curves of the road, as if to show the route is not enough, but that this path among harsh shrubbery and the unpicturesque grey earth are the opposite of what a tourist would seek from a holiday on the Canary Islands. When María is on the beach, the camera closes in on her hands and feet digging into the sand. Close-ups in this film, or even medium close-ups, are nearly always relegated to indoor spaces or night scenes, and it is in indoor spaces and at night that much of the thriller action resides, such as the car accident, or in a later scene when María is attempting to cross the island and unfavourably meets the police detective. These indoor or dark spaces leave room for the thriller, whereas the outdoor spaces and the landscape in daytime further adds to the idea of the insignificance of the humans, making the character study of the art mode as much about place and space as people.

Although originally many art cinema films set out to portray an autonomous woman, such as *Cleo from 5 to 7* (*Cléo de 5 à 7*, Agnès Varda, 1962) and *The Eclipse* (*L'eclisse*, Michaelangelo Antonioni, 1962), *Hierro* examines María in her role as mother almost exclusively. In this role as mother she is autonomous, however, in that there is no husband or father. Films in the Fascist era manufactured a rigid representation of women's identities as focused solely on their roles as wife and mother.[31] Films of the transition were more self-conscious in the portrayal of the mother figure, particularly in the context of the dictatorship's lingering effects, but still often showed women almost exclusively in the role of mother. In the 1980s and 1990s, filmmakers such as Pilar Miró, with her film *The Bird of Happiness* (*El pájaro de la felicidad*, 1993), reinscribed motherhood among newly-found women's issues such as sexual freedom and professional careers.[32] Additionally, films such as *Nobody Will Speak of Us When We're Dead* (*Nadie hablará de nosotras cuando hayamos muerto*, Agustín Díaz Yanes, 1995) and *Alone* (*Solas*, Benito Zambrano, 1999) looked at single mothers in violent domestic situations. The mother has remained a central figure of representation in Spanish film and, contemporary Spain, like many western countries, has more single mothers than in the past, while the extended family has been replaced by the nuclear family to a certain extent.[33] María only says once that she doesn't have a husband, and this is not questioned.

Barbara Creed identifies the archaic mother as the original power, outside of morality and authority, different from the more benign maternal figure in more contemporary representation.[34] Speaking of this archaic mother as represented in horror films, Creed writes that this mother 'is present… as the blackness of extinction… a force that threatens to reincorporate what it once gave birth to'.[35] There are three mothers in the film: María, Julia and Tania. Julia and Mateo have a car accident when she is running away from her husband; María loses the son that she was raising alone; and Tania loses hope of having her own child after her boyfriend leaves her. Julia, by virtue of her injuries, is unable to search for Mateo the way that María is able to search for Diego. María and Tania are closer to what Lynn Paulson calls the 'mama bear'. She writes that it 'is expected that women will instinctually defend their offspring at the cost of their own lives and suffer unbearable grief over childlessness. In the first case, women's violence is sanctioned, and in the second, it is understandable'.[36] María, as natural mother, and Tania, as surrogate mother, fight each other to the death for 'their' child. Their physical fight returns the film to its rural thriller semantics, pitting the 'hillbilly' Tania, insane through loneliness, against the 'urban' María, also driven close to insanity by loneliness. In the confined space of the trailer, the fight scene is in many ways far more violent than many in this type of film, as the women are equally matched physically. Most of the scene plays out with dramatic music, which ends just before María wins the fight; the ensuing silence seems to indicate, however, that there can be no victor in this fight. The film provides a few clues for the spectator: when María sees a photograph of Mateo, she sees it first as Diego; and Diego/Mateo never calls her 'mama'. It is as if the landscape, unwelcoming to her, fosters the illusion; it is only once she is away on the ferry, some distance from the island, that she sees Mateo as himself.

Hierro seeks to combine the genre of the rural thriller, generally considered an American generic form, with the art cinema mode of Europe. It becomes both a study of character psychology and an action thriller driven mainly by women, which is common in European cinema but less so in American cinema. The film seeks to use the landscape not only as a place to investigate issues of the outsider, violence, and the rural/urban divide, but as a character itself, with its own psychology, and the effect it has on the main character. The island itself becomes the outsider, rooted in its peripheral identity, which reflects on the equally peripheral identity of the characters, and their actions, in both the art mode exploration and the thriller narrative.

Sexykiller recycles the semantics of the slasher film through the portrayal of a female protagonist as both the hero and the villain. *Hierro* blends classic Hollywood thriller techniques with the art cinema mode, exploring the identity and loneliness of the mother within a harsh landscape. The engagement of the neo-esperpento in *Sexykiller* marks it as Spanish, but knowledge of esperpento is not necessary for an understanding of the film; *Hierro* has a Spanish location, but is not necessarily identifiable as Spanish, although it is as European. By featuring female protagonists in a non-traditional syntax, both films adapt traditional fantastic genre forms to add to the growing corpus of postnational fantastic cinema.

7

Guillermo del Toro: The Outside Man: *The Devil's Backbone* and *Pan's Labyrinth*

Guillermo del Toro stands out from the other filmmakers in this book by virtue of being the only non-Spaniard, but also as the most famous filmmaker under discussion. His work as both director and as a producer is so distinctive that he is a brand unto himself, as noted in the section on *The Orphanage*. While all of his films are in the fantastic genres, *The Devil's Backbone* and *Pan's Labyrinth* remain unique among his oeuvre in their historical context.

The Devil's Backbone and *Pan's Labyrinth* feature children in confrontation and alliance with monsters, both fantastical and human. The films are set, respectively, during the end and the aftermath of the Spanish Civil War. While historical fantastic films are common, most are presented within fabricated histories, or do not engage with specific historical events. Films that use fantastic elements in conjunction with an examination of political or social issues of the time period in which they are set, such as *It's a Wonderful Life* (Frank Capra, 1946), *The Dead Zone* (David Cronenberg, 1983), and *The Purple Rose of Cairo* (Woody Allen, 1985), are more unusual. The historical context of the above films is not only real, but cinematically important, as is the historical context of *The Devil's Backbone* and *Pan's Labyrinth*. As David Archibald points out, the Spanish Civil War was one of the first conflicts after the introduction of sound to film, and became one of the first wars documented with this new technology.[1] Despite it having ended more than 70 years ago, hardly a year passes without at least one Spanish film that is either set during the war, or references it directly.

Del Toro had made one feature film in his native Mexico (*Cronos*), and one in Hollywood (*Mimic*, 1997), before he directed *The Devil's Backbone*, co-written by Spanish screenwriters Antonio Trashorras and David Muñoz. In an interview, del Toro admits that he had originally conceived his part of the story as set during the Mexican Revolution, but decided that the Spanish Civil War – with what he phrases as a clear division between good (the Republicans) and evil (the Nationalists) – was less ambiguous and more easily understood.[2] Trashorras sees it as a take on the English gothic, and cites his influences as coming from horror television and comics (few of which are Spanish).[3] Michael Atkinson calls del Toro a 'Grimmian, born of an urban-Mexican culture steeped in native-art crafts, poverty, simmering civil discontent, and American pop'.[4] Del Toro claims to work in the universal language of Esperanto, hence his use of horror and fairy tale imagery. In addition, as a Mexican, he remembers that his nation took in exiles from Spain after the civil war.[5] These elements, not necessarily conflicting ones, combine in *The Devil's Backbone* to create historical horror. *Pan's Labyrinth*, (screenplay written solely by del Toro) leans more toward historical fantasy.

The Spanish Civil War is one of the most studied conflicts of the twentieth century. The victory of the Nationalists and subsequent state control of cultural production meant a pro-victor perspective in films during the 1940s and 1950s.[6] Films such as *¡Harka!* (Carlos Arévalo, 1940) and *Raza* (José Luis Sáenz de Heredia, 1942) celebrated Nationalist ideals and demonized Republicans. Others, such as *Dos caminos* (Arturo Ruiz Castillo, 1953), looked at the return of Republican exiles who were now embracing the Nationalist perspective. It was not until Carlos Saura's *Cousin Angelica* (*La prima Angélica*, 1974), that the losing side was portrayed in a favourable light. Politically, after the transition to democracy, there was a pact of forgetting, and those who played a leading role in General Franco's regime benefitted from an implicit amnesty.[7] However, this did not prevent filmmakers from examining the past. In the 1980s, there were many historical dramas about the war from a Republican perspective, such as Manuel Gutiérrez Aragón's *Demons in the Garden* (*Demonios en el jardín*, 1982) and Vicente Aranda's *If They Tell You I Fell* (*Si te dicen que caí*, 1989). Several films about the conflict have also been made elsewhere in Europe and in Hollywood. Marjorie Valleau notes that most of the American films, such as *For Whom the Bell Tolls* (Sam Woods, 1943) and *Confidential Agent* (Herman Shumlin, 1945), focus on the characters' personal lives, whereas European films, such as *The War is Over* (*La guerre est finie*, Alain Resnais, 1966) and *Land and Freedom* (Ken Loach, 1995) emphasize political content and openly identify almost exclusively with the Republicans.[8]

According to Stephen Neale, war films are generally about waging war in the twentieth century; this broad definition includes subcategories such as combat or home front films.[9] It might be more accurate to say that war is a narrative context. Del Toro's films are not the first time that genres or modes outside of either documentary or historical realism have been used to represent war. Art Spiegelman's graphic novel *Maus: A Survivor's Tale* (1987) dramatized the Holocaust and its aftermath in graphic novel form, and Ari Folman's *Waltz with Bashir* (2008) is an animated documentary about the 1982 Israeli-Lebanese war. While the beginning of *Pan's Labyrinth* gives the spectator a specific historical context, *The Devil's Backbone* only references the war in a few lines of dialogue.

Anne Hardcastle writes that, for a generation removed from the trauma of the war, and/or a spectator with limited knowledge of it, a hauntological approach might be a more direct route to understanding that trauma.[10] Jacques Derrida writes that ghosts (in a larger philosophical sense) are the presence of absence, the traces of those who are not allowed to leave a trace.[11] Jo Labanyi argues that in Spanish history this maps onto the ghost of the loser, and notes that 'Latin cultures... tend to choose as their national heroes and heroines... those who lost spectacularly because of their refusal to compromise'.[12] Del Toro's films were released at a time when Spain was confronting the 'ghosts' of the victims of Fascism directly, through the Historical Memory Law, the uncovering of mass graves of the murdered, and founding of groups that collected memories of the war and dictatorship.[13] Yet, as Antonio Lázaro-Reboll also notes, international horror film fans who might have little or no knowledge of the Spanish Civil War embraced the films.[14] This distances them from their historical context, in that context is somewhat irrelevant to understanding and enjoyment of the films. Deborah Shaw notes that Picturehouse, the US distributor, marketed *Pan's Labyrinth* to three groups usually considered separate: arthouse cinema fans, genre audiences, and Latino audiences.[15] The biggest marketing factor was del Toro himself. He appealed to genre audiences because of his previous films *Cronos* and *Hellboy* (2004); *Pan's Labyrinth* would appeal to arthouse cinema fans because of its historical context, and to Latino audiences because of its Hispanic connection.[16]

The Devil's Backbone and *Pan's Labyrinth* are self-reflexive due to their blending of history and the fantastic. This hybridity constructs a distance between the spectator and the events represented, to encourage awareness not only of the process of storytelling, but the engagement with historical representation through the use of the fantastic. Robyn McCallum classifies this as postmodernist historiographic metafiction, mixing fictive and historical modes of representation so as to pose questions about the representation of each.[17] In her work on representations of Holocaust trauma, Marianne Hirsch uses the term postmemory, which is distinguished from memory by generational distance and from history by deep personal connection, so that the 'connection... is mediated... through an imaginative investment and creation'.[18] *The Devil's Backbone* and *Pan's Labyrinth* are marked by the distance between generations who experienced the trauma of the war and Fascism and those who did not. Postmemory is self-reflexive because of this distance. In the films, this self-reflexivity takes the form of the fantastic, which seeks to fill the gap between experience and interpretation.

But the use of historical events by those who did not experience them, directly or indirectly, can also be what Alison Landsberg calls 'prosthetic memory', a form of public cultural memory created by those who were not involved in the original event. For Landsberg, prosthetic memories 'are transportable and therefore challenge more traditional forms of memory that are not premised on claims of authenticity, "heritage" and ownership'.[19] These types of memories occur at a crossroads between the personal and the public. The Spanish Civil War, due to its extensive documentation, the participation of non-Spaniards, and its distance in history, could be classified as open to representation and interpretations via prosthetic memory.

The Devil's Backbone and *Pan's Labyrinth* were created by a younger generation without direct involvement in the conflict, seeking to explore and represent historical events that are now part of larger, cultural memory. They are metafictive texts that seek to represent history through the fantastic, and the fantastic through history. What is presented is a meditation not only on how we view history, but how we view the fantastic.

The Devil's Backbone

A slow close-up on a staircase; one boy bleeding and another crying over him; a bomb dropped from an airplane during a storm; and a voice-over that asks, 'What is a ghost?' So begins *The Devil's Backbone*, the first of del Toro's Spanish Civil War films. It was a success upon release in Spain in 2001, earning over €3 million, and a reasonable success for a foreign-language film in the US, earning almost $800,000. It was co-produced by Tequila Gang, del Toro's company, and Almodóvar's El Deseo. It helped del Toro gain a foothold in the Spanish fantastic film market, a hold onto that he has maintained ever since.

The beginning of the film presents seemingly disparate events that the spectator knows must fit together. That a ghost makes an appearance early in the film from a subjective perspective (i.e. its existence is verified by a POV shot from the ghost) suggests the fantastic. Not long after this, an exposition scene relates the setting of the Spanish Civil War, suggesting a historical dimension. Postmemory lies in the co-existence of these two things: the real and the fantastic, working together in a historical context in a self-reflexive manner to investigate and understand the trauma of violence. The voice-over asks:

> What is a ghost? A tragedy condemned to repeat itself time and again?
> An instant of pain, perhaps. Something dead which seems to be alive.
> An emotion suspended in time. Like a blurred photograph. Like an
> insect trapped in amber.

Only one of the statements offers what might be considered a definition of a ghost as a physical property; the rest are metaphors that describe emotional and physical states. The questions would seem to be asking the spectator to be aware of the different metaphorical meanings of a ghost, and how these different meanings can be related to a historical metafictive perspective.

At the end of the Spanish Civil War in rural Spain, Carlos is brought to an orphanage, run by Carmen and Casares. Jacinto, who grew up in the orphanage, is having an affair with Carmen while secretly trying to steal her supply of gold ingots. On his first night, Carlos sees a ghost, Santi, whom the other boys refer to as 'the one who sighs'. Carlos finds out that Jacinto killed Santi and drowned his body in the cistern. Jacinto reveals his search for the gold to Carmen, and Casares forces him to leave the orphanage. Jacinto returns and ignites the kitchen in order to blow up the safe, killing Carmen and some of the children. Casares dies, and Jacinto locks the remaining children in a closet. The children escape and lure Jacinto to the basement cistern, where they stab him and force him into the water. Carlos and the other boys leave the orphanage.

Any film set in the past brings with it an expectation of historical accuracy: a spectator should be able to recognize the time period through various temporal indicators. While a costume drama might be set in the past with little reference to historical events, a historical drama alludes to or sets itself directly within known and studied events.[20] As noted, *The Devil's Backbone* introduces its time period in an early scene between Carmen, Casares, and two Republican fighters, with a discussion of the war and its impact on the children. The opening montage, with its inclusion of bombs and a drowning boy, and the voice-over meditation on the nature of ghosts, suggests a horror film. These two seemingly opposing perspectives need not be antithetical; instead, they indicate a solution to a possible crisis of representation. In representing the past to an international spectator with little or no historical knowledge, the combination of horror with history makes the film an example of historiographic metafiction; that is to say, a spectator familiar with the semantics of horror can extrapolate and interpret how those semantics are being used to represent the historical past [See

Fig. 7.1 The unexploded bomb, *The Devil's Backbone* (Optimum Releasing, 2002)

Figure 7.1]. The opening montage gives a series of clues in images, and the final statement of the voice-over precedes the opening credits, which are superimposed over images of a misshapen fetus floating in a golden liquid. The final images in particular invite the spectator to interpret the title of the film, given as the last credit. These are the syntactic clues that the spectator must use to interpret the film, through the connection of historical representation and the fantastic.

One genre that often combines the historical and the fantastic is magic realism. It is a branch of the fantastic mainly associated with a literary storytelling mode, and most widely used to refer to works by Latin American writers such as Gabriel García Márquez and Jorge Luis Borges.[21] In works of magic realism, the fantastic exists and is perceived as natural to everyday life.[22] In *The Devil's Backbone*, the orphans readily accept the presence of the ghost as real and natural. Fredric Jameson writes that the 'possibility of magic realism as a formal mode is constitutively dependent on a type of historical raw material in which disjunction is structurally present'.[23] Magic realism is one way of filling in the gaps in history and memory of a culture. In opposition to what Jameson calls the nostalgia film, which generates images and simulacra of the past for consumption, the magic realist film is a mode for examining the past, a 'history with holes'.[24] Rather than the escapism of nostalgia, magic realism seeks to fill the gaps left open by incomplete histories, connecting it with the self-reflexivity of historical metafiction and postmemory, through individuals seeking to recount a trauma to which they were not personally subjected. The ghosts of Santi and Casares are represented as part of the landscape; that is, they are not figments of the imagination. The disjunction present in the story comes from the storyteller's lack of personal experience of the historical time period; it is now a part of prosthetic, collective memory, and the fantastic is utilized by a postmemorial generation to fill in the holes of history. *The Devil's Backbone* is not based on the specific history of a particular orphanage, but rather imagines the experience of war orphans; hence, magic realism seeks to fill in the gaps of history by representing the plight of orphans with its fantastical tale that serves as metaphor for violence and trauma.

The film introduces a disjunction in the opening montage, and the in first scene where the ghost of Santi appears: historical and fantastic images, with no immediate means of reconciliation. The camera focuses on Carlos while a sound cue indicates that he is watching something that will frighten him; the camera then moves to where Carlos is looking, and shows the ghost. Carlos is shown distracted for a moment, and when he looks back, the camera shows the figure of the ghost is gone, but the 'liquid' surrounding him remains. This presentation offers a suggestion of the lingering existence of the fantastic within the real. Joan Mellen writes that in literary magic realism, 'the instances of supernaturalism are intermittent; they arrive and disappear so quickly, so that the reader is always returned to the world of social reality', and readers must have complete faith in the believability of the fantastic moment.[25] Carlos approaches the doorway, then is shown away by the other boys. But the camera lingers to watch, and includes the ghost in the shot. The spectator is reminded of the presence of the fantastic, as though it were in control of the camera, and the following scenes in which the dialogue focuses on exposition of the historical and social reality of the film's setting present the social reality of the narrative. The movement between the historical reality and the fantastic is maintained throughout the film. But more importantly, the fantastic is placed at the centre of the film, as it is part of the real world represented.

In an interview, del Toro said that he sees the characters as entirely Mexican, infused with 'a kind of feast of colours and sensations that could only be found in Mexican culture'.[26] Yet children were connected to historical trauma in earlier Spanish films such as *The Spirit of the Beehive* and *If They Tell You I Fell*. In the latter, the children, who roam the streets of Barcelona, sit among the ruins and tell fantastical tales; they make up stories of those they have known, or only heard about, and often imagine these people as types of monsters. This provides a connection not only between children and monsters, but also to the magic-realist process of integrating the fantastic into the real, especially through the eyes of children connected with the war and its aftermath. The end of *The Devil's Backbone* returns to the voice-over, which is revealed as belonging to the ghost of Casares. It is as if the social reality must now include these ghosts set within history. This is not unlike *The Others*, in which Grace and her children, as ghosts, are isolated in their house, or *The Abandoned*, which leaves Maria trapped on her island. As in these films, the ghosts in *The Devil's Backbone* are trapped in the past, which co-exists with the present.

The questions posed by Casares' ghost are repeated at the end of the film, as if to remind the spectator so that they may reflect on the answers they (presumably) now possess. All of these would suggest that the ghost is not only a metaphor in and of itself (i.e. that Santi's ghost is a metaphor for his unavenged death), but that the term 'ghost' means more than just the spirit of a dead person. Labanyi writes that there is little tradition of ghost stories in Spain (in the sense of ghost as a spectre of the dead).[27] So the film enters into the realm of prosthetic memory: the ghosts are part of a reworking of cultural representation to understand and represent the trauma. They now represent a cultural memory. A ghost as tragedy repeating itself appears in the narrative of the film in Santi's ghost, who haunts the orphanage until his revenge is taken, as well as referring to larger historical implications of the history of twentieth-century Spain, with destruction and chaos, until the dead (the Republicans) are avenged. The ghost as instant of pain: the pain suffered by Santi, and by the children who must now exist within the Fascist state.

Emotions suspended in time might refer to the state the ghosts are in, and the emotions of the losing side of the war, which must be suspended indefinitely. The blurred photograph would appear to be of Santi, who is in a blurred state, and the literal blurred photographs of Jacinto are left floating on the top of the cistern, his resting place, part of history now suspended. Derrida writes that hauntology consists of a dichotomy of first time/repetition: that the ghost, suspended, is repeating its moment of conception, as well as it always being that first moment.[28] Like the moment suspended in time, or the insect trapped in amber, these ghosts represent the trauma of violence, in this context related to the war, and they will inhabit the orphanage in repetition, as permanent reminders of those in history whose story has been buried or forgotten.

According to Ismail Xavier, historical allegories signal the presence of mediation, through 'a cultural artifact… [that] requires specific frames of reference to be read, quite distant from any sense of the "natural".[29] Films such as *Gone with the Wind* (Victor Fleming, 1939), set during the American Civil War, and *Lucía* (Humberto Solas, 1968), covering decades of the history of Cuba, are fictional narratives relating a personal story, set alongside large historical events, and in effect allegorize the historical moment for contemporary and future generations. Different allegorical strategies can provide different ways of thematizing a nation, or a national event, in human history. Del Toro refers to *The Devil's Backbone* as a western gothic allegory, where the violence of Fascism is contrasted with the vulnerability of children, and what starts as a supernatural tale becomes a coming-of-age war film.[30] Adriana Bergero notes that the film is not just a representation of the violence of the Spanish Civil War, but other violent dictatorships and their victims.[31] This is another example of an adaptation of historical allegory to prosthetic memory and postnationalism: a cultural memory specific to Spain can also represent cultural memories of similar traumas in other countries.

The first scene after the opening credits shows a car crossing a barren landscape where there is no shelter but the orphanage. But the first shot of the gate is a graphic match to the first shot of the film, and the doorway leading to the basement cistern. Both doorways are arches, and lead into darkness; both lead to violence. Carlos and Jaime fight there, and Jaime is almost killed. Even in a moment that should be affectionate, when Carmen and Jacinto have sex, the affection is violent, or reminds Carmen of violence. In her moment of death, Casares must remove a shard from her chest, hastening her death. Jacinto is driven off, but he returns to enact more violence that even he cannot escape. When the children leave at the end, they are all injured, and their future is likely to contain more violence. The violence, though, remains firmly in the realm of the historical and the adult characters that inhabit that part of the narration. The violence perpetuates itself in a constant circle of punishment and reparation. Santi is murdered by Jacinto, and so assists in his drowning. Jaime does nothing to stop Jacinto from killing Santi, and so he too is momentarily pushed into the cistern. If at times the camera takes the perspective of the ghost, then the spectator becomes the ghost looking in on the violence of humanity from a critical perspective.

If we look at the film as a story of Carlos' personal destiny, his evolution from boy to man in a time of war, the violence of the war is an allegory for the violence within his mind and body. But it is also an allegory for the violence inflicted upon all children during times of war. The fantastic devices that result from private acts of violence become a critique of public acts of violence. This is not to suggest that there is no violence in the fantastic; rather that, in the case of *The Devil's Backbone*, the suggestion is that the fantastic, when placed in a historical setting, can and/or must be interpreted as allegorical. The narrative experimentation of combining historical trauma with the fantastic is part of the critique; as a postnational film, it is using the Spanish Civil War as an allegory for war and violence in general, interpreted through the fantastic.

Is violence against a child, then, violence against the spectator? As Vicky Lebeau writes:

> At the limits of language, of culture, of knowledge, the child can always
> be used to make the familiar strange, the domestic uncanny, in a way
> that also draws on the attachment to the image of the child as in incite-
> ment to compassion, pity, feeling – above all the future.[32]

The child is a symbol of the future and continuity, as defence against loss of significance. The death of a child is the death of the future. Moreover, children represent
the weakest of society, less able to defend themselves, more vulnerable to excesses
and violence, and, especially in a horror film, more susceptible to danger. In the
case of *The Devil's Backbone*, children are both perpetrators and victims of violence. Their perpetration, admittedly, is brief, and mostly in self-defence. At the
beginning of the film, the impression is given that it is Jaime who killed Santi.
While he seems to regret this alleged crime immediately, the camera moves on
Jaime as though he is a guilty party. When the camera shows Carlos looking at the
ghost of Santi, it also shows Jaime looking at Carlos, to remind the spectator of the
opening of the film, and to implicate him in the appearance of the ghost. Karen
Lury writes that, especially when a story is marked by strange narrative forms, as is
the case in *The Devil's Backbone* with its combination of history and the fantastic),
the 'child figure allows for (or really demands) the side-lining or ignoring of what
is normally considered important, whether this is the intrigues of the adult world
or the facets of the war'.[33] That is partially true in the case of *The Devil's Backbone*.
While the spectator is made aware that there is a war going on, the case of the dead
child, the desires of its ghost, and the centring of the narrative on the children
sidelines the war to only a few scenes. Yet the children do become representative
of the crimes enacted during and after war.

To take an event such as the Spanish Civil War, and add ghosts, seems to be a
violation of the nature of historical representation. The marriage of the fantastic
and the real into a form of historiographic metafiction leads, however, not only to
a new interpretation of historical events, but to new representations of how history
can serve fantasy, how fantasy can serve history, and how postmemory can be the
bridge between the two. *The Devil's Backbone* allows for outside interpretation of
events, and an expansion of the use of the fantastic in Spanish film.

Pan's Labyrinth

There is no doubt that *Pan's Labyrinth* made del Toro a household name, and
this type of film 'his' standard in style and vision. Earning nearly €9 million in
Spain and more than $83 million worldwide, it is currently the fifth most pop-
ular foreign-language film in the United States, having won numerous awards,

including Academy Awards for Cinematography, Make-Up and Art Direction. His name has become synonymous with horror films featuring children or child-like adults, usually involving fairy-tale monsters and trauma.

In *Pan's Labyrinth*, the fairy tale sits alongside historical realism as contrast and counterpoint. Jane Hanley suggests that del Toro is using fairy-tale techniques to interrogate the politics of war and nationhood.[34] Roger Clark and Keith McDonald write that he is harkening back to Spanish Civil War films such as *The Spirit of the Beehive*, as well as borrowing from children's literature and films that evoke a fairy tale mode.[35] But like *The Devil's Backbone*, it is a combination of these, and a metafictive text that self-consciously examines fairy tale imagery and meaning, as well as historical representation. Landsberg writes that prosthetic memory is an alternative method of transmission and dissemination of memory.[36] In the case of *Pan's Labyrinth*, that method is the fantastic. Shaw sees the film as moving freely between art and commercial cinema; a genre film that has the creative control found in art cinema, while still aiming for the wide appeal of commercial cinema through the fantastic.[37] As a postnational film, it draws on the spectator's knowledge of fairy tale semantics, and restructures them in a new syntax that combines the historical and the fantastic.

Ofelia and her mother, Carmen are taken to the countryside in the north of Spain to join Carmen's new husband, Captain Vidal, at an army encampment. Vidal is charged with ridding the area of a group of maquis that continue to rebel against the new government. Ofelia encounters a faun, who claims to represent an underground kingdom whose princess ran to the earth centuries before, and now he is here to help Ofelia return to her state as Princess Moanna. Vidal and his troops ambush and kill several of the maquis and capture one of them, whom Vidal tortures. Carmen dies in childbirth, after which Vidal locks Ofelia in the attic, but she escapes from with her brother to the labyrinth. Vidal finds and kills Ofelia. The rebels destroy the encampment, and kill Vidal. In her death, Ofelia is transported to the underworld as her alter ego, Princess Moanna.

The film gives the location (Spain) and date (1944) in which the film is set. This immediately gives the spectator a historical context with which they are meant to view the film. It is as if the history must be understood first, as though this were the 'true' setting of the film, before the fantastic can be introduced. The description is brief, indicating an expectation that the spectator already knows enough about the Spanish Civil War to understand the context from what is given, with a few key words such as 'rebels' and 'Fascists' providing enough for the spectator to understand where their empathy should lie. The film then shows an image of Ofelia bleeding; the shot is in reverse, and the camera spins in a slow circular motion, indicating that the film will be a kind of flashback. Then, a voice-over begins to tell a story, of a young Princess who ran away from her underground kingdom and forgot who she was. The girl's father, the King, has been awaiting her return. Through a series of masked cuts, the film shows the underground kingdom and then returns to the surface, returning the spectator to the historical setting. Over these intertitles are the sounds of heavy breathing and the humming of a song, possibly a lullaby, which is again reminiscent of the fairy tale. The fantastic and the real remain separate, and only Ofelia sees the fantastic. Mercedes Maroto Camino writes that the colour tones of the fantasy world are associated with the maternal and feminine (red, yellow and dark blue), and are also associated with the Republican flag (red, yellow and purple).[38] The outside world, with its Fascist violence and fantastic dangers, is cold and somewhat cruel; the interior home is warm, but after Carmen dies and Mercedes escapes, it also becomes cold. What is left for Ofelia is the golden world of the underground realm, fantastic yet separate from historical time and space.

The metanarrative of *Pan's Labyrinth* sets out to investigate both fairy tale and historical representation, and how the latter can be seen through the fantastic, through this particular narrative of a particular war. The use of a child at the centre of the split between the historical and the fantastic (in that Ofelia is the only character in both narratives) would suggest an attempt to marry the two concepts into a metanarrative, in that each is allegorical of the other. This relates to Derrida's interpretation of the ghost who lingers because it has been forgotten by history: as del Toro has no personal connection to the war or the Fascist state, he belongs to the generation of postmemory, and is what Hirsch might call an 'adoptive witness'.[39] As a bystander with no direct involvement, he uses the fantastic as a means of relating to this unexperienced history. The maquis are situated the forest, the archetypal location of the fairy tale, connecting them not only to earth and nature, but to the fantastic within the film, though they never have contact with it. That they are victorious at the end of the film is something of a bittersweet conclusion; yet the promise given by the flower suggests not only a return of the fantastic to the world, but also a return of the maquis and the memory of the losing side.

In an interview, del Toro said that he thought of the fairy tale first as the starting point for *Pan's Labyrinth*.[40] This suggests that war and nationhood are being used as allegory for the fairy tale, or more specifically, for the idea of the fairy tale and the implicit role of storytelling in our sense of history and understanding.[41] In this case, there is no attempt to show any possible change or alteration in the course of history; while the maquis might have won this battle, there is nothing to suggest that could have led to a change in Spain's situation. Instead, the combination of the fantastic and the historical real changes the spectator's perception of the situation, leading to a difference perspective not only of the given historical representation, but of the meaning of the allegory represented.

As the film is an engagement between the real and the fantastic, del Toro puts an emphasis on representations of physical sensation in order to gain the audience's attention to the fantastic, highlighting its visceral qualities to engage the senses. The fantastic can thus have an effect that is equal to, or surpasses, the spectator's engagement with the violence of the war. This is fantasy as visual spectacle; fantasy relies heavily on (if not can be defined as) spectacle, as it is through the visual semantics that the spectator understands the fantasy. Ofelia's first magical task engages with the sense of touch: she must remove her clean outfit and crawl through mud. The spectator can see her hand press into the mud, hear the squelch, and imagine the sensation on their own hand. They imagine the bugs crawling on their skin and engage with Ofelia as she pulls them off her arms. In the second task, the spectator can smell and taste the grapes that Ofelia tastes, likely delicious and most definitely forbidden. The spectator is engaged with the fantastic through the senses, and while the narrative is not completely subjective to Ofelia's perspective, the spectator aligns with her through the experience of sensory input. In this case, the metafictive nature of the film works in two ways: the spectator (presumably) has no personal experience of the fantastic; and as Smith points out, few spectators outside of Spain would have known of Republican activities after the Civil War.[42] The spectator thereby relies upon an engagement of the senses for understanding, in line with the mechanisms of prosthetic memory through cultural understanding of war.

Atkinson writes, '[f]rom a child's subjective perspective, a bloody civil conflict appears as it is in its essence, a heavens-fall contest between family victims and neighbouring monsters, in which children underfoot bear the greatest cost'.[43] The first image of the film is a violent one: Ofelia bloody on the ground. The image is in reverse, but this is not necessarily meant to be a sign of hope; rather, that there may be more blood, though not always as a symbol of despair. Maroto Camino writes that in war and horror films, 'blood is often deployed to mark rites of passage, as well as to appeal to our primal fears through an emphasis on the fragility of life'.[44] There is despair when Ofelia, representative of innocence and the future, is seen bleeding at the beginning of the film. At the end, her blood is the rite of passage that opens the gateway to the fantastic underground kingdom to which she can now return. Not all rites of passage are necessarily positive: Carmen hemorrhages and dies in childbirth (though in death she will be reunited with Ofelia); Mercedes spills Vidal's blood before she escapes, which leads to Vidal's killing of Ofelia. The violence must be extreme, both in the historical and fantastic representations, as reflections of each other.

The historical representation of the Spanish Civil War emphasizes this for the spectator. The spectator understands the setting and the conflict as real from the beginning; they accept a child as their representative in the film; the spectator is invested in Ofelia as the connection between the historical and fantastic dimensions, and in those who show her kindness, such as Mercedes. Blood spilt from any of these leads to a resolution in favour of those with whom the spectator aligns themselves. In an interview, del Toro said that, 'you need to know the brutality for the reality of the magic to happen. That's why war is such a perfect backdrop'.[45] Most importantly, the war is an allegory of the fairy tale, an allegory in which a child must play a central role, even within terrible violence. As in *The Devil's Backbone*, the Spanish Civil War setting is somewhat incidental; there are other conflicts that could have been used as backdrop for the same story. This is not to suggest that the use of it as a historical setting is arbitrary; but that the war is in service to the fantastical allegory, rather than the inverse relation. If prosthetic memory is a form of public cultural memory, then the Spanish Civil War can stand in for other wars and violent events that have a traumatic effect on children.

Why does the spectator align with Ofelia? The film is not subjective to her perspective, and it is clear that only she can see the fantastic and therefore arguably it is in her imagination. It begins with the first frame of her, bleeding and dying; as a child, she is innocent, and so whatever may have happened, the spectator is immediately sympathetic to her. She is next encountered in the car, reading a fairy tale book, as any child of her age would; we see her with her mother, who gently chides her for her reading. Grodal writes that popular narratives, such as those that centre on or include the parental-child bond, relate to our cognitive development and inherent instincts, and the spectator understands this bond irrespective of culture.[46] On their first night in the encampment, Carmen asks Ofelia to tell a story to her brother, which she does, much to the unborn child's delight. The establishment of Ofelia as a fairy-tale heroine continues through her first task, when her costume resembles that of *Alice's Adventures in Wonderland* (Lewis Carroll, 1865), and right to the end, where her red shoes are reminiscent of Dorothy's in *The Wizard of Oz* (Victor Fleming, 1939) [See Figure 7.2]. Ofelia's strongest relationships are with her mother, who dies after rejecting Ofelia's attempt at a magical cure, and Mercedes, who attempts to save Ofelia from Vidal. Mercedes even tells Ofelia that she once believed in fairy tales, but has had to put them aside for real life. Perhaps this is why she cannot save Ofelia, for Ofelia must return to the

Fig. 7.2 Ofelia begins her first task, *Pan's Labyrinth* (Optimum Releasing, 2007)

fantastic in order to wait for a time it is safe for her (and what she symbolically represents) to return; that is, when Fascism is defeated. The spectator recognizes, aligns with, and pledges allegiance to Ofelia, as their representative in the film, and by extension with Mercedes, read as an adult version of Ofelia.

The narrative of *Pan's Labyrinth* closely follows Vladimir Propp's taxonomy of the functions of the fairy tale, with Ofelia as heroine. She leaves home, meets a villain, is given a task, encounters misfortune, counteracts it, and defeats the villain. Ofelia's death and return to the underground realm could be interpreted as a happy ending. Vidal is the villain; the Faun is the dispatcher, helper and father; and the underground realm is the prize.[47] The spectator is invited to accept Ofelia's imaginings of the fantastical world through the introduction of the fairy tale concept and Ofelia's perspective early in the film, though the end leaves little room for speculation as to its existence. It is hard not to associate Ofelia with child characters from previous films about the Spanish Civil War, most notably the child protagonist of *Raise Ravens*. In *Raise Ravens*, Ana imagines her mother, who has been dead for some time, speaking to her; the spectator sees this hallucination, and is aware that it is just in Ana's imagination. Her father, who dies at the beginning of the film, is a Fascist serving in the military. Ana and Ofelia both invent a fantasy in order to survive the trauma of parental death; both search for alternative explanation of events, in the form of the fairy-tale narrative, Ana with her dead mother, Ofelia with a fantasy world. And while in both films it is (or seems to be) clear that the girls' imaginings are not real, *Raise Ravens* concludes with Ana abandoning her fantasies for the real world, whereas in *Pan's Labyrinth*, Ofelia remains in the fantasy world through her death.

Children are blank screens onto which the adult spectator can project their anxieties and fears, and yet their subjectivity separates them from the adult world, hence their usefulness in both allegorical and fantastical work. The child protagonist, through whom a spectator may be more willing to accept and understand it, enables the use of the allegorical fantastic. From the opening shot of Ofelia bleeding on the ground, the spectator aligned with her, and invited to view the film as, in part, fairy tale, viewing the other characters as a child in such a story might: as monsters. A conventional narrative would give just the story of Vidal, the maquis, and Ofelia's fractured new home life. The addition of the fantastic, seen only by Ofelia, gives the spectator an alternative way of interpreting history through the fantastic by way of the monstrous. *Pan's Labyrinth* has its share of monsters: some benevolent, some maleficent, some a combination of the two. For Stephen Asma, the monster is a subspecies of the Other, that which is outcast and not viewed as the norm.[48] In the historical representation of the film, it is debatable as to who is the Other: the maquis or the Nationalists. As the nationalists, led by Vidal, are represented as the villains, it might be easy to assume that they are the Other. But in this era of Spain, it is the maquis that are the Other. Even Ofelia could be viewed as a monster: she is both Ofelia and Princess Moanna, a fairy-tale creature. Her consumption of the food at the Pale Man's banquet is both an indication of her human status, in that she requires food, and her transformation, through food consumed in the fantastic realm. The narrative is working to find the connection between the real and the fantastic through the presentation of Ofelia as a benevolent monster who can bridge the gap.

Furthering the reinvention of historical representation, *Pan's Labyrinth* makes the historical implicit, while using historical elements as part of an allegory for larger representations of childhood, violence, war, and maturation. James Clarke writes that fantasy 'allows for allegorical engagement with violence, choice, selfishness and compassion'.[49] It is perhaps only an outsider who could re-engage with the historical drama of one of the most grievous moments in Spain's history, creating a new form in order to interpret and understand the events of the past. *Pan's Labyrinth* is a postnational film that seeks to find new ways to represent violence, war, and their effect on children, through the use of the fantastic.

The Devil's Backbone and *Pan's Labyrinth* become historiographic metafiction in their self-reflexivity of representation of war, trauma, violence, and their effect on children. Post- and prosthetic memory operate in the films through the distance between direct experience and that of subsequent generations, as their director and writers are interpreting a history of which they have no personal knowledge. Through historical metafiction, the films ask the spectator to question not only what is represented, but how it is represented, and how the historical reflects the fantastic, and vice versa. *The Devil's Backbone* and *Pan's Labyrinth* are allegorical meditations on trauma and violence through a historiographically metafictional lens.

8

Franchising the Spanish Fantastic: The *[REC]* Films

One night, Paco Plaza was watching a popular Spanish television programme *Aquí hay tomate* (Telecinco, 2003–8). Widely regarded as *telebasura*, the show ran news stories that tended to the tabloid end of popular information. On this particular episode, the guest was a woman who had once been married to a popular singer. Through him, she had gained her own fame, and the episode focused on the mental health problems she had endured and her subsequent stay in hospital. What struck Plaza was the shooting style the programme used for certain scenes: it was frequently handheld, and gave both a shaky picture and frequently inaudible sound. In an interview, Plaza said, 'these reality shows have a distinct way of filming, [so] that people tend to think that what they see is real'.[1] He and fellow director Jaume Balagueró discussed how disturbed they both were by the form, and how it seemed to create a language that spectators thought reflected reality. Thus was born *[REC]*, which aims to recreate this reality television technique, and present spectators with a story that Plaza would call as ridiculous as the stories shown on *telebasura*, in as disturbing a style as that which those shows used. Whereas del Toro used the fantastic to examine the past, Balagueró and Plaza (like Álex de la Iglesia before them) used the fantastic to examine contemporary Spanish culture and society.

Given a tiny budget and an objective just to have fun with it, no one was more shocked than the directors at the film's success. Produced by Filmax, *[REC]* earned over €8 million in Spain alone, and quickly became a hit with horror fans around the world. The first film would remain the most financially successful of the franchise, with each of the subsequent films earning approximately €5 million, €2 million and €1 million respectively. The first two films were remade in the US under the titles *Quarantine* (John Erick Dowdle, 2008) and *Quarantine 2: Terminal* (John Pogue, 2011); *Quarantine* earned more than $30 million in the US.

[REC]1 and *[REC]2* were directed by both Balagueró and Plaza. *[REC]3: Genesis* (*[REC]3: Génesis*, 2012), purportedly an origin story, was directed and co-written by Plaza, and *[REC]4*, as noted, was directed and co-written by Balagueró. This chapter will focus mainly on the first two films and their representation of the apocalypse and Spanish society through the found footage mode, and will briefly discuss the later films.

Representations of the end of the world frequently show scenes of chaos and barbarism. In the face of pandemics, nuclear war, environmental disaster, giant asteroids, or zombies, civilized society apparently will collapse. The *[REC]* films situate themselves under threat from monsters in the midst of disaster. The films play upon the spectator's reception of visual information. And while the films address an international genre audience as postnational films, they each produce a representation intended as a critique of the religious and media cultures of Spain.

The monsters in the *[REC]* films are infected humans, and while not technically zombies, they display the same behaviour and characteristics, placing them in at least partially in the subgenre of zombie films.[2] With few literary antecedents, the zombie is almost entirely a cinematic creation. The zombie as a monster is generally a human who, because of infection or reanimation from the dead, cannot be reasoned with, appealed to, or dissuaded by logical discourse.[3] Zombies first appeared in film in *White Zombie* (Victor Haleprin, 1932), emerging from a Haitian myth; ethnographically these zombies were victims of voodoo magic, 'soulless corpses revived by witchcraft'.[4] But it was not until the first of George A. Romero's zombie cycle, *Night of the Living Dead* (1968), that the monster gained favour as a horror icon, and the Romero-style zombie has dominated. This kind of zombie is slow-moving and can be killed by destroying the brain, thus meaning that the greater threat frequently comes from other humans. In the *[REC]* films, the 'zombies' are living humans with an infection; the infected represent fear of the other and, for the characters, fear of what they might become: human and not, extending the zombie metaphor. Sarah Lauro and Karen Embry write that the 'terror that comes from an identification of oneself with the zombie is, primarily, a fear of loss of consciousness'; in this case, humanity is defined by cognizance.[5] A zombified state is neither death nor life; one experiences a loss of identification through a lack of self-awareness, and yet one is not dead. There is some question as to whether the infected persist in a state of existence or not; but as our physical state is related to our identity, the loss of consciousness can be seen as death without dying. It is an interruption of the death process without finality, killing the soul while leaving the body alive, the reverse of what is granted by God in Catholic doctrine.

While zombies have been popular in US and UK films, there are only a few Spanish zombie films, such as *Tombs of the Blind Dead* (*La noche del terror ciego*, Amando de Ossorio, 1971) and *The Living Dead at Manchester Morgue* (Jorge Grau, 1974). According to Kyle Bishop, zombie films resurface in times of great political and social unrest; the zombies themselves either represent that unrest, or their manifestation and the ensuing disaster draws attention to political and social problems. Bishop writes, 'zombie narratives manifest the predominant cultural anxieties of their time, anxieties usually repressed or ignored by mainstream media.'[6] In the *[REC]* films, zombies raise anxieties over tabloid television, and the public's insatiable appetite for seemingly superficial stories. The infection that causes people to become monsters has an apparent supernatural origin, but is spread due to human error and negligence. While the films present a secularized, contemporary society, the symbolism and superstition of religion are shown to linger in the collective consciousness. The zombies, then, could represent an updated version of the crisis in Spanish culture seen during the Spanish Civil War: on one side, the fight for a modern, secular, democratic country, and on the other, religion and Fascism. Obviously these do not manifest in the films in the strictest sense; however, what are presented are approaches to dealing with a crisis, with religion and the secular at war. In the *[REC]* films, the zombies raise anxiety over the effects of tabloid television, and the public's insatiable appetite for seemingly superficial stories.

As stated, while the monsters in the *[REC]* films are not technically zombies, they fall within the category due to their collapsing effect on civilized society. In this, they can also be related to literature and artwork involving plague and pestilence. According to Raymond Crawford, most of this type of work shows humans reverting to barbarism and savagery during epidemics.[7] Feelings of fear and evil are projected onto the disease, which is not created by a supernatural force, but comes from humans or nature. Such a rapidly spreading illness leads to lack of ability to contain it, and rapid degradation of civilization. *[REC]* seems to subscribe to this theory, as the disease seems to originate from a dog belonging to one of the tenants. The ending of the film, though, and *[REC]2* suggest a supernatural theory in the form of the devil, spreading person-to-person through the virus and able to speak through the infected.

Jennifer Cooke writes that 'disease is more often than not linked with practices that exclude certain groups from society and so is indicative of deliberately divisive forms of discourse'.[8] The use of a television programme within the film allows for this type of discourse. It shows the tenants revealing their prejudice. One man is concerned about his appearance; a woman constantly interrupts an interview to complain that her husband is trapped outside; several of the tenants blame a Chinese family, and refer to their dietary and hygienic habits as proof that they must be the source of the disease. However, it is revealed that the human source is a child, part of a typical Spanish family. The danger, then, comes (almost) as much from the other tenants as the infected. Spain is a relatively recent multicultural society; the monoculture imposed under Fascism meant that immigration from other nations came to Spain later than to other western nations.[9] Despite its desire to be part of the European community, as a nation with a single culture and religion for so many decades, Spain has shown discrimination and distrust to those of non-European backgrounds.[10] In *[REC] 2* the monster is revealed to be supernatural in origin, necessitating a priest, a symbol of Catholicism, which was at the heart of Spanish monoculturalism.

The *[REC]* films present a high-concept scenario in a classical narrative style, in that there is a causal chain of events based on actions precipitated by the characters and their reactions. Peter Wuss refers to this as a conception-based film structure.[11] The films begin this way, but in the presentation of increasingly frightening events, they move to a perception-based structure, in which goal-oriented actions are hindered, discontinued, or require reorientation. The ways in which they engage with the spectator, that is, how the concepts are presented, shows a metonymic adaptation of the themes and signifiers of horror film. The first two, and the first part of the third of the *[REC]* films, are presented in the found-footage mode. The footage is shot by a news cameraman, a figure of authority in comparison to the amateur bystander behind the camera in previous found-footage films, and the film also places its narration in the context of a reality news magazine, confronting the spectator with their own preconceptions of such programmes. Indeed, while the semantics of both films is horror, their syntax lies in their engagement with the society of the spectacle and role of religion in contemporary Spanish society.

According to Tina Pippin, 'monsters of the apocalypse are of a different species, an animal/human/mineral configuration'; for example, the monsters described in Book of Revelation are freakish hybrids designed to frighten readers.[12] By presenting monsters in a context beyond simply invoking a state of fear in the spectator, the films engage with wider political and social themes. The found footage mode leads to what Murray Smith refers to as central imagining, the process by which the spectator engages with the experiences of the characters.[13] The three processes of central imagining are:

1. Emotional simulation: simulating the emotional states of a character by imagining their experiences from the inside

2. Affective mimicry: mimicking the affective states of characters in a involuntary fashion
3. Automatic responses: reacting in reflex fashion to represented events in the same way as the character

Smith speculates as to whether central imaginings are congruent to the character, or whether they are assimilated into a broader perspective, in which the spectator imagines from outside any single character.[14] An examination of central imagining is key to understanding each film's projected story and subsequent themes and representations.

Each film has syntactic cultural connections to Spain. For *[REC]*, this is the influence of contemporary Spanish television, the new 'religion' of the masses. The *[REC]* films represent Spanish versions of fantastic horror themes, renewed interest in apocalyptic scenarios, and re-engagement with a unique film monster. The semantics are made to reach an international audience through the use of monsters and found footage, but the syntax and underlying themes are both specific to contemporary Spanish culture and understood by a larger postnational genre audience.

[REC] and *[REC]2*

[REC] begins with Ángela, a reporter for a television news magazine, and her cameraman, Pablo, taping a segment following a Barcelona fire crew. The crew is called to an apartment building, where an elderly woman is trapped in her flat. When they arrive, they find other building tenants in the lobby, claiming to have heard screaming. When the policeman tries to help the woman, she bites his neck and attacks others. All retreat screaming to the lobby. When they try to leave the building, they find that some authority has sealed them in. While an intern and the first fireman try to assess the situation, the policeman awakens and then attacks the intern. It soon becomes clear that there is a strange virus being transmitted through saliva that turns its victims into hyper-aggressive monsters. In the penthouse, Ángela and Pablo discover papers and a recording that indicate that someone was experimenting on children. When Pablo switches the camera to night vision, they see a deformed human female, who eventually attacks them. The film ends with Ángela being dragged into the darkness.

[REC]2 begins approximately 15 minutes after the first film ends. Like the first, it begins in the POV of a single camera, showing the inside of a van with a SWAT team destined for the building. The team is introduced to Owen, from the Health

department, who will be giving orders. In the penthouse, the SWAT team discovers that the residents have become violent. One by one, members of the SWAT team are killed. The remaining members discover that Owen is, in fact, a priest, and the source of the virus is the Devil. Meanwhile, three teenagers are playing with their camcorder near the affected building. They find a way into the building, drawing with them a police officer and a resident who was trapped outside, but they are all shortly trapped inside the building when the sewer entrance is welded shut. Two of the youths are killed; the third becomes infected, and Owen proceeds to speak to the demon that possesses him. Ángela, the TV reporter, appears alive with her camera. The remaining four return to the penthouse, where they find a secret chamber. It is then revealed that Ángela has been possessed; she kills the SWAT cameraman and Owen, and obtains release from the building.

The use of found footage as a device for aesthetic expression has been common in documentary and avant-garde cinema since the late 1950s. But it was not until 1980, with *Cannibal Holocaust* (Ruggero Deodato), that the found-footage mode was discovered to be particularly useful in the horror genre, to generate a feeling of fear. Arguably the most famous example of found-footage horror is *The Blair Witch Project* (Daniel Myrick and Eduardo Sánchez, 1999), which spurred a flurry of similar films such as *Cloverfield* (Matt Reeves, 2008) and *Diary of the Dead* (George A. Romero, 2007) that featured amateur cinematographers filming horrific, fantastic events. Before this, Alejandro Amenábar's *Thesis* had examined the snuff film, and the psychological effects of watching violent images presented in found-footage mode. This mode gave filmmakers a new means of cognitive and emotional connection with the spectator. *[REC]* turns the found-footage film into a commentary on Spanish tabloid television, its journalistic presentation and the public's appetite for scandal. *[REC] 2* adapts the form further, expanding it from a single camera to several, and expanding the narrative to issues of political and religious ideology. The *[REC]* films present a representation that conveys the illusion of live experience through found footage. They move beyond the use of found footage as a tool for horror, and repurpose it as a commentary on filmic presentation and spectatorial engagement.

Guy Debord writes that the 'spectacle presents itself as a vast inaccessible reality that can never be questioned'.[15] In other words, if what is shown is presented as 'real', it is not to be doubted, no matter how unbelievable. Indeed, when *The Blair Witch Project* was released, there was speculation as to whether it was a fiction film or a documentary; the film's website cannily suggested that it was the latter. In a culture heavily invested in visual spectacle, the average spectator, confronted with a spectacle of danger or horror in real life or any seemingly unusual event, will frequently bring out their mobile phone and film it, as opposed to watching it with their own eyes, as though it is only through a screen that such images become reality. If, as previously stated, that which was once directly lived is now lived through its representation, recreating a style that mimics the form of *telebasura* forces a spectator to reconsider what is a 'realistic' form of representation. Debord further notes that the 'image is… a historical mutation of the form of commodity fetish'.[16] That is to say, the fetishization of commodities, the idea of human fulfilment coming from what one possesses and accumulates as opposed to who one is, is extended to the spectacular image.[17] The image is no longer a vehicle of information, but another commodity to be consumed.

As Cristina Moreiras Menor notes, once post-dictatorship Spain had integrated into the European marketplace, it began to privilege image and appearance in order to sell itself.[18] Shows such as *La máquina de la verdad* and *Lo que necesitas es amor* (Antena 3, 1993–9) were considered as pushing far past the limits of reasonable excess. *Thesis* came out of this culture, wherein 'spectacle and its appearance have been displaced… by a virtual reality which remains omnipresent in its desperate inaccessibility'.[19] Where *Thesis* used some home movie footage to critique voyeurism in watching the snuff film, *[REC]* expands on this because of advances in technology and audiovisual representation. It presents virtual reality through a found-footage aesthetic, in which the image is both accessible because of the placement of the spectator as a character, and inaccessible through the spectator's inability to control the image. *[REC]* presents the spectator with a familiar format and a character on whose 'eyes' they rely in danger. In *[REC]2*, two types of visual presentation are given: first through the cameras of the SWAT team, as though allowing for an 'inside' observation; and then through the teenagers' camera. The latter form more closely resembles that which the spectator might be expected to produce if they were at the scene. The three types of images provided – amateur, professional, and covert – cover all that might be considered 'real', and give three perspectives on the virtual reality that is both accessible and beyond the spectator's control.

Direct cinema is a form of documentary filmmaking that became popular in the mid-twentieth century. Characterized by long takes, indirect speech and overheard dialogue, it was suited to 'the representation of uneventfulness and of time passing', and was frequently employed in an effort by filmmakers to avoid interference between the subject and the spectator.[20] This relationship is underscored by the technology; even a direct cinema film will be edited, or frame its shots to show only that which the filmmakers wish the spectator to see. But it was a starting point for much of reality television, which claims uncensored access to its subjects.

Tabloid journalism found a niche in these so-called infotainment programs. Since its inception in the late 1980s with such programmes as *Unsolved Mysteries* (NBC/CBS/Lifetime/Spike, 1987–2010) and *America's Most Wanted* (20th Century Fox Television, 1998–2012), reality television has seen rising audience demand. While the popularity of such programmes is not unique to Spain, the Spanish government attempted to legislate it, if not out of existence, at least out of broadcast times when it could be viewed by children.[21] Found-footage aesthetics are similar to and an extension of direct cinema, an attempt to present an unbiased view of a story to the spectator. The spectator's association of the form with documentary, and by extension 'reality', is crucial to an understanding *[REC]* and *[REC] 2* not only as horror, but also as social commentary. Again, the commentary comes from the reflection of contemporary Spanish society, and the characters and their attitude, as well as the source of the virus, are representations of concerns about contemporary Spanish culture. This brings it back to the specifically Spanish syntax of both religion and community, set within the semantics of the found footage format, to create the postnational film.

Daya Kishan Thussu notes that many critics of infotainment programmes refer to them as 'dumbing down' news, emphasizing the trivial, and focusing on crime, celebrity and human-interest stories of a frequently inflammatory or personal nature.[22] Whereas traditional journalism is meant to be objective, tabloid journalism is often viewed as serving 'unrefined tastes for the scandalous and grotesque'.[23] The fictional programme within the narrative of *[REC]*, 'While You're Asleep', sets itself inside a fire station, following the fire crew for a night [See Figure 8.1]. An audience for such a show would likely hope for either a fire or some other emergency that could give them access to the private, and possibly sensational. For the first twenty minutes, this seems to be honoured. The crew goes out on a call, and the spectator is given access through Ángela and Pablo, who are the eyes and ears of the waiting public.

This is expanded in *[REC]2*, with three types of cameras. First, those belonging to the SWAT team: these are covert cameras, ones to which the spectator would normally not have access, adding a sense of intimacy and clandestine information. The second is the teenagers' camera; this reflects the perspective of the average citizen, the desire for fame and access to the forbidden [See Figure 8.2]. At the end of the film, the original camera from *[REC]* is recovered, as if to suggest that *[REC]2* has also been a part of the television programme within the film. The cultural critique lies in the extremities of the situation that is the theme of the films. The audiovisual spectacle is a comment on the cultural obsession with this type of program, and the aesthetic that seeks to replace reality.

Fig. 8.1 Ángela begins her night of reporting, *[REC]* (Contender Entertainment, 2008)

Fig. 8.2 Teenagers wandering the virus-infested building, *[REC]2* (Entertainment One, 2010)

The style of tabloid television can be described in a single term: sensationalism. It brands itself as populist, and depends on heightened emotion and melodrama in order to bridge the gap between news and entertainment. Misha Kavka finds that the conflation of the visual spectacle with reality is linked strongly to television, through its central transmission to the public (which forms social integration), the history of its consumption in the private sphere of the home, and the technology of presence through its constant state in the space of the home.[24] The effect of the style is tension, and that tension finds a comfortable space in horror. What the spectator of 'While You're Asleep' sees is not what would have been broadcast: this is clear from the unedited footage, giving the audience an even greater sense that they are watching the forbidden, such as outtakes in which Ángela expresses boredom, or when the cinematographer spies on the injured security guard. Although this is a feature film intended for spectators to watch in a large space, the style is imitating that of television, and must be understood as that of television.

This episode of 'While You're Asleep' is following fire-fighters; programmes about accident and emergency workers became popular in the 1980s, and viewers were invited to admire the efforts of these so-called heroes.[25] Jessica Fishman writes reality shows featuring law enforcement officers and fire-fighters create a progressive myth of these official agents as heroes battling disturbing forces.[26] By contrast, Richard Kilborn notes that populist myths show everyday people (such as the journalists and a few of the tenants) voluntarily participating as heroes.[27] The films combine these two types of heroism, though it is unclear where the spectator is meant to place their trust, as in the end, all fall victim to the infection. Through this, the films blur the boundaries of the public and the private. John Fiske writes that in tabloid news, especially in infotainment programmes that feature either police or other authority figures, 'the lives of ordinary people enter the public domain of law and order or public safety… in the role of victim'.[28] This is often an exaggeration of the victim's social position, in an effort to maintain ideas of social difference and class.

As tabloid journalism is that which exceeds and transgresses norms, [REC] blurs the lines between different heroic roles. Usually, the style would require both the journalist and the cameraman to be neutral, but they become both hero and victim. The various levels of authority – journalist, firefighter, police, SWAT, priest – come together in this excess of form and content. The public world of everyday heroes comes into the private world of the tenants, and the home of the audience that is theoretically watching this show. But it is Ángela and Owen who remain central to the stories: Ángela, first as representative of tabloid journalism, who attempts to transcend this position to bring the truth through the media, and is then possessed by the virus/ demon; meanwhile Owen, as a priest, represents the ultimate authority of the Church, which in the past controlled spectacle within Spanish society through religious ritual compliance. Now, he falls victim literally to a demon and metaphorically to the spectacle of the post-religious society, which rejects the authority of the Church in favour of audiovisual spectacle. It is interesting to note that, while *Quarantine* is almost identical to *[REC]*, *Quarantine 2* is set in an airport hanger, and engages with the theme of terrorism. This is likely because an American audience would not understand a priest who had authority over government or police officials. This is particular to Spanish culture and its history of the Church's control during the Fascist era.

In his work on film and emotion, Smith contemplates whether POV shots are essential to forming allegiance with a particular character.[29] In *[REC]* and *[REC]2*, all that is given is POV shots, directly from the perspective of a single character in the first film, and from several characters in the second. In *[REC]*, the cameraman is never seen. In *[REC]2*, the camera takes the POV of the members of the SWAT team (all of whom are seen at least once) and the teenagers. Returning to Smith's concept of central imagining, it can be relatively easy for the spectator to imagine the experiences of the character from the inside, as the spectator is literally looking through their eyes. It is also common for spectators to mimic the affective state of characters in horror films, frequently jumping and screaming when scared; this also applies to automatic, reflexive responses. This is further related to two concepts described by Margrethe Bruun Vaage: imaginative empathy, which uses the imagination to enact characters' mental experiences; and embodied empathy, which directly gives the spectator the bodily and affective feeling of the characters.[30] This imagining must occur in the processing of information that is fictional. The spectator watching a horror film that uses the found-footage POV has the capacity to be moved in relation to an apprehension of what is presented, as spectators have learned the stylistic language of such films. Disagreeing with Smith, Jinhee Choi writes that 'a stronger and systematic relation… can be found between the extent of the viewers' knowledge and an activation of certain kinds of imagining'.[31] While less time is spent with each of the individual POVs in the second film, multiple cameras mean that more time is spent with knowledge of the appearance of these characters through whose POV the spectator looks. For Choi, POV shots can, but do not ensure, emotional engagement. Having past knowledge of what has occurred, though, allows the spectator a chance to align themselves with the characters in the second film, knowing what they are about to encounter.

Wuss writes that 'humans… feel the need for "passive control", meaning control in a cognitive sense, the ability, to a certain extent, to foresee what will happen to them and their surroundings'.[32] The spectator plays the role of the character in trying to find a solution to the problem, and the film's tension depends on the spectator's ability to overcome the state of uncertainty. In a film such as *[REC]*, in which chaos reigns, such control would seem to have to be abandoned. Cognitive under-standing is limited due to the POV (though it increases somewhat in the second film with multiple POVs). Kevin Glynn points out that, 'among [tabloid television's] favourite themes are the ubiquity of victimization and the loss of control over the outcome of events, and of one's fate'.[33] That loss of certainty and lack of control are also central to a horror film, and even more so to one that copies the form of reality television in POV. The spectator has emotional engagement with the character who is their eyes, and yet has no control through the limited perspective. The fantastic nature of the story only enhances this uncertainty.

Programmes such as 'While You're Sleeping' purport to be an extension of citizen journalism, through the single camera. As the virus moves from person to person, it moves from camera to camera. It is no coincidence that the first human to exhibit the virus is a girl, that the amateur camera belongs to teenagers, and that the first experimental subjects of the virus are children. They belong to a generation not only attuned to the visual representation of the real, but also to its transnational syntax. The 'old' media, as represented in part by Owen, have a pronounced national syntax, which is corrupt but authoritative. The camera is the most important character: as a symbol of transnational media, accessible by virtually anyone, anywhere, it both feeds the virus and allows it to spread. More importantly, it is the spectator watch-ing through the camera that allows this. At the end of *[REC] 2*, Ángela, positioned midway between amateur and authoritative as a journalist, kills Owen in a symbolic gesture of the growing supremacy of postnational new media. The final shot of the film has the infected Ángela breaking the fourth wall, as if indicating to the spectator that they, too, are infected, or soon will be, by virtue of their spectatorship.

[REC] and *[REC]2* are critical satires of the commodity culture of the sensational image, turning tabloid television, descended from direct cinema, into a demonstration of monstrous engagement, through engagement with monsters. As meta-cinematic horror, it comments as much on the spectator's desire for immediacy and the spec-tacular, as the means through which it is brought to them. While its semantics are those of horror, its syntax presents a reflection and representation of contemporary Spanish society, which is easily translatable beyond national markers for the postna-tional spectator.

[REC]3: Genesis and *[REC]4: Apocalypse*

Contemporary Hollywood plans on many films becoming part of 'franchises', especially if such films are based around characters such as superheroes, or are adaptations of popular novels or comic book series. *[REC]* was not made with the intention of spawning three subsequent films, but such was the success of the first, that Balagueró, Plaza, and, most importantly, Filmax decided to keep going. While the first two films were well received by audiences and critics, the third and fourth films had mixed success critically and at the box office. Plaza was the co-writer and director of the third film, tasked with writing about the origin of the zombie infection. Balagueró took on the final segment, which would (in theory) finish the tale.

*[REC]*3 takes places at the long-awaited wedding of Clara and Koldo. One of the guests is the veterinarian who treated the dog belonging to the infected girl in *[REC]*. He received a bite from the dog; during the wedding reception, the virus takes hold and he begins attacking the other guests. Clara and Koldo are separated in the ensuing chaos, and spend most of the film trying to find each other on the extensive ground of the reception venue. Each must avoid not only the zombies, but also problems with other guests, most of whom are useless in the face of danger. Meanwhile, the demonic nature of the virus is revealed when the chapel offers some guests refuge, and the efforts of a priest keep the zombies at bay with a prayer. Koldo and Clara eventually find each other, but Clara is bitten before they can escape, and at the end, she bites Koldo, and they both are gunned down by security forces.

In effect, this is not a genesis or origin story as had been presumed; rather, it appears to take place at the same time as the events of the first two *[REC]* films. While there is more information about the disease's religious context, nothing more is revealed about how it began. Instead, what is presented is another zombie film, but Plaza gives the spectator some twists. First, the film begins as found footage, mimicking a wedding video. We see a DVD slide show of pictures of Clara and Koldo, from childhood to the early days of their relationship. Then the film moves to a camera operated by Koldo's cousin Adrián, which is acceptably amateur. He interviews the various guests, and meets Atún, the professional videographer. They briefly discuss the quality of video and cinéma vérité, a self-reflexive nod to the first two *[REC]* films. When the outbreak occurs, Koldo is trapped with Adrían, Atún and some of the other guests. When Koldo sees that Atún is still filming (Atún, like Ángela in the first film, is insisting that people will need to see what happened), Koldo attacks him and breaks the camera. The film then switches from found-footage to normal camera (subjective) perspective. Koldo does what many characters should do (and many spectators often wish that characters would do) in the found-footage film: stop the person who insists on filming, because it is a stupid idea that endangers the camera operator's life. Plaza achieves two goals: breaking the series away from its found-footage origins (though whether this was a sound goal is debatable considering how much of the franchise's success was due to its found-footage mode), and allowing the story to take a new direction and find a new formula for the zombie semantic.

While *[REC]3* is set within an enclosed space (as the previous films), the buildings and grounds of a reception venue, the location is more extensive, giving Plaza more range for the story. He plays with specific codes and conventions of weddings: not only the wedding video, but conflicts between the two groups of families and friends, Clara's pregnancy, generational conflict, random sex between strangers, and the priest as mediator. In this case, the priest is not in charge per se, but he does possess the skill to keep the zombies at bay, albeit briefly. Plaza also injects Spanish cultural specificity into the story, as Koldo is Valencian and the wedding takes place in Catalonia. This is a national specificity that might not be understood by spectators outside of Spain, unaware of the nuances of different cultures and languages within Spain and the country's history. Some of the guests have taken refuge in a chapel, apparently only place of safety, relating back to the virus' religious origin and in keeping with a more Spanish view of the (albeit waning) centrality of Catholicism to the national culture. When Koldo leaves the safety of the chapel to find Clara, he puts on the armour and wears the shield of San Jordi, the patron saint of Catalonia.

Arguably, however, Clara is more important and resourceful than Koldo, and a point is made of her heroism. She is willing to pick up a chainsaw, destroy her wedding dress, kill various zombies with said chainsaw, kill one of Koldo's best friends in order to stop him from becoming a zombie, and force Koldo to cut off her arm in a futile effort to halt the zombie infection. While Koldo is given a more traditional aspect, as a 'knight' expected to save his lady, Clara eschews the normal mode of the female character by becoming something of an action hero. While *[REC]3*'s connection to the previous films is arguably loose (in that the only narrative connection is the veterinarian and the general geographical location), it breaks from the found-footage mode and attempts to become a different, yet still original take on, the zombie film.

The first scene of *[REC]4* picks up a few minutes after the end of *[REC]2*. Two SWAT officers, Guzmán and Lucas, enter the apartment building, planting explosive devices. They hear Ángela calling for help; Guzmán tells Lucas to leave, while he attempts to rescue her. In the next scene, Ángela wakes up in a medical bay; she has been taken to a ship in the middle of the ocean, commandeered by officials to try and find a cure for the virus. She is kept there under guard along with Guzmán, Lucas and the lone survivor of the wedding from the previous film. The ship has no means of escape, and the scientists have injected the virus into a test monkey. The monkey is let out of its cage, whereupon the virus spreads to most of the crew. It is revealed that the creature that implanted itself in Ángela at the end of the second film transferred to Guzmán. Ángela and a crew member, Nic, manage to kill him and escape in an inflatable raft just before the ship explodes.

Certainly, the apocalyptic feeling is enhanced by the location. The isolation of the ship in the sea (it is never revealed where exactly it is), the lack of lifeboats, the radio silence, and the pre-emptive means to blow up the ship, give an impression that the ship might be the refuge of the last humans left on earth. The abandonment of found footage in the previous film allowed Balagueró to also let go of the formula, though *[REC]4* is not entirely without technological reflexivity. Nic is analyzing the footage from Ángela's video camera from the first two films, again suggesting that some day, the public will see this, and there are security cameras throughout the ship that both hinder and aid Ángela when she is being chased by the security forces. As in *[REC]*, there is a conflict between official authorities and the public, as the scientists, backed by security forces, try to impede and at one point capture and kill Ángela, who might be an ordinary member of the public at this point, but is still viewed as a journalist in her investigative instincts and behaviour.

Whereas *[REC]3* focused the story on personal relationships as opposed to any conflict between civilians and authority figures, *[REC]4* returns to the more overtly political. In an interview, Balagueró likened the story to George A. Romero's *Day of the Dead* (1985), which was set in an underground bunker run by the military. Romero's film is a criticism of the military industrial complex that allows authority figures widespread latitude to use whatever means necessary without answering for any possible criminal behaviour. As noted, in *[REC]4*, the ship is isolated, not only via the security forces who encode any incoming and outgoing transmissions, but also through its lack of lifeboats. In this case, the scientists are technically in charge, as opposed to a priest, but as in *[REC]2*, they are (in theory at least) supported by the military. This is a subtextual reference to recent news reports of military in conflicts zones around the world that torture and humiliate prisoners of war.

The infection is spread to the crew by a monkey, and the first of its victims is the cook, as if to indicate that innocent bystanders are the first to pay the price for government hubris and negligence. When the security force becomes infected, they represent a double threat, not only from their original orders to keep Ángela and the other civilians in order, but also as the infection causes them to act like out-of-control soldiers whose actions are ignored in favour of what is perceived as a greater good (such as getting rid of Ángela). Dr Ricarte, the lead scientist, makes the decision to destroy the ship, although he intends to escape and save his own skin. While a scientist, he is the main villain of the film, in that his loyalty is to himself and his authority; his alliance with soldiers suggests that, while he might be attempting to find a cure or vaccine for the virus, that virus may still be kept for the military to use as a weapon. In [REC]4, the zombies are not just a product of an experiment with evil forces, but represent the victims of authority, who are sacrificed in the name of experimentation, progress and, as this is early twenty-first-century Spain, austerity. At the conclusion of the film, the escape of Ángela and Nic, and the apparent eradication of the demon worm, seem to suggest that this is the end of the franchise. But with the switch from found-footage to normal perspective, there is always a chance that the franchise could continue.

Given the current popularity and financial importance of franchises and multiverse film storytelling in Hollywood, it is not surprising that other national cinemas might also take part in attempting to elongate the success of a particular film or films. While [REC]3 and [REC]4 might not have duplicated the box office success of the first two films, their expansion of the universe of [REC] and blending of tropes and themes specific to Spain with semantics familiar to genre fans around the world speaks to Filmax's recognition of the power of postnational film, and filmmakers' interest in combining inside and outside influences.

The [REC] franchise has been one of Filmax's biggest successes, and one of the few non-American franchises to have international success. While using culturally-specific Spanish culture, the films are not so specific as to be too obscure for the average fantastic film spectator. The films have added a new and unique dimension to the zombie trope, and have become important markers of the success of Spanish fantastic film in the international market.

9

Nacho Vigalondo: The Illegitimate Inheritor: *Timecrimes* and *Extraterrestrial*

While Guillermo del Toro and Alejandro Amenábar might be more famous among the general film-going public, on the fantastic film festival circuit arguably no filmmaker is more visible than Nacho Vigalondo. He has become a fixture at Fantastic Fest in Austin, anticipated and expected to put on a 'performance' not only professionally, but also personally. But the fans' love comes from a legitimate origin: his films. With ten shorts and three feature films, he is arguably the most prolific filmmaker of his generation (and these numbers do not even include his many film appearances as an actor). His second short, '7:35 in the Morning' ('7:35 de la mañana', 2003), was nominated for the Academy Award for Best Live Action Short in 2005. Vigalondo stands apart from most of his compatriots, working in science fiction as opposed to horror, and growing up free from much of the influence of US films of the 1980s that haunts many contemporary directors.

Vigalondo was born and raised in Cantabria, northern Spain. There was no movie theatre in his town, and while he sometimes watched films on television, he didn't have a VHS player until he was 16 years old. It wasn't until his last year of high school that he started to see films by filmmakers such as Peter Jackson, Sam Raimi, and John Waters, and it was then that he started thinking about the possibility of making films himself. He went to university in Bilbao, where he met his long-time producer, Nahikari Ipiña Sadaba, and also became friends with filmmakers Koldo Serra and Borja Cobeaga; this group would eventually form a company that continues to produce films, both fantastic and in other genres. Nacho officially studied visual communication (journalism and television), and he and his friends started making short films in their spare time.[1]

Vigalondo did not necessarily begin wanting to make films that could be categorized as fantastic: 'I love working with surprises, and absurdity, but within certain parameters. There has to be a balance with realism. I like to work with easy to recognize elements, but then put in something absurd'.[2] One of the signa-tures of Vigalondo's films is the inclusion of certain common generic tropes, and then shooting them against expectation. For example, '7:35 in the Morning' is a musical, but was shot in black and white and with a fairly static camera; 'Choque' (2005) is more serious in narrative, but is a spectacle shot in colour. His short 'Sunday' ('Domingo', 2007) is about a spaceship, but the pivotal moment of revela-tion is denied to the audience; instead, the camera focuses on a bickering couple. Vigalondo has made three shorts for anthology films that could be categorized as horror, but two of them, 'A is for Apocalypse' (2012) and 'Parallel Monsters' (2014), have science fiction elements.

The late 1990s and early 2000s saw a dearth of science fiction cinema, but it is making a comeback, in part due to filmmakers like Duncan Jones, Alex Garland and Vigalondo, and in particular his exploration of the genre via his presentation of unique themes and ideas. What Alejandro Amenábar started with the puzzle film in *Open Your Eyes*, Vigalondo has continued with his features, *Timecrimes*, *Extraterrestrial* (*Extraterrestre*, 2011) and *Open Windows* (2014). All of his films have enjoyed success with long festival circuit runs, though mixed box office suc-cess. In Spain, *Timecrimes* earned less than €300,000, *Extraterrestrial* less than €200,000, and *Open Windows* a little more than €300,000. Vigalondo's popular-ity not only among cinephiles but also among his fans is belied by the fact that his films have not succeeded financially in theatres, despite their popular genre appeal. Nevertheless, Vigalondo remains one of the most prolific and arguably most unique filmmakers of his generation, through his individual syntactical style that mixes genre semantics in inventive ways, particularly with science fiction.

In recent years, the puzzle film has become popular and is often associated with science fiction. While not all puzzle films are science fiction, they often use science fiction devices, and unlike more mainstream science fiction films, in which events have global consequences, *Timecrimes* and *Extraterrestrial* focus on the experi-ences of one man, and how the puzzle has an effect on his life.

In his study of the puzzle film, Warren Buckland first looks at Aristotle's writing on the simple and complex plots. For Aristotle, simple plots are mimetic, arranging events in a single, continuous action; complex plots add qualities of reversal and recognition, with action or an event that runs coun-ter to expectation. But complex plots are still mimetic and unified, as reversal and recognition are made to appear necessary and probable.[3] Thomas Elsaesser refers to these films as mind-game films: the character(s) is being played with, knowingly or unknowingly, and so is the spectator, through the withholding of information.[4] Frequently, the protagonist(s) is mentally unstable, and because of this, the spectator has doubts as to the reliability and communication of the narrative. Some examples of films with withheld information are *Dark City*, *The Sixth Sense*, and *The Others*. Puzzle films can also show events and action in a non-linear order, such as *Memento*, *Donnie Darko*, and *Primer* (Shane Carruth, 2004). Puzzle films bend their narrative contract with the spectator, either by withholding information or by showing events out of chronological sequence, only to dispel the uncertainties at the conclusion.

Timecrimes and *Extraterrestrial* use restricted narration, in that the spectator occupies the same position as the main characters. They are caught in the same sequence of, unstable reality, lack of information and/or time loops, and the spectator only has as much knowledge as the character. The intimate nature of the stories has consequences for the characters' sense of identity. As in *Open Your Eyes*, the hold of causality is swayed by the virtual/dream state. This manifests in *Timecrimes*, in that the dream/virtual state is metaphoric of the displacement cause by time travel. In *Extraterrestrial*, this is seen in the debated identity of the various characters, and the fact that their isolation leaves them in a kind of 'dream' world with no contact with other people. In fact, each of the main characters is, in effect, creating a film of his life, in *Timecrimes* through the recreation of events, and in *Extraterrestrial* through the threat of alien invasion, and the constant change in the characters' back stories.

The semantics of *Timecrimes* and *Extraterrestrial* are informed by the puzzle mode in combination with science fiction. The puzzle film can be considered a postnational mode, as filmmakers utilize it across national borders. Arguably, any film can use the semantics of the puzzle mode while incorporating syntax of its originating culture. This is true of the films in question, which display clear connections to Spanish cultural aesthetics and ideas, as part of the Spanish postnational fantastic.

Timecrimes

Timecrimes is, as the title partially suggests, about time travel. But there are no great historical events or figures, and it takes place within a limited geographical space. While some puzzle films withhold vital information until the end, *Timecrimes* reveals the source of the puzzle in the first third of the film. The puzzle comes from attempting to recreate, or more accurately, create the events that lead to the time loop. While most narrative films follow a cause-and-effect linear plot, *Timecrimes* reverses this to effect-and-cause. Bliss Cua Lim writes that '[f]antastic narratives strain against the logic of clock and calendar, unhinging the unicity of the present by insisting on the survival of the past or the jarring coexistence of other times'.[5] *Timecrimes* aims to create a puzzle by reversing narrative linearity, and creates a mood more commonly found in European cinema. The film is concerned with the emotional and intellectual effects of the fantastic elements than the elements themselves.

In his new house in the Spanish countryside, Héctor receives a phone call seemingly from no one, on a private phone number. When his wife Clara goes into town for groceries, he spies an unconscious naked woman in the forest behind his house. When he attempts to investigate, an unseen assailant attacks him. He climbs a fence and breaks a window to enter a strange building. He bandages his arm, and meanwhile makes contact with someone else in a silo nearby. Héctor gets to the silo, where a man tells him to get into a machine, and he is shut inside. When he emerges, the man tells Héctor that he has travelled back in time. Héctor calls his house, but hears himself answer, and realizes he was the one who made the mysterious phone call. He leaves the building and gets into a car accident. He covers his face with the bandage on his arm, and realizes that he, now known as Héctor 2, was his own assailant. He must recreate the events, including those with the girl, to make Héctor 1 go to the time machine so he can take his place. But in the evening, an accident occurs at his house, and he believes he has accidentally killed Clara. Héctor 2 returns to the silo and travels again to become Héctor 3, in an attempt to correct his mistakes.

In *Timecrimes*, the main character is sent back in time twice; in this, there is concentration on action, as opposed to character. This would seem to opposed traditional European art cinema, which focuses on character development. In his study of structures of identity in film, Jonathan Eig cites Luis Buñuel as the originator of films Eig refers to as 'mindfucks', in which a surprise identity, traditionally reserved for a supporting character, is transferred to the main character, and this information is withheld both from that character and the spectator.[6] In films such as 'An Andalusian Dog' ('Un Chien Andalou', Luis Buñuel and Salvador Dalí, 1929), and *That Obscure Object of Desire* (*Cet obscur objet de désir*, 1977), Buñuel attempted to reconceive traditional ideas of character perception. Eig finds that many mindfuck films, such as *The Sixth Sense* and *The Others*, have little commentary on the social, political, and economic forces that have caused the identity crisis; instead, these are personal journeys. As Eig sees it, where Buñuel was interested in the self-reflexive nature of cinema through altering perceptions of identity, Hollywood films rely on surprises about identity.[7] In *Timecrimes*, little is known about the time-travel device, so for the most part it does eschew larger forces and concentrates on the personal in the science fiction narrative. However,

Vigalondo is also incorporating Buñuel's avant-garde identity crisis on a more lit-eral level: Héctor and the spectator know early that the cause of the events is time travel, and the puzzle derives from the reconstruction of the individual actions.

Buñuel, who had a self-proclaimed love of the instinctive and irrational, used surrealism as a mode of storytelling; updating this for twenty-first century, Vigalondo uses the fantastic. And yet, surrealism is not abandoned; within the fantastic mode, the story presents itself as surreal. William Earle writes that in surrealist art and cinema of the early twentieth century, things are 'set free from their public or scientific connections and places in order to live a life of their own'.[8] In other words, they are designed to play with the spectator's conceptions and perceptions of a comprehensive pattern of reality. This surrealist mode has been recycled through a time-travel narrative that becomes surreal. During Buñuel's time, surrealism was interested in popular culture as a provocation against the bourgeoisie.[9] In a similar fashion, Vigalondo is using a popular cultural form to present a science-fiction/surrealist story of displacement and dislocation.

A traditional narrative film follows a cause-and-effect linearity. The main char-acter is presented in their everyday life, and an event happens that upsets this normality with various negative effects. The film clearly shows each cause and the effect it has, and there is a resolution of the conflict. In the puzzle film, the effect is frequently seen before the cause is known, and the main character is placed in the same unknown as the spectator, and the character and spectator attempt to solve the puzzle 'together'. Other such films are *Primer*, *Groundhog Day* (Harold Ramis, 1993), *Run Lola Run* (*Lola rennt*, Tom Tykwer, 1998), and *Source Code* (Duncan Jones, 2011), which present a character(s) who must solve a mystery of the cause of certain actions or events. While the spectator is watching *Timecrimes* in chronological order, that order is narrowed to the few hours in which the three Héctors co-exist, and so the same time period is shown three times. *Timecrimes* interrupts the process of linear narration, and repeats it from three different per-spectives. The puzzle lies in solving what caused the various effects. According to Gilles Deleuze, we assume that the body is a mathematical point in space, a pure instant or a succession of instances in time, and this affects perception and recol-lection.[10] What is given in this film is three versions of the same body that exist along the same point in time, and part of the puzzle is to understand how these three can co-exist, and have an effect on the other, in order to continue the causal chain of events that will lead to only a single Héctor. It is as if Héctor is the direc-tor of his own film, one in which the causal chain of events has been interrupted by the time machine, and Héctors 2 and 3 must perform their actions in order to maintain the timeline.

As in *Open Your Eyes*, there is a difference between perception and recollection, or at least, how they must be acted upon. As Héctor goes through the time loop, he must perceive an event from a different perspective, and recollect what happened in order to create the events. This is akin to making a film, in which a scene is shot several times, from different camera angles. Time is 'suspended' during this 'filming'; the only references to time are the position of the sun and the sound of thunder. Héctor finds himself performing different actions in each 'reincarnation', which is constantly the present. No clock means that Héctors 2 and 3 must rely upon memory to create the actions that led Héctors 1 and 2 to the effects caused. Henri Bergson writes that real time eludes mathematical treatment; as soon as time moves from one point to another, its previous parts no longer exist.[11] But a living being has duration, a continuous elaboration on the parts given by each moment of time. Héctor might be moving backward along time, but he is not adding or changing anything; rather he is doing what had already been done. His experience is still one of duration, as the time it takes to relive the past is still endured.

Héctor is, in effect, directing his past, reconstructing it almost as a flashback. The flashback is not shown as such, because the spectator has already witnessed it in the first third of the film; the flashback was seen before it was known to be a flashback. Héctor 2 and the spectator must flashback to the first third of the film to remember the sequence of events, in order to create them. After Héctor 2 stabs Héctor 1, he knows that Héctor 1 will run into the woods, at some point stop, and see him. Héctor 2 attempts to recreate the moment several times [See Figure 9.1]. It is not until he stops for a moment that he realizes his mistakes; he is not only director in his film now, but actor, and he must remember his 'lines'. After this, he begins to create events again, speaking to the young man via radio, returning to the silo, and looking at Héctor 1 through the window. Again, this is a kind of flashback that has already been seen from a different Héctor's perspective. Héctor 2 must remember and create his part in this film, as director and actor.

Timecrimes also lends itself to deconstructing cinematic conventions; Susan Hayward writes that deconstructive cinema 'makes visible the codes and conventions of dominant cinema and exposes the function of the cinematic apparatus as an instrument of illusionist representation'.[12] Dominant cinema seeks to provide the spectator with as much information as possible, frequently even beyond that of the characters; the puzzle film goes against this by asking the character(s) and spectator to solve the mystery. In the case of *Timecrimes*, this means creating the film as it is seen/experienced. As deconstructive cinema also refuses the logic of the homogenous filmic space and narrative closure, so the filmic space in *Timecrimes* gives the

Fig. 9.1 Hector 2 takes his position, *Timecrimes* (Mongrel Media, 2007)

same space with the same actions, from a different perspective. And it refuses tradi-tional syntactic narrative closure in that it refuses any change to its timeline; that is to say, while most films that use the time-loop device, such as *Source Code*, *Run Lola Run*, and *Groundhog Day*, see the main character affecting and changing the course of events, Héctor merely re-enacts actions in order to restore himself to his home.

The opening credits play over a car trip, from a large store parking lot in an urban area to the countryside. The camera first offers a backwards perspective as the car drives away from the store, as if indicating to the spectator that this world, the urban/suburban and presumed safety, is being left behind. The camera then moves to shots out the window as the urban becomes rural, and finally to the trail of shopping items that have fallen out of Héctor's car, indicative of the mundanity of everyday life that will soon disappear. It is a common introduction to a char-acter in a traditional classical narrative. Héctor is middle-aged, average-looking, and seemingly psychologically and emotionally stable. He is the everyman, nei-ther overly heroic nor underachieving. Mikhail Bakhtin writes that we never can never see ourselves as whole, because we can never perceive our entire body, and therefore have complete cognition of ourselves; a unitary world of cognition can-not be perceived as a unique concrete whole, because the contemplator does not occupy a perfectly determinate place; he is not unitary.[13] This is literally realized in *Timecrimes*, as Héctor is split into three versions of himself, and three stages

159

of cognition. Héctor 1 has no cognition beyond the strange events happening to him; Héctors 2 and 3 build on this cognition, but neither exists in a unitary world, as each set of cognition acts upon the others. Héctor 1 saw the damaged garbage bin, but didn't know what it meant; Héctor 2 saw the same bin, and thought it was meant to give him his overcoat; Héctor 3 sees it and realizes that he crashed into it, allowing the coat to become visible for Héctor 2. Deleuze writes that perception is the object 'minus everything that does not interest us'.[14] In each incarnation of himself, Héctor perceives that which is important to that particular incarnation. Héctor 2 must perceive only the coat, and not the reason for the overturned bin, and he must perceive the location of the bush to which Héctor 1 looks to see the young woman. Héctor 3, as the last one, has the greatest cognitive understanding: he is both the fullest and darkest version of himself, as if each trip in the time machine, with its greater knowledge, strips him of the identity he had when he first arrived at his home.

Héctor 2 emerges from the time machine soaked in a milky liquid. When he crashes the car on his way back to his home, he takes the bandage off his arm to use for the cut on his head. The mixture of his blood and the liquid turn the bandage pink, and the bandage around his head is far longer than that that would have been on his arm. It is at this point that Héctor 2 realizes that he is his own assailant, and must become a monster in order to recreate the events that lead Héctor 1 to the silo. His exaggerated appearance when he wears the coat, and bandage over his head, fits into the grotesque commonly seen in Spanish literature and art. Vivian Sobchack identifies the body as both the instrument of comprehension and, at times, a prison cell to be endured rather than lived in or enjoyed.[15] Héctor 2 understands his role as monster, once his body is damaged and he puts on his mask; but it is also his prison, as he is trapped in his other lives until nightfall, and he is trapped in his role as a monster in order to reach that time. When he is attempting to convince the young man to put him (Héctor) back in the time machine, he removes his mask as if to attempt to return to his non-monstrous self. Once he becomes Héctor 3, he no longer needs a mask to become a monster, as his injuries now display his monstrosity on his face. Each manifestation becomes more monstrous, not only in body, but in psyche.

While the majority of the film is subjective to Héctor's perspective, there is one important scene that switches the perspective to the young man. At this moment, the spectator is moved outside of Héctor to look at him, as seen from the outside. This is Héctor as he is threatening the young man in order to go back in time and stop the death of Clara. This is what seems to be Héctor's lowest point, a point at which he becomes purposefully violent in order to achieve his goal. According to

Deleuze's interpretation, Bergson sees only a single livable and lived time, and that simultaneity tends to confirm the conception of duration as the virtual coexistence of all degrees of a single identical time.[16] Again, rather than executing this theory through avant-garde style or editing techniques (the editing generally conforms closely to classical Hollywood style continuity and invisibility), Vigalondo instead places it within the narrative. What is shown is a single livable and lived time; but shown three times, from three perspectives of the same person. This is the paradox of coexistence: the past coexists with the present, and Héctor lives the past three times and coexists within it. Each Héctor is a counter-identity, building on the cognition of the last incarnation, displacing him further from his own space and time, even as he attempts to reconstruct it. These counter-identities are the different takes of the film, as Héctor the actor finds the different ways of approaching his role in order to achieve the film he needs to reach the end intact. It could be described as a film that is intertextual of itself, and while all films follow their own (inter)textual logic (in that each part depends on the other), in *Timecrimes* this logic is warped, and keeps referencing its own representations in order to reach its conclusion.

Only one other character in the film is given a name: Clara. The others are nameless, as though the puzzle was a game of chess and they are pawns. The young man (played by Vigalondo, a nod of self-reflexivity), as operator of the time machine, might at first seem to be the co-director of the film, as he guides Héctor 1 and the situation. But to continue with the film analogy, he is more akin to the editor; he admits that it is Héctor 3 who emerges first from the time machine, and it is he who controls the young man's actions towards Héctor 1 and Héctor 2 when he returns to the silo. Héctor 2 tells him what to do when Héctor 1 first arrives at the centre. All of the young man's actions are controlled and conducted, as if he were an editor following the wishes of the director, Héctor.

The young woman is a pawn; she is manipulated by Héctors 2 and 3, and allowed to die, even when Héctor 3 knows he could save her, if only he were willing to change the timeline. This is her position within Héctor's identity, as it grows darker through each trip in the past: while he hides behind his mask, she is forced to strip naked, literally and figuratively, in her body and her ignorance of the double Héctors and the situation. All of this points towards the film's innate pessimism. Once Héctor 3 realizes that it is the young woman whom he accidentally kills, it would appear that his curse is to allow her to die. *Timecrimes* displays some compassion for Héctor, but also something of humour in his situation, though this humour turns darker until it disappears by the end of the film. Noël Carroll writes that 'within a single narrative work, the same grotesque figure can be presented as alternatively horrific or comic, depending upon whether, in context, the fear card is played or not'.[17] In this case, the horror and comedic are combined: as an everyman in a surreal situation, Héctor is comic; as a monster, he is horrific. By the third act, as Héctor's mask is replaced by his facial injuries, humor turns to compassion, when the spectator realizes that Héctor must let the young woman fall to her death in order to maintain the timeline. He knows he will do it, because he already did it.

Unlike *Groundhog Day* or *Run Lola Run*, in both of which the main character lives the same actions several times until he or she gets it 'right', or *Source Code*, in which the main character saves hundreds of lives, *Timecrimes* states categorically that the future cannot be changed, and that bad events will happen because they already have. So while it is semantically linked to the science fiction genre, it is syntactically closer to its deconstructionist and European roots, in that there is no clichéd happy ending. Unlike a Hollywood film involving time travel, there is no rescue, nor is the hero redeemed. The final shot of the film shows Héctor 2 driving to the silo to go back in the time machine. It is almost a suggestion that the day does not end, or again, like the puzzle, there is no other perspective to the end of Héctor 2's timeline, leaving Héctor 3 with the consequences of his actions. Indeed, the story within the film ended earlier, when Héctor 2 went into the time machine to become Héctor 3; Héctor 3 must now face the consequences, which will arrive with the police. Indeed, of all the events that occur within the story, the only one that remains an unknown factor is the police; we know they are coming because sirens are heard, but their arrival is never seen. This leads back to Héctor's experience as 'actor' of this film (his part is not concluded) and its pessimism, as the film reaches a satisfactory, if not happy, conclusion.

As a puzzle film, *Timecrimes* operates within an intimate space of speculation, combining the concept of time travel with a reversal of cause-and-effect narrative. Vigalondo literalizes questions of perception of identity through the time-loop narrative, and asks the spectator not to discover a secret, but to move the pieces of the puzzle alongside the protagonist. Its pessimism belies its semantic generic structure in favour of its syntax, which looks to European surrealism and Spanish grotesque. As a postnational film, it marries this more classical semantic layout with its specific cultural syntax.

Extraterrestrial

Vigalondo's second feature can also lay claim to a science fiction premise, but it is more similar in tone to his short film '7:35 in the Morning' than to *Timecrimes*, in that it is comedic. In fact, it is best described as romantic comedy – with a spaceship. The semantics of science fiction exist, in that there is a spaceship hovering over Madrid (which is only seen unmediated a few times during the film), and there is discussion of possible alien invasion. But this becomes window dressing to the story's focus on the main character's efforts to win the heart of a woman, and how relationships with lovers and neighbours become complicated by misunderstandings and misdirection. Indeed, it is a comedy of errors, where the spaceship and alien invasion are really the least of the characters' worries. Its semantics are also those of youth culture, a culture that has grown up with the cinema of alien invasion and will readily accept the reality of such a situation.

Julio wakes up in a bed with a hangover and no idea where he is or how he got there. The apartment belongs to Julia, whom he doesn't remember. She doesn't remember him either, nor does she recall the night before. He tries to leave, only they discover that the normally busy streets of Madrid are empty. That's because a spaceship is hovering over the city and almost everyone else has fled. The internet isn't working, and the television is only broadcasting emergency information (and only for a short time). Julio ends up hanging around, and when Julia's boyfriend Carlos shows up, she pretends that she found Julio lying in the street and she brought him in out of pity. Julia's neighbour Angel has also stayed in the building, and Julio accidentally reveals his and Julia's one-night stand to him. Julio convinces Carlos that Angel might be an alien to get him kicked out, Carlos goes off by himself and gets locked out of the apartment, and Julio and Julia continue their affair. Julio's deceptions come to a head when Carlos' increasingly violent behaviour forces Julio to pretend to be an alien in disguise.

As stated, both the title of the film and the event that leads to the comedic situation are indicative of science fiction; as Paul Wells writes, 'science fiction is more concerned with the external and macrocosmic'.[18] This is echoed by Vivian Sobchack, who sees science fiction as giving its threats a public and collective aspect.[19] Certainly, an alien spaceship hovering over a major city would normally be represented as an external and macrocosmic event, with at least some of the narrative devoted to the effect of the situation on the larger population. However, in keeping with changing the syntax of common genre semantics, Vigalondo focuses on the personal and microcosmic situation. Julio and Julia are aware of the possible threat, but are far more concerned with Carlos finding out about their affair. When Carlos turns up at the apartment, he talks of seeing other refugees and hearing talk of the possibility of the aliens being in the city, possibly in disguise to try and infiltrate the population, but again, he quickly becomes embroiled in the lies of the affair. Some people have taken over a UHF channel to try and broadcast information to the population about what is really going on, about what the government won't tell them, but never really give out any useful information. No official is ever seen or heard from, and in the second half of the film, Julio and Julia make no attempt to go outside their apartment to find out what is going on.

The addition of the comedic syntax makes the typical science fiction semantics absurd, revealed as more or less a ruse disguising the true nature of the film. As stated, it is, in effect, a romantic comedy of errors. Romantic comedies tend to be stereotyped as made for almost exclusively female audiences, and they tend to follow a formula, at least in Hollywood romcoms, of boy meets girl, boy loses girl, boy regains girl; sometimes the genders are reversed. The narratives of such films usually contain a lot of misdirection, mistaken identity, and misunderstanding, which adds to the comedy. Some comedy subgenres are screwball, as seen in mid-twentieth-century films such as *It Happened One Night* (Frank Capra, 1934) and *Bringing Up Baby* (Howard Hawks, 1938), or sex/cerebral comedies of later decades, such as *Bob and Carol and Ted and Alice* (Paul Mazursky, 1969) and *Annie Hall* (Woody Allen, 1977). The late twentieth century saw the romcom make a comeback in films such as *When Harry Met Sally* (Rob Reiner, 1989) and *You've Got Mail* (Nora Ephron, 1998), and in the early twenty-first century, the somewhat new subgenre of the homme-com, romantic comedies that focus on a male protagonist's perspective, such as *The 40 Year-Old-Virgin* (Judd Apatow, 2005) and *Knocked Up* (Judd Apatow, 2007). *Extraterrestrial* has some elements of the screwball comedy in its absurd situation: Julio makes a drawing of the spaceship, to learn more about the situation, but more as an excuse to remain with Julia, and he makes up the story of the possibility of Angel being an alien in order to stop Carlos from finding out that he (Julio) and Julia had sex. It has some aspects of sex comedy in the affair: after Julio and Julia again begin having sex on the couch, when Carlos comes in she makes up an excuse that she was 'keeping watch' in case something happened with the spaceship. And it shares something with the homme-com, as the story is told from Julio's perspective, and it is the men whose strange behaviour drives most of the story. But it is decidedly un-American in its finale. While Julio does meet Julia and wins her, briefly, then she goes back to Carlos, then to Julio again, Julio must give her up in order to set things right. This is a more European perspective perhaps; in a Hollywood film, even if Julio's lies about being an alien were still believed, Julia would come running to him. But Julio knows his place in this romantic story, and in it, he does not get the girl. As in *Timecrimes*, the ending is feasible, if pessimistic.

Carlos becomes so convinced by Julio's various deceptions about the spaceship and possible alien invasion that he easily believes that Julio is an alien and that his parade float (a giant coffee cup) is some sort of alien shuttle. As in *Timecrimes*, rather than use science fiction semantics to examine implications of the macrocosmic on human life, Vigalondo uses the syntax of the microcosmic, focusing instead on an individual and the absurdity of this particular science fiction scenario. Indeed, it is arguable that not only the spectator, but Julio himself, is unable to untangle his web of deception. Hence, he finally resorts to explaining it all by presenting himself as an alien, in order to fix his mistake of staying at Julia's, and to get Carlos to return to her. In *Timecrimes*, the protagonist is doomed to repeat his deadly mistake; in *Extraterrestrial*, Julio must, and does, fix his mistake. He doesn't do it by telling the truth, of course, but by continuing the deception in order to save Julia. The final shot of the spaceship in the distance suggests that this may not quite be the end of Julio's adventures with science fiction.

Science fiction and puzzle narratives generally centre on information; the characters, and by extension the spectator, learn important information to solve the puzzle. In the case of *Extraterrestrial*, this should, by its science fiction semantics, lead to information about the spaceship and possible aliens; no information is ever really given or uncovered, however. Instead of going into the street to find any authority figure or other people that could help, Julio and Julia set up a camera and watch the image of the spaceship on the television. Carlos claims to have information, but it is never substantiated. Even when a TV station is found to be operating, the host never actually gives any information, or the information is never heard by either the characters or the spectator; instead, most of the broadcast shown and heard is an argument between the host and his producers. When the journalist begins to give information that might be useful, the camera turns back to the characters, keeping Julio and Julia, and by extension their romantic tension, in the foreground, while Carlos, concerned about the spaceship, is kept in the background, and even he does not bother listening to the broadcast. It is in many ways an update on and variation of Buñuel's *The Exterminating Angel* (*El angel exterminador*, 1962), in which characters seemingly accept their fate of entrapment, rather than attempt escape. As stated, the last shot of the film, with Julio and the journalist sitting on a roof looking towards Madrid and the hovering spaceship, suggests that there might be a second part to the film, the missing puzzle piece of the science fiction semantic. But that semantic has been a ruse. As in *Timecrimes*, the science fiction semantics serve the intimate story and the individual reaction to extreme situations, rather than global concerns, expressed as romantic comedy.

While in *Timecrimes*, the time travel technology was only a means to propel the story, in *Extraterrestrial*, technology plays a more significant part. This is likely due its relevance to youth culture in contemporary society (not just in Spain, but in most western countries). When Julio and Julia first notice something is wrong, it's because they can't get a signal on their phones or computer.

Fig. 9.2 The images of the spaceship, *Extraterrestrial* (Icon Home Entertainment, 2014)

When the spaceship is first shown on screen, it is on the television as opposed to an independent shot. Indeed, the characters look at the spaceship more frequently on the television than through the window, as if, in their more televisual lives, it isn't real unless it's on a screen [See Figure 9.2]. When Julio wants to watch Julia sleep, he turns the camera to her so he can watch her on the television. As noted in the previous paragraph, however, even when they have the opportunity to learn information from technology, they ignore it. Once Julio and Julia are isolated, technologically and from the community, they enter this semi-apocalyptic state. How they pass the time is not shown (except they do not make much of an effort to keep the apartment clean). Their peace is disturbed, not by alien invasion or any change in the spaceship, but by Angel, who uses a tennis ball machine to try and get Carlos' attention (this is probably the first time this type of machine has been used in a science fiction film, again marking technology as significant in its absurd usage).

The film becomes the black comedy of Spanish neo-esperpento. It revolves around Julio, as its hero, and the lies he creates to help Julia deceive her Carlos. The situation in which Julio finds himself, as in an esperpento work, passes through irony, cynicism, opportunity, mockery and satire. The film's story uses all of these, as Julio must keep creating lies, exaggerations and distortions of the truth to maintain a relationship with Julia. As esperpento draws attention to itself through its self-conscious distortion of reality into the absurd, the character's lack of attention to the hovering spaceship emphasizes the absurdity of the situation and Julio's lies. The film follows in a tradition of the esperpento in which reality is never directly confronted, and roles are reversed or inverted, especially that of the hero. Julio might be considered similar to Norman in *The Birthday*, the Spanish hero who is 'desgraciado, a social failure, a nobody'. Julio might not be exactly a nobody, but he is this typical Spanish kind of hero: the low mimetic hero. He studies industrial design, which seems of little interest to Julia; he lives with friends of his parents; and his initial encounter with Julia would seem to be out of character enough for him to want to stay.

If this were a Hollywood film, the narrative would likely focus on the space-ship, and Carlos, rather than Julio, would be the hero. Carlos is the kind of hero one would expect in a Hollywood sci-fi film: he is both kind and brave, he crosses the city to find his girlfriend, he seeks answers to the alien invasion, and eventually leaves the apartment to fight for his city and his love. Julio, who would normally be the sidekick, in a Spanish film finds himself the hero. As the esperpentic hero, he distracts from the dramatic reality of possible alien invasion. But that is the essence of its neo-esperpentic absurdity: as the 'reality' of the spaceship and possible alien invasion would normally be the centre of the narrative, it is pushed aside in favour of the absurdity of human relationships, built on a comedic pyramid of lies. The semantics of a high-concept, science fiction film are overlaid by the syntax of Spanish esperpentic absurdity.

While some science fiction films have romantic and/or comedic elements, it is usually the science fiction that is the main component of the story. By adding in an element such as a spaceship, and wrapping a romantic comedy around it, Vigalondo is again pushing genre boundaries. This again shows the postnational Spanish fantastic film, finding elements that can be understood by a spectator from anywhere in the world, and placing them within an unusual context to make a film unique.

Vigalondo's most recent feature film *Open Windows* not only continued on his exploration of difference science fiction semantics, but also heightened his interest in the significance of technology. In *Open Windows*, Nick Chambers, who runs a website dedicated to popular actress Jill Goddard, has won a contest to have dinner with her. He receives a phone call from a man calling himself Cord, who claims to represent the film company, saying that Jill has cancelled. Cord then offers to let Nick spy on Jill via her mobile phone, which he can operate remotely, and to send the audiovisual information to Nick on his computer. Cord then kidnaps Jill and forces Nick to try and save her.

In a unique semantic twist, *Open Windows* is told entirely via a computer screen (for which the projection screen is a substitute). Through multiple 'windows' of various software programmes that show data, images, and video feeds from Skype and other similar software programs, the audience is invited to question how they interpret what they see on their computer screen, all the while experiencing the film as a thriller through its story of a kidnapping. All of Vigalondo's feature films have a common theme: the acquisition and dispensation of information. If *Timecrimes* is about information in the wrong order, and *Extraterrestrial* is about not enough information, then *Open Windows* is about too much information. The narrative of *Open Windows* is more dependent on technology and its affect than Vigalondo's previous films, but remains a puzzle film as well, told through a single character, Nick, who must interpret the clues given to solve the puzzle. Not only is the spectator experiencing the film through the usual mediation of the cinema screen, but also mediated through the superimposition of the computer screen on that cinema screen. At times, with multiple 'windows' open on the screen, the clues are all available for the spectator to put together, as it is these clues that are, in effect, the action of the story, as much as if not more so than the standard action of home invasion and car chases. *Open Windows* is both an homage to thriller directors such as Alfred Hitchcock and Brian De Palma as well as, if not a criticism, then a rethinking, of how the thriller is conceived and represented in a culture where technology makes privacy almost obsolete.

With his numerous short films, *Timecrimes*, *Extraterrestre* and *Open Windows*, Vigalondo can be singled out as one of the most original directors of his generation, not only in his choice of genre, but in how he presents traditional genre semantics in an atypical syntax. His films are at once beholden to the Spanish culture in which he is embedded, while at the same time finding a new syntax of representation that reaches beyond national borders, taking the less typical route of science fiction to a postnational form.

Conclusion

The End of an Era?

The general economic crisis that has gripped Spain for several years has affected all aspects of society and culture, including film. All things considered, the past few years have been good for Spanish films in Spanish cinemas. In 2012, three of the top 10 films in the national box office were Spanish: *The Impossible*, *Tad, The Lost Explorer* (*Las aventuras de Tadeo Jones*, Enrique Gato), and *I Want You* (*Tengo ganas de ti*, Fernando González Molina). Far more were in the top 100 than in previous years, including several fantastic films, such as *Red Lights* (Rodrigo Cortés), *The Body* (*El Cuerpo*, Oriol Paulo) and *[REC]3: Genesis*. However, 2013 was almost the complete opposite, with severe problems in production, distribution, and success, though two horror films, *Mama* (Andrés Mischietti, 2013) and *Witching and Bitching* (*Las brujas de Zugarramurdi*, Álex de la Iglesia, 2013) did well, earning €8 million and €4.8 million respectively. 2014 saw another three films in the top 10 of the box office: *A Spanish Affair* (*Ocho appellidos vascos*, Emilio Martínez Lázaro, 2014), *El niño* (Daniel Monzon, 2014) and *Torrente 5: Operation Eurovegas* (*Torrente 5: Operación Eurovegas*, Santiago Segura, 2014), and *A Spanish Affair 2* (Emilio Martínez Lázaro, 2015) topped the yearly national box office in 2015.

A comparison of statistics between April 2012 and April 2013 showed 45.2 per cent fewer spectators, and a 50 per cent reduction in box office takings. To this was added the worst weekend in Spanish film box office history, 15–16 June 2013, with a revenue of just €2.2 million.[1] This has been at least partially attributed to the increase of the tax on tickets to 21 per cent, one of the highest in Europe. The situation improved a little in 2014, with a 14 per cent increase in cinema admissions and 3 per cent growth in ticket sales. However, the victories seem to be outweighed by the defeats. The increase in cinema admissions is largely due to special promotions by exhibitors with heavily discounted ticket prices, which cannot be sustained in the long-term. There has been a 50 per cent cut in public production funding compared to four years ago, and public broadcaster TVE has collapsed, leaving a shortfall in the traditional funding from television. In addition, Spain has one of the highest rates of film piracy in the world, and even new laws are ineffectual in combating what much of the public sees now as their 'right' to watch films for free.

In an interview, then-president of the Spanish Producer's Association Pedro Pérez said that youth are not going to the cinema as much as in previous years due to high unemployment levels and the rise in ticket prices. According to him, the right-wing government has apparently already changed funding policies from state subsidies to fiscal incentives, which will make it more difficult for feature films (which require more money) to receive state funding unless they can acquire some private investment.[2] Pérez sees the problem of Spanish audiences' disinterest to their national cinema continuing; he attributes this to hostility from the right-wing press in reaction to the subsidising of television broadcasters; much of the press' negative view of the left-wing sensibilities of filmmakers; and a misconception among spectators that most Spanish films are about the Civil War.[3] In a separate interview, Pérez noted that Spanish films make more money abroad than in their own country: in 2012, Spanish films made €150.5 million in theatres outside of Spain, versus €110 million inside.[4] Alta Films, one of the country's major producers and distributors, as well as owner of the Cines Renoir theatre chain, recently closed due to lack of funds, taking with it all but 20 of its 200 screens; the majority of the remainder are in Madrid and Barcelona. In addition, the number of films produced in 2014 decreased by 18 per cent, and it seems that films can only be made if they are high concept/high budget, or low budget. Despite a few exceptions such as *Marshland* (*La isla minima*, Alberto Rodríguez, 2014), a crime thriller set in the early 1980s which earned several Goya awards and took €7.1 million at the Spanish box office, the mid-budget film could all but disappear.

In a masterclass at a film festival in Spain in 2015, Nacho Vigalondo noted that, despite their closeness in age, the generation that includes director Carlos Vermut (*Diamond Flash*, 2011; *Magical Girl*, 2014) have been hit harder than he has by the financial crisis: 'A few years back there was a low-cost festival in Spain that showcased some brilliant titles, such as… *Diamond Flash*, but many were shot in the houses of the directors' parents. That's a paradigm shift'.[5] Unless a filmmaker is making either a middle-of-the-road comedy or drama, or an English-language film with big stars, chances are the budget will be far less than even €1 million, and perhaps not even above five digits.

The Spanish film industry, then, faces cuts in government funding, rising ticket prices, banks unwilling or unable to give out loans, lack of former support from television stations, and a continuing disinterested public. Perhaps the most notable emerging trend is for Spanish filmmakers to make films in English, frequently with American or British stars. While this has happened within Spanish film in the past, it is more common in fantastic film. Many of the filmmakers working in fantastic film began with either a feature or short in Spanish, then – with recognition of their success – moved on to write and/or direct films in English. Such is the case with filmmakers such as Juan Antonio Bayona and his films *The Impossible* and *A Monster Calls*, Rodrigo Cortés and his films *Buried* (2010) and *Red Lights*, and Juan Carlos Medina with *Painless* (*Insensibles*, 2012) and *The Limehouse Golem* (2016). Another case is *Open Windows*, which is in English and features English-language actors. According to Enrique López Lavigne (one of the film's producers), this was in part to secure financing, as state subsidies can no longer be relied on, but also to increase opportunities in the international market, which is now the only viable market for much of Spanish film.[6] This is not to suggest that fantastic films are not being made in Spanish. The popularity of the genre and its variations continues, with films such as *Game of Werewolves* (*Lobos de Arga*, Juan Martínez Moreno, 2011), *Ghost Graduation* (*Promoción fantasma*, Javier Ruiz Caldera, 2012) and *The Last Days* (*Los últimos días*, David Pastor and Àlex Pastor, 2013). Some of these films have had success in their native country; others are more popular abroad. It seems likely, however, that there will be a continued increase in English-language productions. Already, 2015 has seen the release of Amenábar's sixth feature film *Regression*, and *A Monster Calls* is set for release in 2016: both are English-language films with Hollywood stars (Ethan Hawke and Emma Watson in the former; Sigourney Weaver and Liam Neeson in the latter). Certainly, neither film could have been made without the directors' previous popular success, and the support of financing from the US.

So has the Spanish fantastic film era reached its end, or is the end nigh? Probably not; more filmmakers, including a much-needed increase in female directors such as Denise Castro and Alice Waddington, are turning to the fantastic genres to tell their stories. The only deterrent will be lack of funding, but that is a global problem for independent cinema. It could be argued that Spanish fantastic films have anticipated the changes in the national film industry. They are made in both Spanish and English; they often star actors from English-language countries; they use the fantastic genres to reach an international audience; an increasing number of the films are international co-productions; and most take advantage of the film festival circuit as a means of exposure and distribution. It could be that some directors will work on hired projects in Hollywood or the UK in order to work on their own films later, in their own country and language. Some, such as *Open Windows* and *Grand Piano* (Eugenio Mira, 2013), are English-language films, filmed almost entirely in Spain with a Spanish crew, thus generating business in their own nation as well as taking advantage of longstanding relationships between creative teams and crews that have developed locally and nationally.

An analysis of the films studied in this book suggests that a movement from genre to post-genre cinema is simultaneous with a movement from national to postnational cinema. While films still might be regarded within a national cinema, particularly if the majority or all of the talent, production and financing comes from a single country, the increasing use not only of international talent, production and money in a single film, but also the growing intertextuality of cinema, necessitates a postnational, postgenre theoretical approach. This is especially true of fantastic cinema: its elements are increasingly interchangeable, and influences so varied, that even if talent, production, and financing come from within a single nation, international and multiple generic influences must be taken into account. While the new wave of Spanish fantastic film is just one example of this movement, it is arguably the best example, and most clearly articulated because of its unusual history and the rapidity of its growth and popularity. As much of this cinema is produced (at least in part) with money from outside of Spain, stars actors from other nations, and is sometimes in English, it is in many ways leading the shift from national to postnational cinema.

As stated, the majority of the films examined in this book were produced after 2000. This alone shows not only the increase in production, but also the variety of presentation of Spanish fantastic film. The early films – *Mutant Action*, *The Day of the Beast* and *Open Your Eyes* – recycled the esperpento mode, used contemporary Spain and Spanish settings and culture as templates, and found a more postmodernist approach to genre filmmaking. This led to the generic hybridity and heterogeneous approach seen in the later films. The use of the fantastic allows for generic homage; hybridization of American thriller and European art cinema; touches of surrealism and the uncanny; and a return to the essence of horror through an examination of primal fear. In some cases, it leads to a reinterpretation of what can be presented through the fantastic, such as historical events, or adapting presentation through found footage or the puzzle mode, investigating Spanish institutions or cultural iconography.

In the past two decades, contemporary Spanish fantastic film has broken away from the confines of the dominant social realist cinema of its nation to become a driving force, not only as a unique part of the national cinema canon, but as a postnational genre cinema. Some of the films examined in the book have recognizable elements found in previous Spanish art, literature and film; some look almost exclusively to previous cinematic forms and representations from outside of Spain. Some are speaking directly about, or allegorizing, Spanish culture and politics; others have no such aims. There is no single voice in this film movement, but rather a multitude representing different backgrounds, influences (both from home and abroad), and intentions. The films vary from horror to science fiction to fantasy to thriller, and frequently combine these genres. And while the semantics of fantastic films are relatively stable, each film has a different syntax, a different cohesion of fantastic film elements. While many countries have a long history of fantastic film, Spain's lack of it makes this new wave unique and interesting, both in volume and variety. It could be called a perfect storm of knowledge and opportunity. The filmmakers of the new generation have had unprecedented exposure to film, fantastic and otherwise, from around the world, as well as other forms of cultural expression. They then had the opportunity to make their films due to changes in financial assistance and a larger variety of viewing opportunities for a global audience.

As noted, the filmmakers who began their work in the past twenty years are continuing in the fantastic genres, both in Spanish and English, both for national and international audiences. It is perhaps due to increasing access to cinema, via film festivals, the Internet, and VOD, that a movement such as contemporary Spanish fantastic film can be seen and investigated while it is still ongoing. These filmmakers are neither wedded to their Spanish historical past or culture, nor are they completely free of it. As Carlos Heredero notes that the 'most stimulating results [of the new generation of Spanish filmmakers] have been produced… when the new directors have assimilated the forms codified by U.S. cinema in order to utilize them in the service of their own personal discourses'.[7] While I would disagree that it is only US cinema that has codified fantastic film, it is true that these filmmakers have taken and are taking the semantic codes of fantastic film and refashioning them with a new syntax.

From 1992 to the present day, this period of contemporary Spanish fantastic film has been both prolific and varied, in content, form, execution and success. What filmmakers such as Amenábar, Balagueró and de la Iglesia began in the early 1990s has continued with filmmakers such as Bayona, Serra and Vigalondo in the 2000s. While not to be separated from their national roots, their films embrace a postnational cinematic trend which looks to an international film culture, finding influences from around the world, reworking and adapting them. The films are part of a growing trend of postnational cinema, which attempts to access an international audience through the transcultural reach of fantastic film.

Notes

Introduction

1 Barry Keith Grant, 'Genre films and cultural myth', *Film International* 1/1 (2003), p. 28.

2 Rosemary Jackson, *Fantasy: The Literature of Subversion* (London, 1981), p. 7.

3 Vicente Rodríguez Ortega, 'Trailing the Spanish auteur: Almodóvar's, Amenábar's, and de la Iglesia's generic routes in the US market', in J. Beck and V. Rodríguez Ortega (eds), *Contemporary Spanish Cinema and Genre* (Manchester, 2008), p. 53.

4 Antonio Lázaro-Reboll and Andrew Willis, 'Introduction: Film Studies, Spanish cinema, and the question of the popular', in A. Lázaro-Reboll and A. Willis (eds), *Spanish Popular Cinema* (Manchester: Manchester University Press, 2004), p. 1.

5 Equipo Cartelera Turia (eds), *Cine español: cine de subgeneros* (Valencia, 1974).

6 Rúben Gubern, *Historia del cine español* (Madrid, 1995).

7 Núria Triana Toribio, *Spanish National Cinema* (London, 2003), p. 152.

8 Jay Beck and Vicente Rodríguez Ortega (eds), *Contemporary Spanish Cinema and Genre* (Manchester, 2008). Essays such as 'The Fantastic Factory' (Andrew Willis), ' "Now Playing Everywhere": Spanish horror film in the marketplace' (Antonio Lázaro-Reboll), and 'Horror of allegory: *The Others* and its contexts' (Ernesto R. Acevedo-Muñoz) highlight Spanish fantastic film.

9 Jay Beck and Vicente Rodríguez Ortega, 'Introduction', *Contemporary Spanish Cinema and Genre* (Manchester, 2008), p. 1.

10 Andrew Willis, 'The Spanish horror film as subversive text: Eloy de la Iglesia's *La semana del asesino*', in S. J. Schneider and T. Williams (eds), *Horror International* (Detroit: Wayne State University Press, 2005), p. 163.

11 Ann Davies, 'Introduction: The Study of Contemporary Spanish Cinema', in A. Davies (ed.), *Spain on Screen* (Manchester: Manchester University Press, 2011), p. 1.

12 Lázaro-Reboll and Willis, 'Introduction', p. 3.

13 Lázaro-Reboll and Willis, 'Introduction', p. 5.

14 Lázaro-Reboll and Willis, 'Introduction', p. 6

15 Ángel Sala, *Profanando el sueño de los muertos: la historia jamás contada del cine fantástico español* (Monteverde, 2010), p. 10.

16 Triana Toribio, *Spanish National Cinema*, p. 14.

17 Sala, *Profanando el sueño de los muertos*, p. 16.

18 Bernard P.E. Bentley, *A Companion to Spanish Cinema* (Woodbridge, 2008), p. 63.

19 Sala, *Profanando el sueño*, p. 25.

20 Sala, *Profanando el sueño*, p. 31.

21 Antonio Lázaro-Reboll, *Spanish Horror Film* (Edinburgh: Edinburgh University Press, 2012), p. 19.

22 Jaume Balagueró, interview with Shelagh Rowan-Legg, 12 October 2012; Eugenio Mira, interview with Shelagh Rowan-Legg, 7 April 2011.

23 Lázaro-Reboll, 'Screening "Chico": the horror ventures of Narciso Ibáñez Serrador', in A. Lázaro-Reboll and A. Willis (eds), *Spanish Popular Cinema* (Manchester, 2004), p. 155.

24 Augusto M. Torres, 'The film industry: under pressure from the state and television', in H. Graham and J. Labanyi (eds), *Spanish Cultural Studies: An Introduction* (Oxford, 1995), p. 369.

25 Triana Toribio, *Spanish National Cinema*, p. 114.

26 Barry Jordan, 'The Spanish film industry in the 1980s and 1990s', in B. Jordan and R. Morgan-Tamosunas (eds), *Contemporary Spanish Cultural Studies* (London, 1999), p. 181.

27 Peter Evans, 'Back to the future: cinema and democracy', in H. Graham and J. Labanyi (eds), *Spanish Cultural Studies: An Introduction* (Oxford, 1995), p. 326.

28 Bentley, *A Companion*, p. 226. The Civil Guard attempted to block distribution of the film due to its negative portrayal of their activities in the early to mid-twentieth century.

29 Triana Toribio, *Spanish National Cinema*, p. 112; Sally Faulkner, *A History of Spanish Film: Cinema and Society 1910–2010* (London, 2013), p. 160.

30 Faulkner, *A History*, p. 161.

31 Triana Toribio, *Spanish National Cinema*, p. 113.

32 Jordan and Rikki Morgan-Tamosunas, *Contemporary Spanish Cinema* (Manchester, 1998), p. 2.

33 Bentley, *A Companion*, p. 256.

34 Sala, *Profanando el sueño*, p. 204.

35 John Hopewell, '*El corazón del bosque*: mist, myth and history', in P. W. Evans (ed.), *Spanish Cinema: The Auteurist Tradition* (Oxford: Oxford University Press, 1999), p. 166.

36 Rodrigo Cortés, interview with Shelagh Rowan-Legg, 20 November 2011; Miguel Martí, interview with Shelagh Rowan-Legg, 18 April 2011; Paco Plaza, interview with Shelagh Rowan-Legg, 16 August 2011; Nahikari Ipiña, interview with Shelagh Rowan-Legg, 30 July 2011.

37 Jaime Pena, 'Cine español de los noventas: Hoja de reclamaciones', *Secuencias* 16 (2002), p. 48.

38 Mateo Gil, interview with Shelagh Rowan-Legg, 1 December 2011.

39 Mike Hostench, interview with Shelagh Rowan-Legg, 21 April 2011; Adrià Monés, interview with Shelagh Rowan-Legg, 21 April 2011.

40 Adrià Monés, interview with Shelagh Rowan-Legg, 21 April 2011.

41 Bentley, *A Companion*, p. 318.

42 Rafael Cabrera, interview with Shelagh Rowan-Legg, 28 April 2011.

43 Ignacio Escolar, "Cinco grandes mentiras sobre el cine español," *El Diario* 8 October 2013. Available at http://www.eldiario.es/escolar/grandes-mentiras-cine-espanol_6_183791641.html (accessed 27 February 2014).

44 Carlos Heredero and Antonio Santamarina, *Semillas de futuro: cine español, 1990–2001* (Madrid, 2002), p. 47.

45 Enrique López Lavigne, interview with Shelagh Rowan-Legg, 20 February 2013.

46 Carmen Herrero, 'Edgy art cinema: cinephilia and genre negotiations in recent Spanish rural thrillers', *Studies in European Cinema* 7/2 (2010), p. 125.

47 Kenneth Turan, *Sundance to Sarajevo: Film Festivals and the World They Made* (Berkeley, 2002), p. 2.

48 Ibid., 7.

49 Dirk Van Extergem, 'The Brussels International Festival of Fantastic Film', in E. Mathijs and X. Mendek (eds), *Alternative Europe: Eurotrash and Exploitation Cinema since 1945* (London: Wallflower, 2004), p. 217.

50 Mike Hostench, interview with Shelagh Rowan-Legg, 14 January 2015.

51 Gaz Bailey, interview with Shelagh Rowan-Legg, 27 March 2015.

52 Ibid.

53 Stephen Neale, 'Questions of genre', in B.K. Grant (ed.), *Film Genre Reader III* (Austin, 2003), p. 161.

54 Thomas Sobchack, 'Genre films: a classical experience', in B.K. Grant (ed.), *Film Genre Reader II* (Austin, 1995), p. 42.

55 Rick Altman, 'Cinema and genre', in G. Nowell-Smith (ed.), *The Oxford History of World Cinema* (Oxford, 1996), p. 279.

56 Andrew Tudor, 'Genre', in B.K. Grant (ed.), *Film Genre Reader III* (Austin, 2003), p. 7.

57 Raphaëlle Moine, *Cinema Genre*, A. Fox and H. Radner (trans.) (Oxford, 2008), p. 75.

58 Bruce Kawin, 'Children of the light', in B.K. Grant (ed.), *Film Genre Reader II* (Austin, 1995), p. 317.

59 Ibid., p. 319.

60 Tzvetan Todorov, *The Fantastic: A Structural Approach to a Literary Genre*, R. Howard (trans.) (Ithaca, 1975), p. 33.

61 Ibid., p. 44.

62 Jackson, *Fantasy*, p. 3.

63 Ibid., p. 35.

64 Ibid., p. 26.

65 Rick Altman, *Film/Genre* (London, 1999), p. 24.

66 Barry Langford, *Film Genre: Hollywood and Beyond* (Edinburgh, 2005), p. 5.

67 Ibid., p. 18.

68 Altman, *Film/Genre*, p. 219.

69 Ibid., p. 221

70 Willis, 'From the margins to the mainstream: trends in recent Spanish horror film', in A. Lázaro-Reboll and A. Willis (eds), *Spanish Popular Cinema* (Manchester, 2004), p. 240.

71 Jo Labanyi, 'Engaging with ghosts; or, theorizing culture in modern Spain', in J. Labanyi (ed.), *Constructing Identity in Contemporary Spain: Theoretical Debates and Cultural Practices* (Oxford, 2002), p. 9.

72 Ulf Hannerz, 'Where we are and who we want to be', in U. Hedetoft and M. Hjort (eds), *The Postnational Self: Belonging and Identity* (Minneapolis, 2002), p. 227

73 Pietari Kääpä, 'Imaginaries of a global Finland', *Scandinavian-Canadian Studies* 19 (2010), p. 275.

74 Thomas Elsaesser, *European Cinema: Face to Face with Hollywood* (Amsterdam, 2005), p. 13.

75 Tim Bergfelder, 'The nation vanishes: European co-productions and popular genre formula in the 1950s and 1960s', in M. Hjort and S. MacKenzie (eds), *Cinema and Nation* (London, 2000), p. 139.

Chapter 1: Álex de la Iglesia

1 Peter Buse, Triana Toribio and Willis, *The Cinema of Álex de la Iglesia* (Manchester, 2007), p. 9.

2 Marcos Ordóñez, *La bestia anda suelta ¡Álex de la Iglesia lo cuenta todo!* (Madrid, 1997), p. 73. My translation.

3 Norbert Wolf, *Diego Velázquez 1599–1660: The Face of Spain* (London, 1999), p. 53; Juan José Junquera, *The Black Paintings of Goya* (London, 2003), p. 55.

4 Stephen Miller, 'The naturalist novel', in D.T. Geis (ed.), *Cambridge History of Spanish Literature* (Cambridge, 2004), p. 424.

5 Philip Thomson, *The Grotesque* (London, 1972), p. 11.

6 Ibid., p. 11.

7 Nil Santiáñez, 'Great masters of Spanish modernism', in D.T. Geis (ed.), *Cambridge History of Spanish Literature* (Cambridge, 2004), p. 479.

8 Rodolfo Cardona and Anthony N. Zahareas, *Visión del esperpento. Teoría y práctica en los esperpentos de Valle-Inclán* (Madrid, 1970), p. 11. My translation.

9 Anthony N. Zahareas, 'The absurd, the grotesque and the esperpento', in A.N. Zahareas, R. Cardona and S.M. Greenfield (eds), *Ramón del Valle-Inclán: An Appraisal of His Life and Works* (New York, 1968), p. 82.

10 Linda Hutcheon, *A Poetics of Postmodernism* (London, 1998), p. 35.

11 Sala, *Profanando el sueño*, p. 13.

12 Jordi Sánchez Navarro, *Freaks en acción: Álex de la Iglesia o el cine como fuga* (Madrid, 2005), p. 11. Sánchez Navarro's translation.

13 De la Iglesia cited in Ordóñez, *La bestia anda suelta*, p. 107. My translation.

14 Peter L. Podol, 'The grotesque in contemporary Spanish theatre and film', *Modern Language Studies* 15/4 (1985), p. 196.

15 Cristina Moreiras Menor, 'Spectacle, trauma and violence in contemporary Spain', in B. Jordan and R. Morgan-Tamosunas (eds), *Contemporary Spanish Cultural Studies* (London, 1999), p. 135.

16 Ibid., p. 136.

17 Grant, 'Genre films', p. 28.

18 Douglas Pye, 'Movies and tone', in J. Gibbs and D. Pye (eds), *Close-Up 2* (London, 2007), p. 8.

19 Wes D. Gehring, *Parody as Film Genre: 'Never Give a Saga an Even Break'* (Westport, 1999), p. 5.

20 Ibid., p. 6.

21 Hutcheon, *A Theory of Parody: The Teaching of Twentieth Century Art Forms* (London, 1985), p. 6.
22 John Lyon, *The Theatre of Valle-Inclán* (Cambridge, 1983), p. 105. Allegedly Valle-Inclán would later refute this; but de la Iglesia's characters have a puppet-like quality that connects them to this theory of esperpento.
23 Vivian Sobchack, 'The violent dance: a personal memoir of death in the movies', in S. Prince (ed.), *Screening Violence* (London, 2000), p. 122.
24 Santiago Fouz-Hernández and Alfredo Martinez-Expósito, *Live Flesh: The Male Body in Contemporary Spanish Cinema* (London, 2007), p. 67.
25 Rodríguez Ortega, 'Trailing the Spanish auteur', p. 53.
26 Rosanna Maule, *Beyond Auteurism: New Directions in Authorial Film Practices in Spain, France and Italy since the 1980s* (Bristol, 2008), p. 154.
27 Marsha Kinder, *Blood Cinema The Reconstruction of National Identity in Spain.* (Berkeley, 1993), p. 138.
28 Richard Fletcher, 'The early Middle Ages 700–1250', in R. Carr (ed.), *Spain: A History* (Oxford, 2000), p. 63.
29 John Edwards, *The Spanish Inquisition* (Stroud, 1999), p. 67.
30 Stanley G. Payne, *Spanish Catholicism: A Historical Overview* (Madison, 1984), p. 182.
31 Salvador Giner and Sebastián Sarasa, 'Religión y modernidad en España', in R. Diaz-Salazar and S. Giner (eds), *Religión y sociedad en España* (Madrid, 1993), p. 20.
32 David Annandale, 'Dark imperatives: Kant, Sade and Catholicism in Jess Franco's *Exorcism*', in R. Hansen (ed.), *Roman Catholicism in Fantastic Film: Essays on Belief, Spectacle, Ritual and Imagery* (Jefferson, 2011), p. 247.
33 Andrew Greeley, *The Catholic Imagination* (Berkeley, 2000), p. 147.
34 Robert M. Torrance, *The Comic Hero* (Cambridge, 1978), p. 156
35 Paul Julian Smith, 'El día de la bestia', *Sight and Sound* 6/12 (1996), p. 43.
36 Mikhail Bakhtin, *Rabelais and his World*, H. Iswolsky (trans.) (Cambridge, 1968), p. 26.
37 Dean A. Miller, *The Epic Hero* (Baltimore, 2000), p. 275.
38 Ibid., p. 243.
39 Roger R. Rollin, 'The Lone Ranger and Lenny Skutnik: the hero as popular culture', in R.B. Browne (ed.), *The Hero in Transition* (Bowling Green, 1983), p. 18.
40 P. J. Smith, *Television in Spain: from Franco to Almodóvar* (Woodbridge, 2006), p. 1.
41 Manuel Palacio, *Historia de la televisión en España* (Madrid, 2008), p. 171.
42 Umberto Eco, 'The frames of comic "freedom"', in Thomas A. Sebeok (ed.), *Carnival* (Berlin, 1984), p. 13.

Chapter 2: Heroes and Villains

1 Marcel Durán, 'Love at first sight: Spanish surrealism reconsidered', *MLN* 84/2 (1969), p. 330.
2 Robert Lima, *The Dramatic World of Valle-Inclán* (Woodbridge, 2003), p. 137.
3 Torrance, *The Comic Hero*, p. 9.
4 Donald Melbye, *Landscape Allegory in Cinema: From Wilderness to Wasteland* (New York, 2010), p. 73.

5 Faulkner, 'Nostalgia and the middlebrow: Spanish ruralist cinema and Mario Camus' *Los santos inocentes/The Holy Innocents*', in C. Fowler and G. Helfield (eds), *Representing the Rural: Space, Place and Identity in Films About the Land* (Detroit, 2006), p. 37.

6 Evans, 'Cinema, memory and the unconscious', in H. Graham and J. Labanyi (eds), *Spanish Cultural Studies* (Oxford, 1995), p. 307.

7 Melbye, *Landscape Allegory in Cinema*, p. 3.

8 Richard Dyer, *Pastiche* (London, 2007), p. 131.

9 Mikel Alvariño, interview with Shelagh Rowan-Legg, 25 February 2015.

10 Ramón del Valle-Inclán, *Three Plays: Divine Words, Bohemian Lights, Silver Face*, M. Delgado (trans.) (London, 1993), p. 166.

11 'It's My Party', written by John Gluck, Wally Gold and Herb Weiner, 1963.

12 Eco, 'The frames', p. 2.

13 Thomas Lee Snyder, *Sacred Encounters: The Myth of the Hero in the Horror, Science-Fiction and Fantasy Films of George Lucas and Steven Spielberg* (PhD Diss., Northwestern University, 1984), p. 3.

14 Bakhtin, *Rabelais*, p. 10.

15 Hopewell, *Out of the Past: Spanish Cinema After Franco* (London, 1986), p. 60.

16 Northrop Frye, *Anatomy of Criticism* (Princeton, 1957), p. 34.

17 D. Miller, *The Epic Hero*, p. 277.

18 Melbye, *Landscape Allegory*, p. 8.

19 Maria Rovisco, 'Mapping the nation and the countryside in European "films of voyage"', in R. Fish (ed.), *Cinematic Countrysides* (Manchester, 2007), p. 60.

20 Sala, *Profanando el sueño*, p. 275.

21 Faulkner, *Literary Adaptations in Spanish Cinema* (London, 2004), p. 49.

22 Evans, 'Cinema, memory and the unconscious', p. 307.

23 Koldo Serra, interview with Shelagh Rowan-Legg, 11 November 2011

24 María Pilar Rodríguez, 'Dark memories, tragic lives: Representations of the Basque nation in three contemporary films', *Anuario de cine y literatura en español* 3 (1997), p. 134.

25 P. J. Smith, *The Moderns: Time, Space and Subjectivity in Contemporary Spanish Culture* (Oxford, 2000), p. 149.

26 Paddy Woodworth, *The Basque Country: A Cultural History* (Oxford, 2007), p. xiii.

27 Suzanne E. Hatty, *Masculinities, Violence and Culture* (Thousand Oaks, 1999), p. 138.

28 Melbye, *Landscape Allegory*, p. 79.

29 Written by Leonard Cohen, 1974.

Chapter 3: Alejandro Amenábar

1 Rodríguez Ortega, 'Trailing the Spanish auteur', p. 52.

2 Jordan, *Alejandro Amenábar* (Manchester, 2012), p. 23.

3 Elliot Panek, 'The poet and the detective: defining the psychological puzzle film', *Film Criticism* 31/1&2 (2006), p. 65.

4 Ruth Perlmutter, 'Memories, Dreams, Screens', *Quarterly Review of Film and Video* 22.2 (2005), p. 125.

5 Carmen Rabalska, 'A dark desire for the grotesque', in R. Rix and R. Rodríguez-Saona (eds), *Spanish Cinema: Calling the Shots* (Leeds: University of Leeds, 1999), p. 93.

6 Jean-François Lyotard, *The Postmodern Condition: A Report on Knowledge*, G. Bennington and B. Massumi (trans.) (Manchester, 1984), p. 81.

7 Philip Shaw, *The Sublime* (London, 2006), p. 3.

8 Vijay Mishra, *The Gothic Sublime* (Albany, 1994), p. 229.

9 Antonio Sempere, *Alejandro Amenábar: cine en las venas* (Madrid, 2000), p. 85. My translation.

10 P. J. Smith, 'High anxiety: *Abre los ojos/Vanilla Sky*', *Journal of Romance Studies* 4/1 (2004), p. 95.

11 Chris Perriam, 'Alejandro Amenábar's *Abre los ojos/Open Your Eyes* (2007)', in A. Lázaro-Reboll and A. Willis (eds), *Spanish Popular Cinema* (Manchester: Manchester University Press, 2004), p. 212.

12 Diane M. Almeida, *The Esperpento Tradition in the Works of Rámon del Valle Inclán and Luis Buñuel* (Lewiston, 2000), p. 3.

13 Thomas Elsaesser, 'The mind-game film', in W. Buckland (ed.), *Puzzle Films: Complex Storytelling in Contemporary Cinema* (Walden, 2009), p. 17.

14 Perriam, *Stars and Masculinities in Spanish Cinema: From Banderas to Bardem* (Oxford, 2003), p. 175.

15 Bela Balázs, *Theory of the Film: Character and Growth of a New Art*, E. Bone (trans.) (New York, 1970), p. 63.

16 Bahktin, *Art and Answerability: Early Philosophical Essays*, M. Holquist and V. Liapunov (eds), V. Liapunov (trans.) (Austin, 1990), p. 27.

17 Henri Bergson, *Matter and Memory*, N.M. Paul and W.S. Palmer (trans.) (New York, 1988), p. 25.

18 Jean-Louis Baudry, 'Ideological effects of the basic cinematic apparatus'; 'The apparatus: metapsychological approaches to the Impression of Reality in Cinema', in P. Rosen (ed.), *Narrative, Apparatus, Ideology* (New York, 1986), p. 287; p. 305.

19 N. Katherine Hayles, *How We Became Posthuman: Virtual Bodies in Cybernetics, Literature and Informatics* (Chicago, 1999), p. 2.

20 Ibid., p. 247.

21 Ernesto R. Acevedo-Muñoz, 'Horror of allegory: *The Others* and its contexts', in J. Beck and V. Rodríguez Ortega (eds), *Contemporary Spanish Cinema and Genre* (Manchester, 2008), p. 202.

22 Fred Botting, 'In gothic darkly: heterotopia, history, culture', in D. Punter (ed.), *A Companion to the Gothic* (Oxford, 2000), p. 3.

23 Andrew Smith, 'Hauntings', in C. Spooner and E. McEvoy (eds), *The Routledge Companion to the Gothic* (New York, 2007), p. 148.

24 Sala, *Profanando el sueño, p.* 46.

25 Rodríguez Ortega, 'Trailing the Spanish auteur', p. 51.

26 Christine Gledhill, 'The melodramatic field: an investigation', in C. Gledhill (ed.), *Home is Where the Heart is: Studies in Melodrama and the Woman's Film* (London, 1987), p. 33.

27 Rodríguez Ortega, 'Trailing the Spanish auteur', p. 51.

28 Aviva Briefel, 'What some ghosts don't know: spectral recognizance and the horror film', *Narrative* 17/1 (January 2009), p. 97.

29 Mishra, *The Gothic Sublime*, p. 33.

30 This was also the opening phrase of the BBC radio programme 'Listen with Mother', which broadcast between 1950 and 1982. It is not known if Amenábar knew of it. https://en.wikipedia.org/wiki/Listen_with_Mother#.22Are_you_sitting_comfortably.3F.22 (Accesses 20 February 2016).

31 Lyotard, 'The sublime and the avant-garde', in A. Benjamin (ed. and trans.) *The Lyotard Reader* (Oxford: Basil Blackwell, 1989), p. 203.

32 Dani Cavallaro, *The Gothic Vision: Three Centuries of Horror, Terror and Fear* (London, 2002), p. 131.

33 Stella Bruzzi, *Bringing Up Daddy: Fatherhood and Masculinity in Post-War Hollywood* (London, 2005), p. 44.

34 Maria Purves, *The Gothic and Catholicism: Religion, Cultural Exchange and the Popular Novel, 1795–1829* (Cardiff, 2009), p. 3.

35 Cavallaro, *The Gothic Vision*, p. 63.

36 Ismael Ibáñez Rosales, 'Otherness in *The Others*: haunting the Catholic other, humanizing the self', in R. Hansen (ed.), *Roman Catholicism in Fantastic Film* (Jefferson, 2011), p. 276.

Chapter 4: The Haunting of Houses

1 Gaston Bachelard, *The Poetics of Space*, M. Jolas (trans.) (Boston, 1994), p. 4.

2 Piera Scuri, *Design of Enclosed Spaces* (New York, 1995), p. 80.

3 Barry Curtis, *Dark Places: The Haunted House in Film* (London, 2008), p. 28.

4 Sigmund Freud, *The Uncanny*, D. McLintock (trans.) (London, 2003), p. 123.

5 Todorov, *The Fantastic*, p. 44.

6 Tom Gunning, 'Uncanny reflections, modern illusions: sighting the modern optical uncanny', in J. Collins and J. Jervis (eds), *Uncanny Modernity* (New York, 2008), p. 69.

7 Anthony Vidler, *The Architectural Uncanny: Essays in the Modern Unhomely* (Cambridge, 1992), p. 4.

8 http://www.imdb.com/search/keyword?keywords=haunted-house (accessed 20 February 2016).

9 Sala, *Profanando el sueño*, p. 274.

10 Willis, 'The Fantastic Factory: the horror genre and contemporary Spanish cinema', in J. Beck and V. Rodríguez Ortega (eds), *Contemporary Spanish Cinema and Genre* (Manchester, 2008), p. 41.

11 Jackson, *Fantasy*, p. 8.

12 Todorov, *The Fantastic*, p. 47.

13 Duncan Wheeler, 'The representation of domestic violence in Spanish cinema', *Modern Language Review* 107.2 (2012), p. 440.

14 Gilles Deleuze, *Cinema 2: The Time-Image*, H. Tomlinson and R. Galeta (trans.) (Minneapolis, 1989), p. 38.

15 Ibid., p. 37.

16 Ibid., p. 39.
17 William Earle, *Surrealism in Film: Beyond the Realist Sensibility* (New Brunswick, 2011), p. 35.
18 Bliss Cua Lim, *Translating Time: Cinema, the Fantastic and Temporal Critique* (Durham, 2009), p. 12.
19 Curtis, *Dark Places*, p. 33.
20 Lim, *Translating Time*, p. 12.
21 Otto Rank, *The Double: A Psychoanalytical Study*, H. Tucker Jr. (trans.) (Chapel Hill, 1971), p. 50.
22 Nicholas Royle, *The Uncanny: An Introduction* (Manchester, 2002), p. 75.
23 Marianne Hirsch, *Family Frames: Photography Narrative and Postmemory* (Cambridge, 1997), p. 5.
24 Avery F. Gordon, *Ghostly Matters: Haunting and the Sociological Imagination* (Minneapolis, 2008), p. xvi.
25 Charles Gant, 'Tell no one it's subtitled', *Sight and Sound* 18/4 (2008), p. 13.
26 P. J. Smith, *Spanish Practices: Literature, Cinema, Television* (Oxford, 2012), p. 62.
27 Ibid., p. 70.
28 Cavallaro, *The Gothic Vision*, p. 68.
29 Devendra P. Varma, *The Gothic Flame* (New York, 1957), p. 211.
30 Curtis, *Dark Places*, p. 7.
31 Ibid., p. 34.
32 Ibid., p. 15.
33 Bachelard, *The Poetics of Space*, p. 19.
34 P. J. Smith, *Spanish Practices*, p. 75.
35 Gledhill, 'The melodramatic field', p. 30.
36 Davies, 'The final girl and the monstrous mother of *El orfanato*', in A. Davies (ed.), *Spain on Screen: Developments in Contemporary Spanish Cinema* (London, 2011), p. 80.
37 Claire Colebrook, *Irony* (London, 2004), p. 1.

Chapter 5: Jaume Balagueró

1 Noël Carroll, *The Philosophy of Horror: or Paradoxes of the Heart* (New York, 1990), p. 127.
2 Ibid., p. 130.
3 Ibid., p. 99.
4 Willis, 'From the margins', p.246.
5 Carroll, 'The paradox of suspense', in P. Vordered, H.J. Wolff and M. Friedricksen (eds) *Suspense: Conceptualizations, Theoretical Analyses, and Empirical Explorations* (Mahwah, 1996), p. 71.
6 Richard J. Gerrig, 'The resilience of suspense', in P. Vordered, H.J. Wolff and M. Friedricksen (eds) *Suspense: Conceptualizations, Theoretical Analyses, and Empirical Explorations* (Mahwah, 1996), p. 94.

7 Lothar Mikos, 'The experience of euspense: Between Fear and Pleasure', in P. Vordered, H.J. Wolff and M. Friedricksen (eds) *Suspense: Conceptualizations, Theoretical Analyses, and Empirical Explorations* (Mahwah, 1996), p. 38.

8 Julio Ángel Olivares Merino, 'Naming the ghost within: filmic defamiliarization in Jaume Balagueró's *Nameless (Los sin nombre)*', *Film International* 17 (2005), p. 29.

9 Carroll L. Fry, *Cinema of the Occult: New Age, Satanism, Wicca and Spiritualism in Film* (Bethlehem, 2008), p. 92.

10 Michael Fleming, 'Themes of madness', in M. Fleming and R. Manville (eds), *Images of Madness: The Portrayal of Insanity in the Feature Film* (Rutherford, 1985), p. 17.

11 Jason Horsley, *The Secret Life of Movies: Schizophrenic and Shamanic Journeys in American Cinema* (Jefferson, 2009), p. 7.

12 Jacqueline Noll Zimmerman, *People like Ourselves: Portrayals of Mental Illness in the Movies* (Lanham, 2003), p. xv.

13 Patrick Fuery, *Madness and Cinema: Psychoanalysis, Spectatorship and Culture* (Basingstoke, 2004), p. 28.

14 Ibid., p. 27.

15 Vidler, *The Architectural Uncanny*, p. 17.

16 Barbara Creed, *Phallic Panic: Film, Horror, and the Primal Uncanny* (Carleton, 2005), p. 153.

17 Kate Hebblethwaite and Elizabeth McCarthy, 'Introduction', in K. Hebblethwaite and E. McCarthy (eds), *Fear: Essays on the Meaning and Experience of Fear* (Dublin, 2007), p. 9.

Chapter 6: The Spanish Fantastic Woman

1 David Greven, *Representations of Femininity in American Genre Cinema: The Woman's Film, Film Noir and Modern Horror* (Basingstoke, 2013), p. 12.

2 Ibid.

3 Ibid., p. 87.

4 Wheeler, 'The representation', p. 444.

5 Ibid., p. 479.

6 Carol J. Clover, *Men, Women, and Chainsaws: Gender in the Modern Horror Film* (London, 1992), p. 42.

7 Gerard C. Wood, 'Horror film', in ed. Wes D. Gehring (ed.), *Handbook of American Film Genres* (New York, 1988), p. 218.

8 Danny Shipka, *Perverse Titillation: The Exploitation Cinema of Italy, Spain and France, 1960–1980* (Jefferson, 2011), p. 9.

9 Hutcheon, *Poetics*, p. 26.

10 Ibid., p. 35.

11 Linda Williams, 'When a woman looks', in B.K. Grant (ed.), *The Dread of Difference: Gender and the Horror Film* (Austin, 1996), p. 22.

12 Written by Claus Norreen and Soren Nystrom Rasted, 1997.

13 Yvonne Tasker, *Spectacular Bodies: Gender, Genre and the Action Cinema* (London, 1993), p. 16.

14 Marc O'Day, 'Beauty in motion: gender, spectacle and action babe cinema', in Y. Tasker (ed.), *Action and Adventure Cinema* (London, 2004), p. 203.

15 Clover, *Men, Women*, p. 48.

16 Ibid., p. 44.

17 Peter Conrad, *Islands: A Trip Through Time and Space* (London, 2009), p. 65.

18 David Bordwell, 'The art cinema as a mode of practice', in C. Fowler (ed.), *The European Cinema Reader* (London, 2002), p. 94.

19 Ibid., p. 95.

20 Ibid., p. 95.

21 Neale, 'Art cinema as institution', *Screen* 22/1 (1981), p. 13.

22 Ibid., p. 11.

23 Ibid., p. 34.

24 Rosalind Galt and Kurt Schoonover, 'Introduction: the impurity of art cinema', in R. Galt and K. Schoonover (eds), *Global Art Cinema: New Theories and Histories* (Oxford, 2010), p. 6.

25 András Bálint Kovács, *Screening Modernism: European Art Cinema, 1950–1980* (Chicago, 2007), p. 72.

26 Ibid., p. 72.

27 Mark Betz, *Beyond the Subtitle: Remapping European Art Cinema* (Minneapolis, 2009), p. 95.

28 Conrad, *Islands*, p. 6.

29 Ian D. Copestake, 'Madness and the sea in the american literary imagination', in V.P. Messier and N. Batra (eds), *This Watery World: Humans and the Sea* (Mayaguez, 2007), p. 24.

30 Gabe Ibáñez, interview with Shelagh Rowan-Legg, 4 August 2011.

31 Maria José Gámez Fuentes, *Cinematergrafía: la madre en el cine y la literatura de la democracia* (Castellón, 2004), p. 44.

32 Ibid., p. 164.

33 Tiffany Trotman, 'Introduction', in T. Trotman (ed.), *The Changing Spanish Family: Essays on New Views in Literature, Cinema and Theatre* (Jefferson, 2011), p. 2.

34 Creed, *The Monstrous-Feminine: film, feminism, psychoanalysis* (London, 1993), p. 27.

35 Ibid., p. 28.

36 Lynn Edith Paulson, 'Mama bears, bitches and monsters: motherhood and violence in popular film', in E. Cole and J. Hernderson Daniel (eds), *Featuring Females: Feminist Analysis of Media* (Washington, 2005), p. 136.

Chapter 7: Guillermo del Toro

1 David Archibald, *The War that Won't Die: The Spanish Civil War in Cinema* (Manchester, 2012), p. 20.

2 Kimberly Chun, 'What is a ghost? an interview with Guillermo del Toro', *Cineaste* XXVIII/2 (Spring 2002), p. 29.

3 Antonio Trashorras, interview with Shelagh Rowan-Legg, 11 November 2011.

4 Michael Atkinson, 'Moral horrors in Guillermo del Toro's *Pan's Labyrinth*', *Film Comment* XLIII/1 (2007), p. 50.

5 P. J. Smith, '*Pan's Labyrinth*', *Film Quarterly* 60/4 (2007): p. 4.

6 Martin Hurcombe, 'Mi guerra, tu guerra: claiming the Spanish Civil War in literature and film', *Journal of War and Culture Studies* 1/1 (2008), p. 28.

7 Davies, *Spanish Spaces*, p. 21.

8 Marjorie A. Valleau, *The Spanish Civil War in American and European Films* (Ann Arbor, 1978), p. 148. My research has uncovered only two post-transition films that show the war from the Nationalist side (though not necessarily sympathetically): *Frozen Silence* (*Silencio en la nieve*, Gerardo Herrero, 2011) and *There Be Dragons* (Roland Joffé, 2011).

9 Neale, *Genre and Hollywood* (London, 2000), p. 125.

10 Anne Hardcastle, 'Ghosts of the past and present: hauntology and the Spanish Civil War in Guillermo del Toro's *The Devil's Backbone*', *Journal of the Fantastic in the Arts* 15/2 (2005), p. 119.

11 Jacques Derrida, *Specters of Marx: The State of the Debt, the Work of Mourning and the New International*, P. Kamuf (trans.) (New York, 1994), p. xix.

12 Labanyi, 'Engaging with ghosts', p. 6.

13 Lázaro-Reboll, *Spanish Horror Film*, p. 256.

14 Lázaro-Reboll, 'The transnational reception of *El espinazo del diablo*', *Hispanic Research Journal* 8/1 (2007), p. 46.

15 Deborah Shaw, *The Three Amigos: The Transnational Filmmaking of Guillermo del Toro, Alejandro González Iñarritu and Alfonso Cuarón* (Manchester, 2013), p. 68.

16 Ibid., p. 78.

17 Robyn McCallum, 'Very advanced texts: metafictions and experimental work', in P. Hunt (ed.) *Understanding Children's Literature: Key Essays from the International Companion Encyclopedia of Children's Literature* (London, 1999), p. 148.

18 Hirsch, *Family Frames*, p. 22.

19 Alison Landsberg, *Prosthetic Memory: The Transformation of American Remembrance in the Age of Mass Culture* (New York, 2004), p. 19.

20 Robert Burgoyne, *The Hollywood Historical Film* (Oxford, 2008), p. 4.

21 For example, *One Hundred Years of Solitude* by Gabriel García Márquez, and *The Library of Babel* by Jorge Luis Borges.

22 Alejo Carpentier, 'Baroque and the marvelous real', in L. Parkinson Zamora and W.B. Faris (eds), *Magic Realism: Theory, History, Community* (Durham, 1995), p. 102.

23 Fredric Jameson, *Signatures of the Visible* (New York, 1992), p. 138.

24 Ibid., p. 137.

25 Joan Mellen, *Magic Realism* (Farmington Hills, 2000), p. 59.

26 Antonio Santamarina, 'Un sugerente melodrama gótico', *Dirigido por* (2001), p. 23. My translation.

27 Labanyi, 'Engaging with ghosts', p. 1.

28 Derrida, *Specters of Marx*, p. 10.

29 Ismail Xavier, 'Historical allegory', in T. Miller and R. Stam (eds), *A Companion to Film Theory* (Oxford, 1999), p. 333.

30 Del Toro cited in Chun, 'What is a ghost?', p. 29.

31 Adriana J. Bergero, 'Espectros, escalofríos y discursividad herida en *El espinazo del diablo*: El gótico como cuerpo-geografía cognitiva-emocional de quiebre', *MLN* 125/2 (2010), p. 435.
32 Vicky Lebeau, *Childhood and Cinema* (London, 2008), p. 176.
33 Karen Lury, *The Child in Film: Tears, Fears and Fairy Tales* (London, 2010), p. 110.
34 Jane Hanley, 'The walls came down: fantasy and power in *El laberinto del fauno*', *Studies in Hispanic Cinema* 4/1 (2007), p. 38.
35 Roger Clark and Keith McDonald, 'A Constant Transit of Finding: Fantasy as Realization in *Pan's Labyrinth*', *Children's Literature in Education* 41/1 (2010), p. 54.
36 Landsberg, *Prosthetic Memory*, p. 2.
37 D. Shaw, *The Three Amigos*, p. 68.
38 Mercedes Maroto Camino, *Film, Memory and the Legacy of the Spanish Civil War: Resistance and Guerilla 1936–2010* (London, 2011), p. 121.
39 Hirsch, 'The generation of postmemory', *Poetics Today* 29/1 (2008), p. 107.
40 Mark Kermode, 'Girl interrupted', *Sight and Sound* XVI/12 (2006), p. 21.
41 Clark and McDonald, 'A constant transit', p. 53.
42 P.J. Smith, '*Pan's Labyrinth*', p. 5.
43 Atkinson, 'Moral Horrors', p. 52.
44 Maroto Camino, *Film, Memory*, p. 12.
45 Kermode, 'Girl interrupted', p. 22.
46 Torben Grodal, *Embodied Visions: Evolution, Emotion, Culture and Film* (Oxford, 2009), p. 6.
47 Vladimir Propp, *Morphology of the Folk Tale*, L. Scott (trans.) (Austin, 1968), p. 26.
48 Stephen Asma, *On Monsters: An Unnatural History of Our Worst Fears* (Oxford, 2009), p. 252.
49 James Clarke, 'Young hearts and minds in a time of sound and fury', in J. Slater (ed.), *Under Fire: A Century of War Movies* (Hershan, 2009), p. 199.

Chapter 8: Franchising the Spanish Fantastic

1 Paco Plaza, interview with Shelagh Rowan-Legg, 16 August 2011.
2 Strictly speaking, zombies are dead humans, reanimated, who feed off the flesh of the living. The infected humans in these films are living victims of a virus. Other films in this subgenre include *28 Days Later* (Danny Boyle, 2002) and *Resident Evil* (Paul W.S. Anderson, 2002).
3 Kyle William Bishop, *American Zombie Gothic: The Walking Dead in Popular Culture* (Jefferson, 2010), p. 20.
4 Ibid., p. 12.
5 Sarah Jane Lauro and Karen Embry, 'A zombie manifesto: the nonhuman condition in the era of advanced capitalism', *Boundary 2* 35/1 (2008), p. 90.
6 Bishop, *American Zombie Gothic*, p. 26.
7 Raymond Crawford, *Plague and Pestilence in Literature and Art* (Oxford, 1914), p. 8.
8 Jennifer Cooke, *Legacies of Plague in Literature, Theory and Film* (Basingstoke, 2009), p. 3.

9 David Corkill, 'Race, immigration and multiculturalism in Spain', in B. Jordan and R. Morgan-Tamosunas (eds), *Contemporary Spanish Cultural Studies* (London, 1999), p. 48.

10 Ibid., p. 56.

11 Peter Wuss, *Cinematic Narration and its Psychological Impact* (Newcastle, 2009), p. 38.

12 Tina Pippin, *Apocalyptic Bodies: The Biblical End of the World in Text and Image* (London, 1999), p. 88.

13 Murray Smith, 'Imagining from the inside', in R. Allen and M. Smith (eds), *Film Theory and Philosophy* (Oxford, 1997), p. 415.

14 Ibid., p. 415.

15 Guy Debord, *Society of the Spectacle*, K. Knabb (trans.) (Eastbourne, 2009), p. 26.

16 Ibid., p. 8.

17 Ibid., p. 27.

18 Moreiras Menor, 'Spectacle, trauma and violence', p. 135.

19 Ibid., p. 139.

20 Anita Biressi and Heather Nunn, *Reality TV: Realism and Revelation* (London, 2005), p. 38.

21 P. J. Smith, *Television in Spain*, p. 115.

22 Daya Kishan Thussu, *News as Entertainment: The Rise of Global Infotainment* (Los Angeles, 2007), p. 9.

23 Kevin Glynn, *Tabloid Culture: Trash Taste, Popular Power, and the Transformation of American Television* (Durham, 2000), p.7.

24 Misha Kavka, *Reality Television, Affect and Intimacy* (New York, 2008), p. 8.

25 Richard Kilborn, *Staging the Real: Factual TV Programming in the Age of Big Brother* (Manchester, 2003), p. 55.

26 Jessica Fishman, 'The populace and the police: models of social control in reality-based crime television', *Critical Studies in Mass Communication* 16/3 (1999), p. 269.

27 Kilborn, *Staging the Real*, p. 68.

28 John Fiske, 'Popularity and the politics of information', in P. Dahlgren and C. Sparks (eds), *Journalism and Popular Culture* (London, 1992), p. 48.

29 Smith, M., *Engaging Characters: Fiction, Emotion and the Cinema* (Oxford, 1995), p. 75.

30 Margrethe Bruun Vaage, 'Fiction film and the varieties of empathic engagement', in P.A. French and H.K. Weltstein (eds), *Film and the Emotions* (Oxford, 2010), p. 163.

31 Jinhee Choi, 'Leaving it up to the imagination', *The Journal of Aesthetics and Art Criticism* 63/1 (2005), p. 17.

32 Wuss, *Cinematic Narration*, p. 109.

33 Glynn, *Tabloid Culture*, p. 7.

Chapter 9: Nacho Vigalondo

1 Nacho Vigalondo, interview with Shelagh M. Rowan-Legg, 1 May 2011

2 Ibid., 17 April 2015.

3 Warren Buckland, 'Introduction: puzzle plots', in W. Buckland (ed.), *Puzzle Films: Complex Storytelling in Contemporary Cinema* (Walden, 2009), p. 2.

4 Elsaesser, 'The mind-game film', p. 14.

5 Lim, *Translating Time*, p. 11.

6 Jonathan Eig, 'A beautiful mind(fuck): Hollywood Structures of Identity', *Jumpcut: A Review of Contemporary Media* 46 (2003). Available at http://www.ejumpcut.org/archive/jc46.2003/eig.mindfilms/text.html (accessed 2 July 2012).

7 Ibid.

8 Earle, *Surrealism in Film*, p. 35.

9 Michael Richardson, *Surrealism and Cinema* (Oxford, 2006), p. 30.

10 Gilles Deleuze, *Bergsonism*, H. Tomlinson and B. Habberjam (trans.) (New York, 1988), p. 25.

11 Henri Bergson, *The Creative Mind: An Introduction to Metaphysics*, M.L. Anderson (trans.) (New York, 2002), p. 12.

12 Susan Hayward, *Cinema Studies: The Key Concepts* (London, 2000), p. 80.

13 Bakhtin, *Art and Answerability*, p. 23.

14 Deleuze, *Bergsonism*, p. 25.

15 V. Sobchack, '"Is any body home?" embodied imagination and visible evictions', in H. Naficy (ed.), *Home, Exile, Homeland: Film, Media and the Politics of Place* (New York, 1999), p. 46.

16 Deleuze, *Bergsonism*, p. 85.

17 Carroll, 'The grotesque today: preliminary notes toward a taxonomy', in F.S. Connelly (ed.), *Modern Art and the Grotesque* (Cambridge, 2003) p. 305.

18 Paul Wells, *The Horror Genre: From Beelzebub to Blair Witch* (London, 2000), p. 8.

19 V. Sobchack, *Screening Space: The American Science Fiction Film* (New Brunswick, 1987), p. 30.

Conclusion

1 Sergio Ríos Pérez, 'The Spanish box-office hits the bottom (or not)', *Cineuropa* (20 June 2013). Available at http://cineuropa.org/nw.aspx?t=newsdetail&l=en&did=240223 (accessed 5 August 2013).

2 P. J. Smith, 'Spanish cinema roundup', *Film Quarterly* 66.1 (2012). Available at http://www.filmquarterly.org/2013/04/spanish-cinema-roundup/ (accessed 5 August 2013).

3 Ibid. According to Smith, in the last decade, only 1.4 per cent of films have been about the war.

4 Alfonso Rivera, 'Pedro Pérez, President of the FAPAE', *Cineuropa* (18 June 2013). Available at http://cineuropa.org/it.aspx?t=interview&l=en&did=240191 (accessed 5 August 2013).

5 Hopewell, 'Vigalondo, Vermut rip it up in Mar del Plata', *Variety*, 27 November 2014. Available at http://variety.com/2014/film/news/vigalondo-vermut-rip-it-up-in-mar-del-plata-1201366340/ (accessed 2 July 2015).

6 López Lavigne, interview, 20 February 2013.

7 Carlos Heredero, 'New creators for the new millennium: transforming the directing scene in Spain', *Cineaste* 29/1 (2003), p. 36.

Bibliography

Acevedo-Muñoz, Ernesto R., 'Horror of allegory: *The Others* and its contexts', in J. Beck and V. Rodríguez Ortega (eds), *Contemporary Spanish Cinema and Genre* (Manchester, 2008).

Águilar, Carlos, *Cine fantástico y de terror español 1900–1983* (San Sebastián, 1999).

___ *Cine fantástico y de terror español 1984–2004* (San Sebastián, 2005).

Almeida, Diane M., *The Esperpento Tradition in the Works of Ramón del Valle-Inclán and Luis Buñuel* (Lewiston, 2000).

Altman, Rick, 'Cinema and genre', in G. Nowell-Smith (ed.), *The Oxford History of World Cinema* (Oxford, 1996).

___ *Film/Genre* (London, 1999).

Alvariño, Mikel, interview with Shelagh Rowan-Legg, 25 February 2015.

Annandale, David, 'Dark imperatives: Kant, Sade and Catholicism in Jess Franco's *Exorcism*', in R. Hansen (ed.), *Roman Catholicism in Fantastic Film: Essays on Belief, Spectacle, Ritual and Imagery* (Jefferson, 2011).

Archibald, David, *The War that Won't Die: The Spanish Civil War in Cinema* (Manchester, 2012).

Asma, Stephen, *On Monsters: An Unnatural History of Our Worst Fears* (Oxford, 2009).

Atkinson, Michael, 'Moral horrors in Guillermo del Toro's *Pan's Labyrinth*', *Film Comment* XLIII/1 (2007), pp. 50–53.

Bachelard, Gaston, *The Poetics of Space*, M. Jolas (trans.) (Boston, 1994).

Bailey, Gaz, interview with Shelagh Rowan-Legg, 27 March 2015.

Bakhtin, Mikhail, *Art and Answerability: Early Philosophical Essays*, M. Holquist and V. Liapunov (eds), V. Liapunov (trans.) (Austin, 1990).

___ *Rabelais and his World*, H. Iswolsky (trans.) (Cambridge, 1968).

Balagueró, Jaume, interview with Shelagh Rowan-Legg, 12 October 2012.

Balázs, Bela, *Theory of the Film: Character and Growth of a New Art*, E. Bone (trans.) (New York, 1970).

Bálint Kovács, András, *Screening Modernism: European Art Cinema, 1950–1980* (Chicago, 2007).

Barrie, J.M., *Peter Pan and Wendy* (Dorking, 2004)

Baudry, Jean-Louis, 'The apparatus: metapsychological approaches to the impression of reality in cinema', in P. Rosen (ed.), *Narrative, Apparatus, Ideology* (New York, 1986).

___ 'Ideological effects of the basic cinematic apparatus', in P. Rosen (ed.), *Narrative, Apparatus, Ideology* (New York, 1986).

Beck, Jay and Vicente Rodríguez Ortega (eds), *Contemporary Spanish Cinema and Genre* (Manchester, 2008).

___ 'Introduction', in J. Beck and V. Rodríguez Ortega (eds), *Contemporary Spanish Cinema and Genre* (Manchester, 2008).

Bentley, Bernard P.E., *A Companion to Spanish Cinema* (Woodbridge, 2008).

Bibliography

Bergero, Adriana J., 'Espectros, escalofríos y discusividad herida en *El espinazo del diablo*: El gótico como cuerpo-geografía cognitiva-emocional de quiebre', *MLN* 125/2 (2010), pp. 433–456.

Bergfelder, Tim, 'The nation vanishes: European co-productions and popular genre formula in the 1950s and 1960s', in M. Hjort and S. MacKenzie (eds), *Cinema and Nation* (London, 2000).

Bergson, Henri, *Matter and Memory*, N.M. Paul and W. S. Palmer (trans.) (New York, 1988).

___ *The Creative Mind: An Introduction to Metaphysics*, M.L. Andison (trans.) (New York, 2002).

Betz, Mark, *Beyond the Subtitle: Remapping European Art Cinema* (Minneapolis, 2009).

Biressi, Anita and Heather Nunn, *Reality TV: Realism and Revelation* (London, 2005).

Bishop, Kyle William, *American Zombie Gothic: The Walking Dead in Popular Culture* (Jefferson, 2010).

Bordwell, David, 'The art cinema as a mode of practice', in C. Fowler (ed.), *The European Cinema Reader* (London, 2002).

Botting, Fred, 'In gothic darkly: heterotopia, history, culture', in D. Punter (ed.), *A Companion to the Gothic* (Oxford, 2000).

Briefel, Aviva, 'What some ghosts don't know: spectral recognizance and the horror film', *Narrative* 17/1 (2009), pp. 95–108.

Bruun Vaage, Margrethe, 'Fiction film and the varieties of empathetic engagement', in P.A. French and H.K. Weltstein (eds), *Film and the Emotions* (Oxford, 2010).

Bruzzi, Stella, *Bringing Up Daddy: Fatherhood and Masculinity in Post-War Hollywood* (London, 2005).

Buckland, Warren, 'Introduction: puzzle plots', in W. Buckland (ed.), *Puzzle Films: Complex Storytelling in Contemporary Cinema* (Walden, 2009).

Burgoyne, Robert, *The Hollywood Historical Film* (Oxford, 2008).

Buse, Peter, Núria Triana Toribio and Andy Willis, *The Cinema of Álex de la Iglesia* (Manchester, 2007).

Cabrera, Rafael, interview with Shelagh Rowan-Legg, 28 April 2011.

Calderón de la Barca, Pedro, *Life is a Dream*, W.E. Colfrod (trans.) (Woodbury, 1958).

Campbell, Ramsay, *The Nameless* (London, 1981).

Cardona, Rodolfo and Anthony N. Zahareas, *Visión del esperpento. Teoría y práctica en los esperpentos de Valle-Inclán* (Madrid, 1970).

Carpentier, Alejo, 'The baroque and the marvelous real', in L. Parkinson Zamora and W.B. Faris (eds), *Magic Realism: Theory, History, Community* (Durham, 1995).

Carroll, Lewis. *Alice's Adventures in Wonderland and Other Tales* (New York, 2015).

Carroll, Noël, *The Philosophy of Horror: or Paradoxes of the Heart* (New York, 1990).

___ 'The paradox of suspense', in P. Vordered, H.J. Wolff and M. Friedricksen (eds) *Suspense: Conceptualizations, Theoretical Analyses, and Empirical Explorations* (Mahwah, 1996).

___ 'The grotesque today: preliminary notes toward a taxonomy', in F.S. Connelly (ed.), *Modern Art and the Grotesque* (Cambridge, 2003).

Cavallaro, Dani, *The Gothic Vision: Three Centuries of Horror, Terror and Fear* (London, 2002).

Choi, Jinhee, 'Leaving it up to the imagination', *The Journal of Aesthetics and Art Criticism* 63/1 (2005), pp. 17–25.

Bibliography

Chun, Kimberly, 'What is a ghost? an interview with Guillermo del Toro', *Cineaste* XXVIII/2 (2002), pp. 28–31.

Clark, Roger and Keith McDonald, 'A constant transit of finding: fantasy as realization in *Pan's Labyrinth*', *Children's Literature in Education* 41/1 (2010), pp. 52–63.

Clarke, James, 'Young hearts and minds in a time of sound and fury', in J. Slater (ed.), *Under Fire: A Century of War Movies* (Hersham, 2009).

Clover, Carol J., *Men, Women, and Chainsaws: Gender in the Modern Horror Film* (London, 1992).

Colebrook, Claire, *Irony* (London, 2004).

Conrad, Peter, *Islands: A Trip Through Time and Space* (London, 2009).

Cooke, Jennifer, *Legacies of Plague in Literature, Theory and Film* (Basingstoke, 2009).

Copestake, Ian D. 'Madness and the sea in the American literary imagination', in V.P. Messier and N. Batra (eds), *This Watery World: Humans and the Sea* (Mayaguez, 2007).

Corkhill, David, 'Race, immigration and multiculturalism in Spain', in B. Jordan and R. Morgan-Tamosunas (eds), *Contemporary Spanish Cultural Studies* (London, 1999).

Cortés, Rodrigo, interview with Shelagh Rowan-Legg, 20 November 2011.

Crawford, Raymond, *Plague and Pestilence in Literature and Art* (Oxford, 1914).

Creed, Barbara, *The Monstrous-Feminine: film, feminism, psychoanalysis* (London, 1993).

___ *Phallic Panic: Film, Horror, and the Primal Uncanny* (Carleton, 2005).

Curtis, Barry, *Dark Places: The Haunted House in Film* (London, 2008).

Davies, Ann, 'The final girl and monstrous mother of *El orfanato*', in A. Davies (ed.), *Spain on Screen: Developments in Contemporary Spanish Cinema* (London, 2011).

___ *Spanish Spaces: Landscape, Space and Place in Contemporary Spanish Culture* (Liverpool, 2012).

De Cervantes Saavedra, Miguel, *Don Quixote*, E. Grossman (trans.) (London, 2004).

Debord, Guy, *Society of the Spectacle*, K. Knabb (trans.) (Eastbourne, 2009).

Del Valle-Inclán, Ramón, *Three Plays: Divine Words, Bohemian Lights, Silver Face*, M. Delgado (trans.) (London, 1993).

Deleuze, Gilles, *Bergsonism*, H. Tomlinson and B. Habberjam (trans.) (New York, 1988).

___ *Cinema 2: The Time-Image*, H. Tomlinson and R. Galeta, (trans.) (Minneapolis, 1989).

Derrida, Jacques, *Specters of Marx: The State of the Debt, the Work of Mourning, and the New International*, P. Kamuf (trans.) (New York, 1994).

Durán, Marcel, 'Love at first sight: Spanish surrealism reconsidered', *MLN* 84/2 (1969), pp. 330–334.

Dyer, Richard, *Pastiche* (London, 2007).

Earle, William, *Surrealism in Film: Beyond the Realist Sensibility* (New Brunswick, 2011).

Eco, Umberto, 'The frames of comic "freedom"', in T.A. Sebeok (ed.), *Carnival* (Berlin, 1984).

Edwards, John, *The Spanish Inquisition* (Stroud, 1999).

Eig, Jonathan, 'A beautiful mind(fuck): Hollywood structures of identity', *Jumpcut: A Review of Contemporary Media* 46 (2003). Available at http://www.ejumpcut.org/archive/jc46.2003/eig.mindfilms/text.html (accessed 2 July 2012).

Elsaesser, Thomas, *European Cinema: Face to Face with Hollywood* (Amsterdam, 2005).

___ 'The mind-game film', in W. Buckland (ed.), *Puzzle Films: Complex Storytelling in Contemporary Cinema* (Walden, 2009).

Bibliography

Equipo Cartelera Turia (eds), *Cine español: cine de subgeneros* (Valencia, 1974).

Evans, Peter, 'Back to the future: cinema and democracy', in H. Graham and J. Labanyi (eds), *Spanish Cultural Studies: An Introduction* (Oxford, 1995).

___ 'Cinema, memory and the unconscious', in H. Graham and J. Labanyi (eds), *Spanish Cultural Studies: An Introduction* (Oxford, 1995).

Faulkner, Sally, *Literary Adaptations in Spanish Cinema* (London, 2004).

___ 'Nostalgia and the middlebrow: Spanish ruralist cinema and Mario Camus' *Los santos inocentes/The Holy Innocents*', in C. Fowler and G. Helfield (eds), *Representing the Rural: Space, Place and Identity in Films About the Land* (Detroit, 2006).

___ *A History of Spanish Film: Cinema and Society 1910–2010* (London, 2013).

Fishman, Jessica, 'The populace and the police: models of social control in reality-based crime television', *Critical Studies in Mass Communication* 16/3 (1999), pp. 268–288.

Fiske, John, 'Popularity and the politics of information', in P. Dahlgren and C. Sparks (eds), *Journalism and Popular Culture* (London, 1992).

Fleming, Michael, 'Themes of madness', in M. Fleming and R. Manville (eds), *Images of Madness: The Portrayal of Insanity in the Feature Film* (Rutherford, 1985).

Fletcher, Richard, 'The early Middle Ages 700–1250', in R. Carr (ed.), *Spain: A History* (Oxford, 2000).

Fouz-Hernández, Santiago and Alfredo Martínez-Expósito, *Live Flesh: The Male Body in Contemporary Spanish Cinema* (London, 2007).

Freud, Sigmund, *The Uncanny*, David McLintock (trans.) (London, 2003).

Fry, Carroll L., *Cinema of the Occult: New Age, Satanism, Wicca, and Spiritualism in Film* (Bethlehem, 2008).

Frye, Northrop, *Anatomy of Criticism* (Princeton, 1957).

Fuery, Patrick, *Madness and Cinema: Psychoanalysis, Spectatorship and Culture* (Basingstoke, 2004).

Galt, Rosalind and Kurt Schoonover, 'Introduction: the impurity of art cinema', in R. Galt and K. Schoonover (eds), *Global Art Cinema: New Theories and Histories* (Oxford, 2010).

Gámez Fuentes, María José, *Cinematergrafía: la madre en el cine y la literatura de la democracia* (Castellón, 2004).

Gant, Charles, 'Tell no one it's subtitled', *Sight & Sound* 18/4 (2008), p. 13.

Gehring, Wes D., *Parody as Film Genre: 'Never Give a Saga an Even Break'* (Westport, 1999).

Gerrig, Richard J., 'The resilience of suspense', in P. Vordered, H.J. Wolff and M. Friedricksen (eds), *Suspense: Conceptualizations, Theoretical Analyses, and Empirical Explorations* (Mahwah, 1996).

Gil, Mateo, interview with Shelagh Rowan-Legg, 1 December 2011.

Giner, Salvador and Sebastián Sarasa, 'Religión y modernidad en España', in R. Díaz-Salazar and S. Giner *Religión y sociedad en España* (Madrid, 1993).

Gledhill, Christine, 'The melodramatic field: an investigation', in C. Gledhill (ed.), *Home is Where the Heart Is: Studies in Melodrama and the Woman's Film* (London, 1987).

Glynn, Kevin, *Tabloid Culture: Trash Taste, Popular Power, and the Transformation of American Television* (Durham, 2000).

Gordon, Avery F., *Ghostly Matters: Haunting and the Sociological Imagination* (Minneapolis, 2008).

Bibliography

Grant, Barry Keith, 'Genre films and cultural myth', *Film International* 1/1 (2003), pp. 27–35.

Greeley, Andrew, *The Catholic Imagination* (Berkeley, 2000).

Greven, David, *Representations of Femininity in American Genre Cinema: The Woman's Film, Film Noir and Modern Horror* (Basingstoke, 2013).

Grodal, Torben, *Embodied Visions: Evolution, Emotion, Culture and Film* (Oxford, 2009).

Gubern, Rúben, *Historia del cine español* (Madrid, 1995).

Gunning, Tom, 'Uncanny reflections, modern illusions: sighting the modern optical uncanny', in J. Collins and J. Jervis (eds), *Uncanny Modernity* (New York, 2008).

Hanley, Jane, 'The walls came down: fantasy and power in *El laberinto del fauno*', *Studies in Hispanic Cinema* 4/1 (2007), pp. 35–45.

Hannerz, Ulf, 'Where we are and who we want to be', in U. Hedetoft and M. Hjort (eds), *The Postnational Self: Belonging and Identity* (Minneapolis, 2002).

Hardcastle, Anne, 'Ghosts of the past and present: hauntology and the Spanish Civil War in Guillermo del Toro's *The Devil's Backbone*', *Journal of the Fantastic in the Arts* 15/2 (2005), pp. 119–131.

Hatty, Suzanne E., *Masculinities, Violence and Culture* (Thousand Oaks, 1999).

Hayles, N. Katherine, *How We Became Posthuman: Virtual Bodies in Cybernetics, Literature and Informatics* (Chicago, 1999).

Hayward, Susan, *Cinema Studies: The Key Concepts* (London, 2000).

Hebblethwaite, Kate and Elizabeth McCarthy, 'Introduction' in K. Hebblethwaite and E. McCarthy (eds), *Fear: Essays on the Meaning and Experience of Fear* (Dublin, 2007).

Heredero, Carlos, 'New creators for the new millennium: transforming the directing scene in Spain', *Cineaste* 29/1 (2003), pp. 32–37.

Heredero, Carlos, and Antonio Santamarina, *Semillas de futuro: cine español, 1990–2001* (Madrid, 2002).

Herrero, Carmen, 'Edgy art cinema: cinephilia and genre negotiations in recent Spanish rural thrillers', *Studies in European Cinema* 7/2 (2010), pp. 123–134.

Hirsch, Marianne, *Family Frames: Photography Narrative and Postmemory* (Cambridge, 1997).

___ 'The generation of postmemory', *Poetics Today* 29/1 (2008), pp. 103–108.

Hopewell, John, *Out of the Past: Spanish Cinema After Franco* (London, 1986).

___ '*El corazón del bosque*: mist, myth and history', in P.W. Evans (ed.), *Spanish Cinema: The Auteurist Tradition* (Oxford, 1999).

___ 'Vigalondo, Vermut rip it up at Mar del Plato', *Variety*, 27 November 2014. Available at http://variety.com/2014/film/news/vigalondo-vermut-rip-it-up-in-mar-del-plata-1201366340/ (accessed 2 July 2015).

Horsley, Jason, *The Secret Life of Movies: Schizophrenic and Shamanic Journeys in American Cinema* (Jefferson, 2009).

Hostench, Mike, interview with Shelagh Rowan-Legg, 21 April 2011.

Hurcombe, Martin, 'Mi guerra, tu guerra: claiming the Spanish Civil War in literature and film', *Journal of War and Culture Studies* 1/1 (2008), pp. 25–30.

Hutcheon, Linda, *A Theory of Parody: The Teaching of Twentieth Century Art Forms* (London, 1985).

___ *A Poetics of Postmodernism* (London, 1998).

Ibáñez, Gabe, interview with Shelagh Rowan-Legg, 4 August 2011.

Bibliography

Ibáñez Rosales, Ismael, 'Otherness in *The Others*: haunting the Catholic other, humanizing the self', in R. Hansen (ed.), *Roman Catholicism in Fantastic Film: Essays on Belief, Spectacle, Ritual and Imagery* (Jefferson, 2011).

Ipiña Sadaba, Nahikari, interview with Shelagh Rowan-Legg, 30 July 2012.

Jackson, Rosemary, *Fantasy: The Literature of Subversion* (London, 1981).

Jameson, Fredric, *Signatures of the Visible* (New York, 1992).

Jordan, Barry, 'The Spanish film industry in the 1980s and 1990s', in B. Jordan and R. Morgan-Tamosunas (eds), *Contemporary Spanish Cultural Studies* (London, 1999).

___ *Alejandro Amenábar* (Manchester, 2012).

Jordan, Barry, and Rikki Morgan-Tamosunas, *Contemporary Spanish Cinema* (Manchester, 1998).

Junquera, Juan José, *The Black Paintings of Goya* (London, 2003)

Kääpä, Pietari, 'Imaginaries of a global Finland', *Scandinavian-Canadian Studies* 19 (2010), pp. 262–283.

Kavka, Misha, *Reality Television, Affect and Intimacy* (New York, 2008).

Kawin, Bruce 'Children of the light', in B.K. Grant (ed.), *Film Genre Reader II* (Austin, 1995).

Kermode, Mark, 'Girl interrupted', *Sight and Sound* XVI/12 (2006), pp. 20–24.

Kilborn, Richard, *Staging the Real: Factual TV Programming in the Age of Big Brother* (Manchester, 2003).

Kinder, Marsha, *Blood Cinema: The Reconstruction of National Identity in Spain* (Berkeley, 1993).

Kishan Thussu, Daya, *News as Entertainment: The Rise of Global Infotainment* (Los Angeles, 2007).

Labanyi, Jo, 'Engaging with Ghosts; or, Theorizing Culture in Modern Spain', in J. Labanyi (ed.), *Constructing Identity in Contemporary Spain: Theoretical Debates and Cultural Practices* (Oxford, 2002).

Landsberg, Alison, *Prosthetic Memory: The Transformation of American Remembrance in the Age of Mass Culture* (New York, 2004).

Langford, Barry, *Film Genre: Hollywood and Beyond* (Edinburgh, 2005).

Lauro, Sarah Jane and Karen Embry, 'A zombie manifesto: the nonhuman condition in the era of advanced capitalism', *Boundary 2* 35/1 (2008), pp. 85–108.

Lázaro-Reboll, Antonio, 'Screening "Chico": the horror ventures of Narciso Ibáñez Serrador', in A. Lázaro-Reboll and A. Willis (eds), *Spanish Popular Cinema* (Manchester, 2004).

___ 'The Transnational Reception of *El espinazo del diablo*', *Hispanic Research Journal*, 8/1 (2007), pp. 39–51.

___ *Spanish Horror Film* (Edinburgh, 2012).

Lázaro-Reboll, Antonio, and Andrew Willis, 'Introduction: Film Studies, Spanish cinema, and the question of the popular', in A. Lázaro-Reboll and A. Willis (eds), *Spanish Popular Cinema* (Manchester: Manchester University Press, 2004), p. 1.

Lebeau, Vicky, *Childhood and Cinema* (London, 2008).

Lim, Bliss Cua, *Translating Time: Cinema, the Fantastic and Temporal Critique* (Durham, 2009).

Lima, Robert, *The Dramatic World of Valle-Inclán* (Woodbridge, 2003).

Lopez, Diego and David Pizarro, *Silencios de pánico: Historia del cine fantástico y de terror español 1897-2010* (Barcelona, 2013).

Bibliography

López Lavigne, Enrique, interview with Shelagh Rowan-Legg, 20 February 2013.

Lury, Karen, *The Child in Film: Tears, Fears and Fairy Tales* (London, 2010).

Lyon, John, *The Theatre of Valle-Inclán* (Cambridge, 1983).

Lyotard, Jean-François, *The Postmodern Condition: A Report on Knowledge*, G. Bennington and B. Massumi (trans.) (Manchester, 1984).

___ 'The sublime and the avant-garde' in A. Benjamin (ed. and trans.) *The Lyotard Reader* (Oxford: Basil Blackwell, 1989), p. 203.

Maroto Camino, Mercedes, *Film, Memory and the Legacy of the Spanish Civil War: Resistance and Guerilla 1936–2010* (London, 2011).

Martí, Miguel, interview with Shelagh Rowan-Legg, 18 April 2011.

Maule, Rosanna, *Beyond Auteurism: New Directions in Authorial Film Practices in France, Spain and Italy since the 1980s* (Bristol, 2008).

McCallum, Robyn, 'Very advanced texts: metafictions and experimental work', in P. Hunt (ed.) *Understanding Children's Literature: Key Essays from the International Companion Encyclopedia of Children's Literature* (London, 1999).

Melbye, Donald, *Landscape Allegory in Cinema: From Wilderness to Wasteland* (New York, 2010).

Mellen, Joan, *Magic Realism* (Farmington Hills, 2000).

Mikos, Lothar, 'The experience of suspense: between fear and pleasure', in P. Vordered, H.J. Wolff and M. Friedricksen (eds), *Suspense: Conceptualizations, Theoretical Analyses, and Empirical Explorations* (Mahwah, 1996).

Miller, Dean A., *The Epic Hero* (Baltimore, 2000).

Miller, Stephen, 'The naturalist novel', in D.T. Geis (ed.), *Cambridge History of Spanish Literature* (Cambridge, 2004).

Mira, Eugenio, interview with Shelagh Rowan-Legg, 7 April 2011.

Mishra, Vijay, *The Gothic Sublime* (Albany, 1994).

Moine, Raphaëlle, *Cinema Genre*, A. Fox and H. Radner (trans.) (Oxford, 2008).

Monés, Adrià, interview with Shelagh Rowan-Legg, 21 April 2011.

Moreiras Menor, Cristina, 'Spectacle, trauma and violence in contemporary Spain', in B. Jordan and R. Morgan-Tamosunas (eds), *Contemporary Spanish Cultural Studies* (London, 1999).

Neale, Stephen, 'Art Cinema as Institution', *Screen* 22/1 (1981), pp. 11–39.

___ *Genre and Hollywood* (London, 2000).

___ 'Questions of Genre' in B.K. Grant (ed.), *Film Genre Reader III* (Austin, 2003).

Noll Zimmerman, Jacqueline, *People like Ourselves: Portrayals of Mental Illness in the Movies* (Lanham, 2003).

O'Day, Marc, 'Beauty in motion: gender, spectacle and action babe cinema', in Y. Tasker (ed.), *Action and Adventure Cinema* (London, 2004).

Ordóñez, Marcos. *La bestia anda suelta ¡Álex de la Iglesia lo cuenta todo!* (Madrid, 1997).

Olivares Merino, Julio Ángel, 'Naming the ghost within: filmic defamiliarization in Jaume Balagueró's *Nameless* (*Los sin nombre*), *Film International* 17 (2005), pp. 28–33.

Palacio, Manuel, *Historia de la televisión en España* (Madrid, 2008).

Palacios, Jesús, 'Los últimos días de la bestia: cine fantástico español ante el nuevo milenio', in H.J. Rodríguez (ed.), *Miradas para un nuevo milenio: fragmentos para una historia futura del cine español* (Madrid, 2006).

Bibliography

Panek, Elliot, 'The poet and the detective: defining the psychological puzzle film', *Film Criticism* 31/1-2 (2006), pp. 62–88.

Paulson, Lynn Edith, 'Mama bears, bitches and monsters: motherhood and violence in popular film', in E. Cole and J. Henderson Daniel (eds), *Featuring Females: Feminist Analysis of Media* (Washington, 2005).

Payne, Stanley G., *Spanish Catholicism: A Historical Overview* (Madison, 1984).

Pena, Jaime, 'Cine español de los noventa: Hoja de reclamaciones', *Secuencias* 16 (2002), pp. 38–54.

Perlmutter, Ruth, 'Memories, Dreams, Screens', *Quarterly Review of Film and Video* 22.2 (2005), pp. 125–134.

Perriam, Chris, *Stars and Masculinities in Spanish Cinema: From Banderas to Bardem* (Oxford, 2003).

___ 'Alejandro Amenábar's *Abre los ojos/Open Your Eyes*', in A. Lázaro-Reboll and A. Willis (eds), *Spanish Popular Cinema* (Manchester, 2004).

Pippin, Tina, *Apocalyptic Bodies: The Biblical End of the World in Text and Image* (London, 1999).

Plaza, Paco, interview with Shelagh Rowan-Legg, 16 August 2011.

Podol, Peter L., 'The grotesque mode in contemporary Spanish theatre and film', *Modern Language Studies* 15/4 (1985), pp. 194–207.

Propp, Vladimir *Morphology of the Folk Tale*, L. Scott (trans.) (Austin, 1968).

Purves, Maria, *The Gothic and Catholicism: Religion, Cultural Exchange and the Popular Novel, 1785–1829* (Cardiff, 2009).

Pye, Douglas, 'Movies and tone', in J. Gibbs and D. Pye (eds), *Close-Up 2* (London, 2007).

Rabalska, Carmen, 'A dark desire for the grotesque', in R. Riz and R. Rodriguez-Saona (eds), *Spanish Cinema: Calling the Shots* (Leeds, 1999).

Radcliffe, Ann, *The Mysteries of Udolpho: A Mystery Story* (London, 2013).

Rank, Otto, *The Double: A Psychoanalytical Study*, H. Tucker Jr. (trans.) (Chapel Hill, 1971).

Richardson, Michael, *Surrealism and Cinema* (Oxford, 2006).

Ríos Pérez, Sergio, 'The Spanish box-office hits the bottom (or not)', *Cineuropa*, 20 June 2013. Available at http://cineuropa.org/nw.aspx?t=newsdetail&l=en&did=240223 (accessed 5 August 2013).

Rivera, Alfonso, 'Pedro Pérez, President of the FAPAE', *Cineuropa*, 18 June 2013. Available at http://cineuropa.org/it.aspx?t=interview&l=en&did=240191 (accessed 5 August 2013).

Rodríguez, María Pilar, 'Dark memories, tragic lives: representations of the Basque nation in three contemporary films', *Anuario de cine y literatura en Español* 3 (1997), pp. 129–144.

Rodríguez Ortega, Vicente. 'Trailing the Spanish auteur: Almodóvar's, Amenábar's, and de la Iglesia's generic routes in the US market', in J. Beck and V. Rodríguez Ortega (eds), *Contemporary Spanish Cinema and Genre* (Manchester, 2008).

Rollin, Roger R., 'The Lone Ranger and Lenny Skutnik: The hero as popular culture', in R.B. Browne (ed.), *The Hero in Transition* (Bowling Green, 1983).

Rovisco, Maria, 'Mapping the nation and the countryside in European "films of voyage"', in R. Fish (ed.), *Cinematic Countrysides* (Manchester, 2007).

Royle, Nicholas, *The Uncanny: An Introduction*, (Manchester, 2002).

Bibliography

Sala, Ángel, *Profanando el sueño de los muertos: la historia jamás contada del cine fantástico español* (Pontevedra, 2010).

Sánchez Navarro, Jordi, *Freaks en acción: Álex de la Iglesia o el cine como fuga* (Madrid, 2005).

Santamarina, Antonio, 'Un sugerente melodrama gótico', *Dirigido por* (2001), pp. 22–24.

Santiáñez, Nil, 'Great masters of Spanish modernism', in D.T. Geis (ed.), *Cambridge History of Spanish Literature* (Cambridge, 2004).

Scuri, Piera, *Design of Enclosed Spaces* (New York, 1995).

Sempere, Antonio, *Alejandro Amenábar: cine en las venas* (Madrid, 2000).

Serra, Koldo, interview with Shelagh Rowan-Legg, 11 November 2011.

Shaw, Deborah, *The Three Amigos: The Transnational Filmmaking of Guillermo del Toro, Alejandro González Iñarritu and Alfonso Cuarón* (Manchester, 2013).

Shaw, Philip, *The Sublime* (London, 2006).

Shipka, Danny, *Perverse Titillation: The Exploitation Cinema of Italy, Spain and France, 1960–1980* (Jefferson, 2011).

Smith, Andrew, 'Hauntings', in C. Spooner and E. McEvoy (eds), *The Routledge Companion to the Gothic* (New York, 2007).

Smith, Murray, *Engaging Characters: Fiction, Emotion and the Cinema* (Oxford, 1995).

___ 'Imagining from the inside', in R. Allen and M. Smith (eds), *Film Theory and Philosophy* (Oxford, 1997).

Smith, Paul Julian, 'El día de la bestia', *Sight and Sound* 6/12 (1996), p. 43.

___ *The Moderns: Time, Space and Subjectivity in Contemporary Spanish Culture* (Oxford, 2000).

___ 'High Anxiety: *Abre los ojos/Vanilla Sky*', *Journal of Romance Studies* 4/1 (2004), pp. 91–102.

___ *Television in Spain: From Franco to Almodóvar* (Woodbridge, 2006).

___ 'Pan's Labyrinth', *Film Quarterly* 60/4 (2007), pp. 4–9.

___ *Spanish Practices: Literature, Cinema, Television* (Oxford, 2012).

___ 'Spanish Cinema Roundup', *Film Quarterly* 66.1 (2012). Available at http://www.film-quarterly.org/2013/04/spanish-cinema-roundup/ (accessed 5 August 2013).

Snyder, Thomas Lee, *Sacred Encounters: The Myth of the Hero in the Horror, Science Fiction and Fantasy Films of George Lucas and Steven Spielberg*. PhD Diss., Northwestern University, 1984.

Sobchack, Thomas, 'Genre films: a classical experience', in B.K. Grant (ed.), *Film Genre Reader II* (Austin, 1995).

Sobchack, Vivian, *Screening Space: The American Science Fiction Film* (New Brunswick, 1987).

___ '"Is any body home?" embodied imagination and visible evictions', in H. Naficy (ed.), *Home, Exile, Homeland: Film, Media and the Politics of Place* (New York, 1999).

___ 'The violent dance: a personal memoir of death in the movies', in S. Prince (ed.), *Screening Violence* (London, 2000).

Spielgelman, Art, *Maus: A Survivor's Tale* (London, 1987).

Stone, Rob, *Spanish Cinema* (New York, 2001).

Tasker, Yvonne, *Spectacular Bodies: Gender, Genre and the Action Cinema* (London, 1993).

Thomson, Philip, *The Grotesque* (London, 1972).

Todorov, Tzvetan, *The Fantastic: A Structural Approach to a Literary Genre*, R. Howard (trans.) (Ithaca, 1975).

Bibliography

Torrance, Robert M., *The Comic Hero* (Cambridge, 1978).

Torres, Augusto M., 'the film industry: under pressure from the state and television', in H. Graham and J. Labanyi (eds), *Spanish Cultural Studies: An Introduction* (Oxford, 1995).

Trashorras, Antonio, interview with Shelagh Rowan-Legg, 11 November 2011.

Triana Toribio, Núria, *Spanish National Cinema* (London, 2003).

Trotman, Tiffany, 'Introduction', in T. Trotman (ed.), *The Changing Spanish Family: Essays on New Views in Literature, Cinema and Theatre* (Jefferson, 2011).

Tudor, Andrew, 'Genre', in B.K. Grant (ed.), *Film Genre Reader III* (Austin, 2003).

Turan, Kenneth, *Sundance to Sarajevo: Film Festivals and the World They Made* (Berkeley, 2002).

Valleau, Marjorie A., *The Spanish Civil War in American and European Films* (Ann Arbor, 1978).

Van Extergem, Dirk, 'The Brussels International Festival of Fantastic Film', in E. Mathjis and X. Mendek (eds), *Alternative Europe: Eurotrash and Exploitation Cinema since 1945* (London, 2004).

Varma, Devendra P., *The Gothic Flame* (New York, 1957).

Vidler, Anthony, *The Architectural Uncanny* (Cambridge, 1992).

Vigalondo, Nacho, interview with Shelagh Rowan-Legg, 1 May 2011.

Walpole, Horace, *The Castle of Otranto: A Gothic Novel* (London, 2011).

Wells, Paul, *The Horror Genre: From Beelzebub to Blair Witch* (London, 2000).

Wheeler, Duncan, 'The representation of domestic violence in Spanish cinema', *Modern Language Review* 107/2 (2012), pp. 438–500.

Williams, Linda, 'When a woman looks', in B.K. Grant (ed.), *The Dread of Difference: Gender and the Horror Film* (Austin, 1996).

Willis, Andrew, 'From the margins to the mainstream: trends in recent Spanish horror film', in A. Lázaro-Reboll and A. Willis (eds), *Spanish Popular Cinema* (Manchester, 2004).

___ 'The Spanish horror film as subversive text: Eloy de la Iglesia's *La semana del asesino*', S.J. Schneider and T. Williams (eds), in *Horror International* (Detroit: Wayne State University Press, 2005), p. 163.

___ 'The Fantastic Factory: the horror genre and contemporary Spanish cinema', in J. Beck and V. Rodríguez Ortega (eds), *Contemporary Spanish Cinema and Genre* (Manchester, 2008).

Wolf, Norbert, *Diego Velázquez 1599–1660: The Face of Spain* (London, 1999).

Wood, Gerald C., 'Horror film', in W.D. Gehring (ed.), *Handbook of American Film Genres* (New York, 1988).

Woodworth, Paddy, *The Basque Country: A Cultural History* (Oxford, 2007).

Wuss, Peter, *Cinematic Narration and its Psychological Impact* (Newcastle, 2009).

Xavier, Ismail, 'Historical allegory', in T. Miller and R. Stam (eds), *A Companion to Film Theory* (Oxford, 1999).

Zahareas, Anthony N., 'The absurd, the grotesque and the esperpento', in A.N. Zahareas, S. Greenfield and R. Cardona (eds), *Ramón del Valle-Inclán: An Appraisal of His Life and Works* (New York, 1968).

Filmography

'7:35 in the Morning' ('7:35 de la mañana', Nacho Vigalondo, 2003)

20 Centimetres (*20 centímetros*, Ramón Salazar, 2005)

28 Days Later (Danny Boyle, 2002)

28 Weeks Later (Juan Carlos Fresnadillo, 2007)

The 40 Year-Old-Virgin (Judd Apatow, 2005)

'A is for Apocalypse' (Nacho Vigalondo, 2012)

The Abandoned (Nacho Cerdà, 2006)

'Aftermath' (Nacho Cerdà, 1997)

Agora (Alejandro Amenábar, 2009)

Airbag (Juanma Bajo Ulloa, 1997)

'Alicia' (Jaume Balagueró, 1994)

Alien (Ridley Scott, 1979)

Alien Predator (Deran Sarafian, 1985)

Aliens (James Cameron, 1986)

All About My Mother (*Todo sobre mi madre*, Pedro Almodóvar, 1999)

Alone (*Solas*, Benito Zambrano, 1999)

America's Most Wanted (20th Century Fox Television, 1998–2012)

American Psycho (Mary Harron, 2000)

The Amityville Horror (Stuart Rosenberg, 1979)

Ana and the Wolves (*Ana y los lobos*, Carlos Saura, 1973)

'An Andalusian Dog' ('Un Chien Andalou', Luis Buñuel and Salvador Dalí, 1929)

Anguish (Bigas Luna, 1987)

Annie Hall (Woody Allen, 1977)

Aquí hay tomate (Telecinco, 2003–2008)

'The Awakening' (Nacho Cerdà, 1990)

The Awful Dr Orlof (*Gritos en la noche*, Jesús Franco, 1961)

The Backwoods (Koldo Serra, 2006)

Balarrasa (José Antonio Nieves Conde, 1951)

The Bird of Happiness (*El pájaro de la felicidad*, Pilar Miró, 1993)

The Birthday (Eugenio Mira, 2006)

Black Christmas (Rob Clark, 1974)

The Black Siren (*La sirena negra*, Carlos Serrano de Osma, 1947)

Filmography

Blade Runner (Ridley Scott, 1982)

The Blair Witch Project (Daniel Myrick and Eduardo Sánchez, 1999)

Blinkers (*Salir pitando*, Álvaro Fernández Armero, 2007)

The Bloody Judge (Jesús Franco, 1970)

Bob and Carol and Ted and Alice (Paul Mazursky, 1969)

The Body (*El Cuerpo*, Oriol Paulo, 2012)

The Breakfast Club (John Hughes, 1985)

Bringing Up Baby (Howard Hawks, 1938)

Buffy the Vampire Slayer (Fran Rubel Kuzui, 1992)

Buried (Rodrigo Cortés, 2007)

'La Cabeza' (Alejandro Amenábar, 1991)

Cannibal Holocaust (Ruggero Deodato, 1980)

Carrie (Brian de Palma, 1976)

Carriers (David Pastor and Àlex Pastor, 2009)

Casper (Brad Silberling, 1995)

The Castle of Fu-Manchu (Jesús Franco, 1968)

Charlie's Angels (ABC, 1976–1981)

'Choque' (Nacho Vigalondo, 2005)

Cleo from 5 to 7 (*Cléo de 5 à 7*, Agnès Varda, 1962)

Close Encounters of the Third Kind (Steven Spielberg, 1977)

Cloverfield (Matt Reeves, 2008)

Club Virginia Orchestra (*Orquesta Club Virginia*, Manuel Iborra, 1992)

Confidential Agent (Herman Shumlin, 1945)

Cronos (Guillermo del Toro, 1993)

Cousin Angelica (*La prima Angélica*, Carlos Saura, 1974)

Cows (*Vacas*, Julio Medem, 1992)

The Cuenca Crime (*El crimen de Cuenca*, Pilar Miró, 1979)

Dark City (Alex Proyas, 1998)

Darkness (Jaume Balagueró, 2002)

The Day of the Beast (*El día de la bestia*, Álex de la Iglesia, 1995)

Day of the Dead (George A. Romero, 1985)

Dead Mother (*La madre muerta*, Juanma Bajo Ulloa, 1993)

The Dead Zone (David Cronenberg, 1983)

Deliverance (John Boorman, 1972)

Demons in the Garden (*Demonios en el jardín*, Manuel Gutiérrez Aragón, 1982)

La dernière sorcière (Segundo de Chomón, 1906)

The Devil's Backbone (*El espinazo del diablo*, Guillermo del Toro, 2001)

Diary of the Dead (George A. Romero, 2007)

'Días sin luz' (Jaume Balagueró, 1995)

Diamond Flash (Carlos Vermut, 2012)

Donnie Darko (Richard Kelly, 2001)

Don't Look Now (Nicholas Roeg, 1973)

Dos caminos (Arturo Ruiz Castillo, 1953)

Dracula (Tod Browning, 1931)

Dying of Laughter (*Muertos de risa*, Álex de la Iglesia, 1999)

Earth (*Tierra*, Julio Medem, 1996)

The Eclipse (*L'eclisse*, Michaelangelo Antonioni, 1962)

Embrujo (Carlos Serrano de Osma, 1947)

E.T. the Extra-Terrestrial (Steven Spielberg, 1982)

The Exorcist (William Friedkin, 1973)

The Exterminating Angel (*El angel exterminador*, Luis Buñuel, 1962)

Extraterrestrial (*Extraterrestre*, Nacho Vigalondo, 2011)

Eyes Without a Face (*Les yeux sans visage*, Georges Franju, 1960)

'Fade' (Eugenio Mira, 2000)

Father Coplillas (*El padre Coplillas*, Ramón Comas, 1968)

Faust: Love of the Damned (Brian Yuzna, 2001)

The Fisher King (Terry Gilliam, 1992)

For Whom the Bell Tolls (Sam Woods, 1943)

Fragile (Jaume Balagueró, 2005)

Friday the 13th (Sean S. Cunningham, 1980)

Frozen Silence (*Silencio en la nieve*, Gerardo Herrero, 2011)

Game of Werewolves (*Lobos de Arga*, Juan Martínez Moreno, 2011)

'Genesis' (Nacho Cerdà, 1998)

Ghost Graduation (*Promoción fantasma*, Javier Ruiz Caldera, 2012)

Gimlet (José Luis Acosta, 1995)

Gone with the Wind (Victor Fleming, 1939)

The Goonies (Richard Donner, 1985)

Grand Piano (Eugenio Mira, 2013)

Groundhog Day (Harold Ramis, 1993)

Halloween (John Carpenter, 1978)

Hannibal (NBC, 2013–2015)

¡Harka! (Carlos Arévalo, 1940)

The Haunted Mansion (Rob Minkoff, 2003)

The Haunting (*No-Do*, Elio Quiroga, 2009)

Hellboy (Guillermo del Toro, 2004)

Hierro (Gabe Ibáñez, 2009)

Filmography

'Himenóptero' (Alejandro Amenábar, 1992)

Historias para no dormir (TVE-1, 1966–1968)

'El hombre Esponja' ('Sponge Man', Juan Antonio Bayona, 2002)

El hotel eléctrico (Segundo de Chomón, 1908)

Horror Express (Eugenio Martín, 1972)

House (*Hausu*, Nobuhiko Obayashi, 1977)

The House that Screamed (*La residencia*, Narciso Ibáñez Serrador, 1969)

The Hunger Games (Gary Ross, 2012)

The Hunt (*La caza*, Carlos Saura, 1966)

I Spit on Your Grave (Meir Zarchi, 1971)

I Want You (*Tengo ganas de ti*, Fernando González Molina)

If They Tell You I Fell (*Si te dicen que caí*, Vicente Aranda, 1989)

The Impossible (Juan Antonio Bayona, 2012)

In a Glass Cage (*Tras el cristal*, Agustí Villaronga, 1987)

The Innocents (Jack Clayton, 1961)

Intruders (Juan Carlos Fresnadillo, 2011)

It Happened One Night (Frank Capra, 1934)

It's a Wonderful Life (Frank Capra, 1946)

Jesus Christ Superstar (Norman Jewison, 1973)

Justino (*Justino, un asesino de la tercera edad*, Santiago Aguilar and Luis Guridi, 1994)

Kill Bill (Quentin Tarantino, 2003)

Killer Tongue (Alberto Sciamma, 1996)

King of the Hill (*El rey de la montaña*, Gonzalo López-Gallego, 2007)

Knocked Up (Judd Apatow, 2007)

Land and Freedom (Ken Loach, 1995)

The Last Days (*Los últimos días*, David Pastor and Àlex Pastor, 2013)

Last House on the Left (Wes Craven, 1972)

Last Year in Marienbad (*L'année dernière á Marienbad*, Alain Resnais, 1961)

Let's Scare Jessica to Death (John D. Hancock, 1971)

The Limehouse Golem (Juan Carlos Medina, 2016)

The Living Dead at Manchester Morgue (Jorge Grau, 1974)

Lo que necesitas es amor (Antena 3, 1993–1999)

The Lost Boys (Joel Schumacher, 1987)

Lovers (*Amantes*, Vicente Aranda, 1990)

Lovers of the Arctic Circle (*Los amantes del Círculo Polar*, Julio Medem, 1998)

Lucía (Humberto Solas, 1968)

Filmography

'Luna' (Alejandro Amenábar, 1995)

The Mad Monkey (Fernando Trueba, 1989)

Magical Girl (Carlos Vermut, 2014)

'Máma' (Pablo Berger, 1988)

Mama (Andrés Mischietti, 2013)

La máquina de la verdad (Telecinco, 1992–1994)

Marshland (*La isla minima*, Alberto Rodríguez, 2014)

Martyrs (Pascal Laugier, 2008)

La melodía misteriosa (Juan Fortuny, 1955)

Memento (Christopher Nolan, 2000)

Mimic (Guillermo del Toro, 1997)

'Mirindas asesinas' (Álex de la Iglesia, 1991)

'Mis vacaciones' (Juan Antonio Bayona, 1999)

Mission: Impossible (CBS, 1966–1973)

A Monster Calls (Juan Antonio Bayona, 2016)

Mutant Action (*Acción Mutante*, Álex de la Iglesia, 1993)

The Nameless (*Los sin nombre*, Jaume Balagueró, 1999)

Night of the Living Dead (George A. Romero, 1968)

Night of the Sunflowers (*La noche de los girasoles*, Jorge Sánchez-Cabezudo, 2006)

Nights of the Werewolf (*Las noches del Hombre Lobo*, René Govar, 1968)

Nikita (*La Femme Nikita*, Luc Besson, 1990)

El niño (Daniel Monzon, 2014)

Nobody Will Speak of Us When We're Dead (*Nadie hablará de nosotras cuando hay-amos muerto*, Agustín Díaz Yanes, 1995)

The Nun (Luis de la Madrid, 2005)

El ojo de cristal (Antonio Santillán, 1955)

Only Me (*Sólo mía*, Javier Balaguer, 2001)

Open Windows (Nacho Vigalondo, 2014)

Open Your Eyes (*Abre los ojos*, Alejandro Amenábar, 1997)

The Omen (Richard Donner, 1976)

Operación mantis (Paul Naschy, 1984)

The Orphanage (*El orfanato*, Juan Antonio Bayona, 2007)

The Other Side of the Bed (*El otro lado de la cama*, Emilio Martínez Lázaro, 2002)

The Others (Alejandro Amenábar, 2001)

Painless (*Insensibles*, Juan Carlos Medina, 2012)

Pan's Labyrinth (*El laberinto del fauno*, Guillermo del Toro, 2006)

'Parallel Monsters' (Nacho Vigalondo, 2014)

Pascual Duarte (Ricardo Franco, 1976)

Passages (*Pasajes,* Daniel Calparsoro, 1996)

The Phantom of the Opera (Arthur Lubin, 1943)

Poachers (*Furtivos,* José Luis Borau, 1975)

Poltergeist (Tobe Hooper, 1982)

Primer (Shane Carruth, 2004)

Psycho (Alfred Hitchcock, 1968)

The Purple Rose of Cairo (Woody Allen, 1985)

Quarantine (John Erick Dowdle, 2008)

Quarantine 2: Terminal (John Pogue, 2011)

Raise Ravens (*Cría cuervos,* Carlos Saura, 1976)

Raza (José Luis Sáenz de Heredia, 1942)

Rebecca (Alfred Hitchcock, 1940)

[REC] (Jaume Balagueró and Paco Plaza, 2007)

[REC]2 (Jaume Balagueró and Paco Plaza, 2009)

[REC]3: Genesis (*[REC]3: Génesis,* Paco Plaza, 2012)

[REC]4: Apocalypse (*[REC]4: Apocalipsis,* Jaume Balagueró, 2014)

Red Lights (Rodrigo Cortés, 2012)

Regression (Alejandro Amenábar, 2015)

Repulsion (Roman Polanski, 1965)

Resident Evil (Paul W. S. Anderson, 2002)

Romasanta: The Werewolf Hunt (Paco Plaza, 2004)

Rosemary's Baby (Roman Polanski, 1968)

Run, Lola, Run (*Lola rennt,* Tom Tykwer, 1998)

The Sadist of Notre Dame (*El exorcista diabólico,* Jesús Franco, 1971)

Scream (Wes Craven, 1997)

The Sea Inside (*Mar adentro,* Alejandro Amenábar, 2004)

Se7en (David Fincher, 1995)

Sexykiller (*Sexykiller: morirás para ella,* Miguel Martí, 2008)

The Shining (Stanley Kubrick, 1980)

The Silence of the Lambs (Jonathan Demme, 1991)

The Sixth Sense (M. Night Shyamalan, 1999)

Sleep Tight (*Mientras duermes,* Jaume Balagueró, 2012)

Slugs (Juan Piquer, 1987)

Some Kind of Wonderful (Howard Deutch, 1987)

Source Code (Duncan Jones, 2011)

A Spanish Affair (*Ocho appellidos vascos,* Emilio Martínez Lázaro, 2014)

A Spanish Affair 2 (*Ocho appellidos catalan*, Emilio Martínez Lázaro, 2015)
The Spiral Staircase (Robert Siodmak, 1945)
The Spirit of the Beehive (*El espíritu de la colmena*, Victor Erice, 1973)
Stand By Me (Rob Reiner, 1986)
Star Knight (Fernando Colomo, 1985)
Star Wars Episode IV: A New Hope (George Lucas, 1977)
Straw Dogs (Sam Peckinpah, 1971)
'Sunday' ('Domingo', Nacho Vigalondo, 2007)
Sunday Carnival (*Domingo de carnaval*, Edgar Neville, 1945)
Tad, The Lost Explorer (*Las aventuras de Tadeo Jones*, Enrique Gato, 2012)
Take My Eyes (*Te doy mis ojos*, Icíar Bollaín, 2003)
Taxi Driver (Martin Scorsese, 1976)
Terminator 2: Judgment Day (James Cameron, 1991)
Texas Chainsaw Massacre (Tobe Hooper, 1974)
That Obscure Object of Desire (*Cet obscur objet de désir*, Luis Buñuel, 1977)
There Be Dragons (Roland Joffe, 2011)
Thesis (*Tesis*, Alejandro Amenábar, 1996)
Timecrimes (*Los cronocrímenes*, Nacho Vigalondo, 2007)
Tombs of the Blind Dead (*La noche del terror ciego*, Amando de Ossorio, 1971)
Torrente, The Dumb Arm of the Law (*Torrente, el brazo tonte de la ley*, Santiago Segura, 1998)
Torrente 5: Operation Eurovegas (*Torrente 5: Operación Eurovegas*, Santiago Segura, 2014)
The Tower of the Seven Hunchbacks (*La torre de los siete jorobados*, Edgar Neville, 1944)
True Detective (HBO, 2014–)
Unsolved Mysteries (NBC/CBS/Lifetime/Spike, 1987–2010)
Vanilla Sky (Cameron Crowe, 2001)
Vertigo (Alfred Hitchcock, 1958)
Village of the Damned (Wolf Rilla, 1960)
Waltz with Bashir (Ari Folman, 2008)
The War is Over (*La Guerre est finie*, Alain Resnais, 1966)
What Have I Done to Deserve This? (*¿Qué he hecho yo para merecer esto!*, Pedro Almodóvar, 1984)
When Harry Met Sally (Rob Reiner, 1989)
White Zombie (Victor Haleprin, 1932)
Who Can Kill a Child? (*¿Quién puede matar a un niño?*, Narciso Ibáñez Serrador, 1976)

Filmography

The Wicker Man (Robin Hardy, 1973)

Witching and Bitching (*Las brujas de Zugarramurdi*, Álex de la Iglesia, 2013)

The Wizard of Oz (Victor Fleming, 1939)

A Woman Under the Influence (John Cassavetes, 1974)

Women on the Verge of a Nervous Breakdown (*Mujeres al borde de un ataque de nervios*, Pedro Almodóvar, 1988)

You've Got Mail (Nora Ephron, 1998)

Index

207

Index

Index

Index

Index

Index

212

Index

Index